firm day-old bread for ₁d crumbs (4 or 5 slices ₂e 2 cups). Break into ₃es and grind crust and ₁n the electric blender, ₂rumble by hand until ₃ fine.

To marinate—soak or steep meats or other foods in a marinade (seasoned liquid) to impart flavor and, in some instances, to tenderize.

To crush garlic, give it a good whack with the side of a cleaver, heavy knife or any heavy, flat implement. No need to peel.

To whip heavy cream, the cream, bowl, and beater should be cold, preferably chilled. Whip until the beater leaves light traces on the surface of the cream and a bit of cream lifted and dropped will just retain its shape.

To reduce—simply boil a liquid over a high heat until the amount left is what the recipe specifies.

To dice—cut into fairly small, even pieces.

To baste—spray, spoon, or brush a liquid or melted fat over food while it cooks.

To score—make shallow cuts or slashes. In this instance use a small, sharp paring knife to crosshatch the surface.

To dice or chop scallions (green onions)—peel off any withered skin and cut off the long roots. Take as much of the scallions, including the green top as you think you'll need. Slice lengthwise, four times. Then slice across into small dice.

Live clams, like oysters, open, once cooked. If they don't, they were dead before cooking and must be discarded.

To shell an egg the easy way, tap all over with the back of a knife until it is "mapped." Then, holding the egg in the palm of your hand, peel off the shell and inner skin. If small shell particles cling to the egg, dip the egg in cold water.

There are two types of scallops: the tiny, sweet, tender bay scallops and the large, less sweet sea scallops. If you are using sea scallops, cut them in half.

The button mushrooms, the least expensive, are best in cooked dishes. Mushrooms need not be peeled.

Other Books by Helen McCully

NOBODY EVER TELLS YOU THESE THINGS
ABOUT FOOD AND DRINK

THE OTHER HALF OF THE EGG
(with Jacques Pépin)

THE CHRISTMAS PONY
(with Dorothy Crayder)

COOKING WITH
HELEN McCULLY BESIDE YOU

COOKING
WITH
HELEN McCULLY
BESIDE YOU

by HELEN
McCULLY

RANDOM HOUSE

NEW YORK

Library of Congress Catalog Card Number: 79–102296

Printed by Universal Lithographers, Lutherville-Timonium, Maryland.
Bound by L. H. Jenkins Inc., Richmond, Virginia.

Illustrations by Donna Marie Pasino
Typography and binding design by Kenneth Miyamoto

FIRST PRINTING

TO

Camille Davied Rose and Kate Titus Yutzy

CONTENTS

EQUIPMENT

INTRODUCTION

If you believe that some people are "born" cooks, help yourself to a few grains of salt. It simply isn't true. What is true is that some people are born with an aptitude—a penchant, let us say—for cooking and as a consequence learn to cook more easily and more imaginatively than others. The facts are, if you like to eat, you can learn to cook and what's more learn to be a good cook. Not, perhaps, another Escoffier but you can be a pleasure to yourself and give pleasure to all who come and sit at your table.

"There is one thing to remember in all of cookery: the time to get ready is before you start." This remark by Craig Claiborne, an old friend and the witty, knowledgeable Food Editor of The New York Times, struck me as making great good sense and it is, in an important way, the essence of this book.

Anyone who has cooked for a long time, as I have, knows that planning and organization are half the battle. One of the reasons cooks, and not necessarily those who are new, young or inexperienced, sometimes get themselves into hot water is because they don't wash, trim, chop, dice, mince or whatever the recipe says to do before they start "cooking." Nothing is more infuriating than to discover you've forgotten to melt the chocolate when the cake batter is ready to go in the pan. Reading all the way through all recipes before you start and taking all the little preliminary "cooking" steps can help to forestall such dumb mistakes.

This book is designed for all cooks. It is a learning book (it seems to me I learn something each time I cook) but at the same time it is a constant reminder. Ticklers parallel every recipe throughout the book to jog the cook's memory on basic principles while he or she is actually cooking. Take a look at one recipe and you will see that we have italicized the tickler to emphasize it for you. Those few cooking principles that are too long to fit on the page can be found at the back of the book on the page indicated.

Since I have a memory akin to a sieve, I constantly check myself and I wouldn't think of cooking anything—no matter how simple the dish or how many times I've made it—without running through the recipe before I start.

Menus and the logistics of getting everything on the dinner table at the right time, cooked, hot, and in proper sequence, seem to be the bêtes noires of many a cook, sometimes even experienced ones. This book is planned to help lick those problems. To that end each menu has a cooking schedule indicating exactly what steps to take and when and how to take them. To make cooking as easy, comfortable and efficient as possible, each recipe starts off with a list of the equipment needed to make that particular dish. In a country as gadget-minded as the United States, I suspect many a housewife is lured down the gadget path and as a result has cupboards cluttered with "things." Out of experience, some bitter, I strongly recommend you buy only the equipment you need and that you buy the best there is. Better, I say, to put your dollars into a fine casserole that, given proper care, will last you a lifetime than to splurge on a 3-rib roast that will be gone tomorrow. Throughout this book you will find illustrations of most of the major small, but important, pieces of cooking equipment. With these efficient, modern tools at hand, cooking is no longer work but fun. Good fun.

I hope you have good fun when you cook with me and—good luck.

H. McC.

New York, 1970

POULTRY

CHICKEN

ROAST STUFFED CHICKEN

Whole Baked Tomatoes   *Potatoes Dauphinois*

Vanilla Ice Cream   *Hot Chocolate Sauce*

Coffee

YOUR COOKING SCHEDULE: The chicken can be stuffed early in the day, or even the day before, then covered with foil, Saran, or a polyethylene bag, and refrigerated. But it must be brought to room temperature a couple of hours before it is to be roasted—which means if dinner is to be served at 7 o'clock, the chicken must be taken out of the refrigerator about 3:30 P.M. The chocolate sauce can be finished ahead, sealed with Saran, and kept at room temperature. Reheat over hot water about 10 minutes before serving. The potatoes can be made ready for baking any time during the day, then tucked into the oven along with the chicken. The tomatoes can be stuffed ahead (do not refrigerate them) then baked after the chicken and potatoes come from the oven. The ice cream should be moved from the freezer to the refrigerator about one half hour before serving, unless you belong to that school that likes hard ice cream.

3

ROAST STUFFED CHICKEN

EQUIPMENT:
French chef's knife; measuring cups and spoons; peppermill; electric blender; saucepan; metal skewers; white string; roasting pan with a rack; kitchen fork; bulb baster or large metal spoon.

INGREDIENTS:

1 ready-to-cook roasting chicken	Half a lemon

STUFFING:

¾ cup (1½ sticks) butter (about)	1 teaspoon thyme
1 onion, *peeled* and *minced*	2½ cups fine, dry *bread crumbs*
1 rib celery, *chopped*	Salt
15 to 20 parsley sprigs, *minced*	*Freshly ground* pepper

In buying chicken figure on about 1 pound per person. Roasting chickens weigh from 4 to 5½ pounds.

To peel, slice, mince, or dice onions, garlic, and shallots the easy way—see directions on page 306.

To mince celery ribs—make 3 or 4 cuts down the entire length, leaving the top intact. Holding the rib together, use a heavy French chef's knife to cut across it.

To mince parsley—hold the blade of a heavy French chef's knife at both ends and chop with rapid up-and-down motions, pulling the ingredients back into a pile with the knife as you work.

Preheat the oven to 350° (or moderate) for 15 minutes before placing the chicken in to roast.

Rub the inside of the chicken with the cut side of half a fresh lemon. Set bird aside.

Melt 6 tablespoons of the butter in a saucepan. Add the onion and ½ cup water. Cook over moderate heat until all the water has boiled away and the onion is limp and transparent. Combine with the celery, parsley, thyme, bread crumbs, 2 tablespoons of the butter (melted), and salt and pepper to *taste*. The stuffing should be moist but not soggy.

Stuff the chicken, fasten the opening with the metal skewers and *truss*. Place on a rack in a roasting pan. Rub the entire surface of the chicken well with the remaining butter, softened. Sprinkle lightly with salt and pepper.

Roast in the preheated oven, uncovered, for 1 hour and 20 to 30 minutes.

Use firm day-old bread for bread crumbs (1 slice makes ¼ cup). Break into pieces and grind crust and all in the electric blender or crumble by hand until very fine.

Use a peppermill for this. Freshly ground pepper is more vibrant than already-ground pepper. Both black and white peppercorns are available, the former being somewhat lustier.

Learn to taste. This makes sense, since one person's salt-and-pepper tolerance can be quite different from another's.

To truss—see directions on page 306.

To baste—spray, spoon, or brush a liquid or melted fat over food while it cooks.

Baste every 15 minutes with pan juices, using a bulb baster or long metal spoon. If there is not sufficient juice, add more melted butter. Test for doneness: The juices should run clear yellow when a drumstick is pierced at the thickest part with a fork and the leg should feel soft when squeezed.

Allow the chicken to "rest" 15 to 20 minutes after it comes from the oven. This allows juices to settle and makes carving easier.

Unstuffed Roasted Chicken: Rub the inside of the bird with the cut side of a lemon, salt, pepper, ½ teaspoon of dried thyme; tuck in a few stalks of parsley. Truss and roast at same temperature as for stuffed chicken, although for a slightly shorter time. Test for doneness as above.

GIBLET GRAVY

EQUIPMENT:
Medium saucepan with a cover; large metal spoon; sieve; wire whisk.

Very popular with Americans, Giblet Gravy is best used when the accompanying vegetables are not "saucy." In short, when a gravy or sauce seems in order.

Giblets include the gizzard, heart, and liver. The liver, delicate and delicious can be used in a special way (see page 261). Freeze, then wrap properly for later use.

INGREDIENTS:

Giblets	1 or 2 stalks parsley
⅓ cup dry white wine	1 onion
1 teaspoon salt	2 cloves
3 or 4 peppercorns	1 carrot, coarsely chopped

In saucepan, combine the neck and giblets (except the liver) with ⅔ cup water and the wine. Add salt; peppercorns; parsley; onion (skin on), cut in half, stuck with the cloves; and the carrot.

To simmer—cook liquid just below boiling (185°) so that it just shivers.

Bring to boil, then boil for 1 minute. With spoon, skim off any scum that rises to the surface. Cover, reduce heat to *simmer*, and cook for 1 hour.

Strain the broth through a fine sieve, then *reduce* to 1 cup. *Taste* for salt and pepper. When the chicken is roasted, add the pan juices to the broth.

If you are accustomed to slightly thickened gravy, make a beurre manié by working into a paste 1 tablespoon of flour with 1 of butter. Drop into the sauce in little bits and cook, whipping constantly with a wire whisk, until slightly thickened. Pour into a heated sauceboat to serve.

To reduce—simply boil liquid over a high heat until the amount left is what the recipe specifies.

Learn to taste. This makes sense, since one person's salt-and-pepper tolerance can be quite different from another's.

WHOLE BAKED TOMATOES

EQUIPMENT:
Baking pan just large enough to accommodate tomatoes; paring knife; peppermill; pastry brush; French chef's knife; bulb baster or large metal spoon.

INGREDIENTS:
6 firm, ripe tomatoes, all of a size

Freshly ground pepper

Olive oil

Minced parsley

Salt

Use a peppermill for this. Freshly ground pepper is more vibrant than already-ground pepper. Both black and white peppercorns are available, the former being somewhat lustier.

Preheat the oven to 400° (hot).

Brush baking pan lightly with olive oil. Set aside for the moment.

Using a sharp paring knife, cut out the stem ends of the tomatoes, making as small a hole as possible. Sprinkle salt and pepper into the opening. Brush the tomatoes all over with oil, then place in the prepared pan, stem side down.

Bake for 10 minutes or until the skins just begin to show signs of breaking. No longer or the tomatoes will burst. Using a bulb baster or spoon, baste once or twice with the pan juices. When cooked, place on a warm serving platter and sprinkle with the minced parsley. Serve at once.

To mince parsley—hold the blade of a heavy French chef's knife at both ends and chop with rapid up-and-down motions, pulling the ingredients back into a pile with the knife as you work.

POTATOES DAUPHINOIS

EQUIPMENT:

Measuring cups and spoons; peppermill; vegetable peeler; grater; 1½-quart baking dish attractive enough to go to the table; large, heavy saucepan; small, sharp knife; Saran.

INGREDIENTS:

2 cups milk	6 cloves garlic, peeled
½ cup (1 stick) butter	1 cup heavy cream
Salt	3 tablespoons freshly grated Swiss
Freshly ground white pepper	cheese, about
4 large Idaho baking potatoes	

Use a peppermill for this. Freshly ground pepper is more vibrant than already-ground pepper. Both black and white peppercorns are available, the former being somewhat lustier.

Preheat the oven to 425° (hot) 15 minutes before baking the potatoes.

Butter baking dish well and set aside.

Combine in saucepan the milk, butter, and salt and pepper to *taste*. Place over moderate heat and bring to a boil slowly. Take off the heat.

Learn to taste. This makes sense, since one person's salt-and-pepper tolerance can be quite different from another's.

Peel the potatoes with a vegetable peeler; wash and dry thoroughly. Do not soak in water or you will lose the starch the dish needs. Slice fairly thin, dropping the slices into the hot milk as you work, so they won't discolor. When all the potatoes have been added, add the garlic and cream. Again, bring up to a boil slowly and *simmer* about 15 minutes or until the potatoes feel slightly resistant when tested with the point of a small sharp knife. Pour into the prepared casserole. (The potatoes can be prepared in advance to this point, sealed with Saran, and set aside.)

To simmer—cook liquid just below boiling (185°) so that it just shivers.

Sprinkle generously with grated cheese and bake in the preheated oven until the potatoes are tender, the sauce has thickened slightly, and the cheese has melted and turned golden. Approximately 10 to 15 minutes. Serves 6.

CHOCOLATE SAUCE

EQUIPMENT:
Measuring cups and spoons; double boiler; wooden spatula.

INGREDIENTS:

1 package (6-ounce size) semisweet chocolate pieces

2 squares (1-ounce size) unsweetened chocolate

3 tablespoons strong powdered instant coffee

1 cup heavy cream

2 tablespoons Cognac or rum (optional)

Melt chocolate over hot—not boiling—water, because if steam rises, then condenses, the chococlate will tighten and become unmanageable. Should this happen, add 2 tablespoons of vegetable shortening and work into the chocolate until it becomes soft again.

Combine the two chocolates and the instant coffee in the top of a double boiler. *Melt* over hot water. Remove from the heat and stir with a wooden spatula until smooth. Gradually stir in the cream and Cognac until smooth. Makes 1½ cups. Serve hot over ice cream.

Refrigerated, securely covered in a jar, this sauce keeps most successfully. To reheat, place jar, uncovered, in a pan of hot water over very low heat. When hot, stir until smooth.

———— ◆ ————

FRIED CHICKEN

Mashed Potatoes   *Milk Gravy*

Bibb Salad with White Grapes, Garlic Dressing

Brownies   *Coffee*

YOUR COOKING SCHEDULE: Since the chicken needs to stand in the cream mixture for 8 hours, it would make sense to start it the day before. A few hours more won't make one iota of difference in the cooked chicken. The lettuce must be washed considerably in advance so that it is thoroughly dry.

The garlic dressing actually improves if made somewhat ahead but, as always, the salad should be tossed just before it is eaten. The Brownies certainly can be baked early in the day or the day before.

About forty minutes before dinner is to be served, bring the chicken from the refrigerator and coat it. At approximately the same time, start the potatoes. Meanwhile, cut and arrange the Brownies on a suitable serving dish. Obviously, the gravy is a last-minute job.

FRIED CHICKEN

EQUIPMENT:
Measuring cups and spoons; peppermill; 2-cup measuring cup or pitcher; large polyethylene bag; bowl or pan; garbage bag; cake rack; large, heavy skillet; candy thermometer; tongs; paper towels; baking sheet; wire whisk.

INGREDIENTS:
2 ready-to-cook 2½ pound broiler-fryer chickens, cut into frying pieces
1 cup heavy cream
2 teaspoons salt
2 teaspoons *freshly ground* black pepper

1 teaspoon Tabasco
1 cup all-purpose flour, plus 2 tablespoons
1 pound lard
½ cup (1 stick) butter

Use a peppermill for this. Freshly ground pepper is more vibrant than already-ground pepper. Both black and white peppercorns are available, the former being somewhat lustier.

Combine the cream, 1 cup cold water, 1 teaspoon of the salt, 1 teaspoon of the pepper and the Tabasco in measuring cup or pitcher. Pour into a large polyethylene bag. Add the chicken pieces, squeeze out all air, and tie securely. Place in a pan or bowl in case of leakage and refrigerate for at least 8 hours. Turn whenever you think of it so chicken will be well bathed.

When it comes time to fry the chicken, combine 1 cup of the flour with the remaining salt and pepper in a heavy bag (a fresh garbage bag is just the ticket). Lift the chicken pieces from the cream mixture, shake off any excess but do not dry. Drop the pieces, a few at a time, into the bag of seasoned flour and shake until each piece is well coated. Place on a cake rack and allow to dry for about 1 hour. Set the cream mixture aside to use in making the gravy.

Melt the lard and butter in the skillet. Heat to 325° on a candy thermometer. Place the chicken pieces, a few at a time (don't crowd the pan) skin side down in the hot fat and cook until golden. About 10 minutes. Turn with tongs, taking care not to break the crust, and cook on the second side 7 to 8 minutes. Do not overcook. As the pieces are cooked, lift from the skillet onto a baking sheet lined with a couple of layers of paper towels to drain. Place in a low, keep-warm (140°) oven until serving time. Serves 5 to 6.

To make the gravy: Pour off all but 2 tablespoons of the fat from the skillet. Stir in the remaining 2 tablespoons of the flour until smooth. Then add the reserved cream mixture and cook, whipping constantly with a wire whisk until smooth and slightly thickened.

MASHED POTATOES

EQUIPMENT:
Vegetable peeler; 2 generous saucepans with covers; small sharp knife; potato ricer; wooden spatula or electric beater.

Allow about 1½ medium, mature potatoes per person. Peel with a vegetable peeler or paring knife, then quarter. The pieces should be approximately all of a size so they will all finish cooking at the same time. Drop into saucepan of boiling water, enough to cover. Add the lid. Cook over moderate heat until tender when pierced with the point of a small sharp knife. Drain at once and dry quickly by shaking the pan over high heat.

Learn to taste. This makes sense, since one person's salt-and-pepper tolerance can be quite different from another's.

Force the potatoes through a ricer into a dry saucepan. Add a few lumps of butter, salt and pepper to *taste*, and a few tablespoons of hot cream. Beat vigorously with a wooden spatula or an electric beater until very smooth. If they are not to be used immediately, set aside uncovered. To reheat, cover and place over hot water, beating occasionally to prevent a skin forming on top.

One of the best of the convenience products is instant potatoes. These can well be substituted for "boiling your own." Season and keep warm as directed.

BIBB SALAD WITH WHITE GRAPES, GARLIC DRESSING

EQUIPMENT: French chef's knife.

The combination of tender Bibb with sweet white grapes and garlic dressing is delicious. The proportions depend on how many you are serving. About 8 grapes, washed, then pulled off the stems and dried would be enough for 1 person. Make a Sauce Vinaigrette (page 44) and add one small clove garlic finely *minced*. Combine the washed, dry fresh greens with the grapes, then toss in the dressing.

To wash Bibb, slosh the heads up and down in warm, not too hot, water so the leaves wilt and release any dirt that has crept into their little indentations. Then drop the heads into a basin of very cold water to tighten the heads up again. To dry, shake off as much water as possible, then wrap the heads, root side turned up, in fresh dish towels and chill in the hydrator of refrigerator.

To peel, slice, mince, or dice onions, garlic, and shallots the easy way, see directions on page 306.

RICH BROWNIES

EQUIPMENT:

Measuring cups and spoons; mixing bowl; flour sifter; 8-inch square baking pan; double boiler; rotary or electric beater; wooden spatula; cake rack; metal spatula.

INGREDIENTS:

½ cup (1 stick) butter

2 squares (1-ounce size) unsweetened chocolate

1 cup sugar

2 eggs

½ cup *sifted* all-purpose flour

½ teaspoon salt

1 cup coarsely chopped walnuts

½ teaspoon vanilla

To measure sifted flour properly, spoon it—after sifting—into a dry measuring cup well above the top, then level or cut off with the edge—not the flat surface—of a metal spatula or knife. Do not shake flour down.

Preheat the oven to 350° (or moderate) for 15 minutes before baking the brownies.

Grease the pan and set aside.

Melt the chocolate in the double boiler top over hot water. In a bowl, cream or work the remaining butter until soft and fluffy, using your hands or an electric beater. Gradually work in the sugar. Add the eggs, one at a time, beating very hard with a rotary or electric beater after each addition. Combine the flour and salt in a sifter and sift straight into the mixture. Stir in with a wooden spatula. Finally, thoroughly mix in the nuts, melted chocolate, and vanilla.

Pour into the prepared pan and bake in the preheated oven for 25 to 30 minutes. Properly baked the brownies are soft to the touch when pressed lightly.

Cool in the pan set on a cake rack. Cut into 16 even squares in the pan. Lift out carefully with a metal spatula.

To grease a pan—crumple up a little waxed paper, scoop up a bit of butter and coat the bottom and sides of the pan generously.

Melt chocolate over hot—not boiling—water because if steam rises, then condenses, the chocolate will tighten and become unmanageable. Should this happen, add 2 tablespoons of vegetable shortening and work into the chocolate until it becomes soft again.

———◆·◆———

Gazpacho

BROILED CHICKEN   *Creamed Mushrooms*

Orange and Onion Salad

Crème Brulée   *Coffee*

YOUR COOKING SCHEDULE: The Gazpacho must be made in time to allow for a good long chilling. So make it in the morning or even the day before. The chicken should be at room temperature before broiling. If it has been refrigerated, allow about 1 hour before you prepare it, and 25 minutes all told to broil it. The mushrooms can be all but finished (see recipe) any time during the day. The crème of the Crème Brulée can be prepared, if more convenient, a day ahead, then finished long enough before serving to chill in the refrigerator—about two hours. The salad can be prepared shortly before dinner or, if earlier in the day, refrigerated and protected by a covering of Saran or foil. But add the dressing just before taking it to the table.

Although the menu does not call for bread, your family may like it. If so, serve a good French or Italian bread, sliced rather thick, presented in a napkin-lined bowl. Nice for mopping up the good sauces.

GAZPACHO

EQUIPMENT:

Electric blender; measuring cups and spoons; sharp paring knife; large mixing bowl; wooden spatula; vegetable peeler; French chef's knife; small spoon; 2 medium-size bowls.

As a first course, a cup of Gazpacho is sufficient, but if served on a hot summer's day for lunch—a very good idea, too—a big bowlful is delicious, followed by cheese, perhaps, and fruit.

INGREDIENTS:

6 very large, very ripe tomatoes
2 tablespoons white wine vinegar
1 cup fresh white bread *crumbs*

3 large cloves garlic, *peeled* and *minced*
1 teaspoon salt
4 tablespoons olive oil

To peel, slice, mince, or dice onions, garlic, and shallots the easy way—see directions on page 306.

GARNISH:

1 ripe tomato, in small cubes
1 large cucumber

3 or 4 green onions, chopped fine
2 large green peppers, diced

Bread crumbs are most easily made in the electric blender. Lacking that, crumble day-old, firm bread with your hands, crust and all, until very fine. Commercial bread crumbs are too dry for this recipe.

To peel tomatoes—cover with boiling water for a minute or so, or actually boil for 10 seconds. Cut out the stem end with a sharp paring knife, then peel off the skin. To seed—slice in half crosswise. Squeeze gently to extract the seeds.

Peel and *seed* the tomatoes. Chop coarsely and set aside. Sprinkle the vinegar over the bread crumbs in the mixing bowl; add the garlic, salt, and olive oil and work together with a wooden spatula to make a smooth paste. Combine with the tomatoes in the container of the electric blender and blend at high speed until smooth. Add about 1 to 2 cups of ice water, depending on how thin you like your Gazpacho, and refrigerate. It must be very cold when served.

Peel the cucumber with a vegetable peeler. With chef's knife slice in half and scoop out the seeds with a spoon. Dice into small cubes. Slice the ends off the peppers, slice in two, remove the ribs and seeds. Dice. Place each in a separate bowl.

To serve, place each of the chopped garnishes in a small serving bowl, so each person can help himself. Serves 4 to 6.

BROILED CHICKEN

EQUIPMENT:

Measuring cups and spoons; peppermill; heavy French chef's knife; tongs or 2 large spoons; bulb baster or large metal spoon; 2-pronged kitchen fork.

INGREDIENTS:

2 ready-to-cook 2½-pound broiler-fryers
½ cup (or 1 stick) butter, *softened*

Freshly ground white pepper
2 tablespoons kosher salt
Minced parsley

Figure on ½ broiler per person and have the butcher quarter them and cut out the backbone.

To soften butter—take it from the refrigerator an hour or so before using.

Remove broiling pan before lighting the broiler, or the chicken pieces will stick.

Use a peppermill for this. Freshly ground pepper is more vibrant than already-ground pepper. Both black and white peppercorns are available, the former being somewhat lustier.

To mince parsley—hold the blade of a heavy French chef's knife at both ends and chop with rapid up-and-down motions, pulling the ingredients back into a pile with the knife as you work.

Preheat the *broiler* to the highest point for 15 minutes before broiling the chicken.

Bring the chicken pieces to room temperature if they have been refrigerated. Allow about 1 hour.

Coat the individual pieces, on both sides, with as much butter as will cling to them. Best done with your hands.

Lay skin side down on the cold broiler rack. Sprinkle lightly with freshly ground pepper, then sprinkle with half the salt.

Place in the broiler about 4 inches from the heating unit and broil for 15 minutes; then turn, using tongs or 2 spoons so as not to break the skin, sprinkle with freshly ground pepper and the remaining salt, and broil for 10

To baste—spray, spoon, or brush a liquid or melted fat over food while it cooks.

minutes on the skin side. *Baste* the chicken every 5 minutes throughout the entire broiling time, using the remaining butter first, then the pan drippings. A bulb baster is ideal for this because it sucks up the pan juices and you can spray them over the chicken. It's more efficient than a spoon.

To test for doneness—pierce the fleshy part of the legs or thigh with the fork. The juice that comes out should be a clear yellow. If tinged with pink, broil a few minutes longer. Perfectly cooked, the chicken is moist and succulent inside, crisp and brown on the outside.

Arrange the chicken pieces on a hot, serving platter. Spoon all the delicious drippings and brown crustiness from the broiling pan over them. Sprinkle with the minced parsley and serve immediately. Serves 4.

VARIATIONS:

Garlic butter: Mince I small clove of garlic and, with your hands, mix into the softened butter along with a good squeeze of fresh lemon juice.

Tarragon butter: With your hands, mix into the softened butter about 1½ teaspoons dried tarragon, crumbled.

Marinated chicken: Combine 1 cup olive oil, ½ cup white vinegar, 6 green onions (scallions), tops and bulbs, minced very fine, 1 tablespoon salt, and 1 teaspoon freshly ground white pepper. Pour into a polyethylene bag. Add the chicken pieces, tie bag securely, and place in a pan in case of leakage. *Marinate* 2 or 3 hours, turning the bag frequently so the chicken will be well saturated. Follow broiling instructions, basting with the marinade, rather than with butter.

To marinate—soak or steep meats or other foods in a marinade (seasoned liquid) to impart flavor and, in some instances, to tenderize.

CREAMED MUSHROOMS

EQUIPMENT:
Can opener; measuring cups and spoons; peppermill; lemon squeezer; medium kitchen bowl; medium heavy saucepan; wooden spatula; Saran.

INGREDIENTS:

1 can (4-ounce size) sliced mushrooms

2 tablespoons (or ¼ stick) butter

1½ tablespoons flour

1 cup heavy cream

Juice ½ lemon

Freshly ground white pepper

Salt

2 tablespoons dry vermouth or white wine

Use a peppermill for this. Freshly ground pepper is more vibrant than already-ground pepper. Both black and white peppercorns are available, the former being somewhat lustier.

Open the can of mushrooms and drain off all the liquor into the bowl. Set aside.

Make a roux by heating the butter in the saucepan and stirring in the flour until smooth. Then cook over a low heat, stirring constantly with a wooden spatula for 3 to 4 minutes. Do not allow the roux to brown.

Add the liquor from the mushrooms, the cream, lemon juice, salt and pepper to *taste*. Bring up to a boil stirring constantly, until the sauce has thickened slightly. Can be prepared in advance to this point, sealed with Saran and set aside.

Learn to taste. This makes sense, since one person's salt-and-pepper tolerance can be quite different from another's.

A few minutes before dinnertime, add the mushrooms and bring up to a boil again. Do not cook further. Just before serving, stir in the wine. Serves 4.

Also good served with cold braised beef, cold roast turkey or chicken, or cold fresh tongue. Can be used too as a filling for omelets, over toast as a tasty luncheon dish or for Sunday breakfast.

ORANGE AND ONION SALAD

EQUIPMENT:

Measuring spoons; peppermill; small paring knife; electric blender or mortar and pestle; very sharp stainless-steel knife; medium kitchen bowl; lemon squeezer; wire whisk.

INGREDIENTS:

2 large red Italian onions	Salt
2 large navel oranges	*Freshly ground* white pepper
4 tablespoons olive oil	*Rosemary*, ground
1 tablespoon lemon juice	

Peel the onions, then with the stainless-steel knife, slice as thin as possible. Next, peel the orange. Slice the *peeled* oranges very thin, on the bias; in other words, at a 45° angle. Sliced in this fashion, the membrane between the sections is minimized. Work over a bowl to catch any juices.

Arrange the onion and orange slices alternately on a flat serving platter.

Combine with the oil and lemon juice any orange juice you salvaged. Add salt, pepper, and rosemary to *taste*. Whip together with a wire whisk. Pour over the salad just before serving. Serves 4.

To peel, slice, mince, or dice onions, garlic, and shallots the easy way—see directions on page 306.

To peel or section citrus fruits (oranges, lemons, grapefruit)—see directions on page 307.

Learn to taste. This makes sense, since one person's salt-and-pepper tolerance can be quite different from another's.

Use a peppermill for this. Freshly ground pepper is more vibrant than already-ground pepper. Both black and white peppercorns are available, the former being somewhat lustier.

If ground rosemary is not available, pulverize the spiky dried leaves in the electric blender or pound them in a mortar and pestle.

CRÈME BRULÉE

EQUIPMENT:

Measuring cups and spoons; saucepan; mixing bowl; electric or rotary beater; wire whisk; 1-quart baking dish attractive enough to go to the table; roasting pan; small kitchen knife; foil.

INGREDIENTS:

2 cups heavy cream	⅛ teaspoon salt
4 egg *yolks*	1 teapsoon vanilla
2½ tablespoons sugar	Brown sugar

If you haven't mastered the trick of separating egg yolks from egg whites, see directions on page 305.

To scald milk or cream— heat it to the boiling point, when it will wrinkle on top.

Preheat the oven to 350° (or moderate) for 15 minutes before putting the custard in the oven.

Scald the cream in the saucepan.

In the mixing bowl, beat the egg yolks vigorously with an electric or rotary beater until very thick and creamy. Beat in the sugar and salt. Then add the hot cream very slowly, stirring constantly with a wire whisk. Finally stir in the vanilla. Pour into baking dish. Place the baking dish in a roasting pan. Add enough hot water to reach to two-thirds the depth of the dish.

Bake in the preheated oven for 1 hour or until *done*.

Remove from the oven and refrigerate. The crème can be prepared to this point the day before, covered with foil when cold, and refrigerated.

To finish the Crème Brulée (pronounced krem broo-lay) sift a layer of brown sugar, to a depth of ⅓ inch, over the cold crème, place in a preheated broiler, 4 to 5 inches from heating unit, until the sugar melts and forms a hard, crunchy crust that you can tap with your fingernail.

This takes only a minute or two, so don't even close the oven door. Chill in the refrigerator before serving.

Test by the standard method for baked custards. If the custard is to be served cold, insert the blade of a knife 1 inch from the outside edge; if it is to be served hot, insert the knife 1 inch from the center. With both tests the knife blade should come out clean; that is, without any mixture clinging to it.

———— ◆ ————

POACHED CHICKEN WITH LEMON SAUCE

Buttered Noodles   *Onions in Casserole*
(page 111)

Cucumber Salad, Swedish Style

Apple Ping   *Coffee*

YOUR COOKING SCHEDULE: The chicken should go on the stove about 2½ hours before dinnertime. If you have two ovens, you can bake the Apple Ping almost anytime at all, depending on whether you intend to serve it warm or at room temperature. Most people like it best slightly warm. Otherwise, it must come out of the oven in time to allow you to cook the onions, which need about an hour to bake. Use the noodle recipe on p. 111, omitting the poppy seeds. The cucumber salad needs a mellowing period in the refrigerator. Therefore, it can be made way ahead, even days.

POACHED CHICKEN WITH LEMON SAUCE

EQUIPMENT:
Heavy French chef's knife; kitchen string; large kettle with a cover; large metal spoon; strainer; long wooden spoon.

A poached chicken is the basis for many a good meal. It can be served at once with boiled potatoes and baked onions. It is the raison d'être for Chicken Aspic as well as for real Chicken Salad, Chicken Curry, Chicken Pie, and Chicken Hash. Small quantities of cooked chicken (about 2 cups, chopped) can be turned into Chicken Mousse or a Chicken Soufflé. The broth, with rice and vegetables added, can be used as a sturdy soup or clarified to make jellied soup; finally it can be strained and frozen to use in recipes calling for chicken stock. Freeze in small quantities (about a pint) to make it easier to use when needed.

INGREDIENTS:

1 5-to-6 pound stewing *chicken*	6 stalks parsley (about)
Chicken neck	1 bay leaf
2 onions, *skin on*, split, stuck with 4 cloves	6 to 8 peppercorns
1 large carrot, coarsely chopped	1 teaspoon salt
3 ribs celery with leaves, coarsely *chopped*	1 teaspoon thyme

Truss the chicken if the butcher has not already done it. Place, breast side down, in the kettle, with all ingredients except the *thyme*. Cover with cold water and bring to a boil slowly. Skim off with a large metal spoon any scum

Do not choose a stewing chicken (a mature female chicken) that weighs less than 5 pounds. Also called hens or fowl, they are less tender, also less expensive than roasting chickens. Properly poached, however, they yield delicious meat.

Don't bother to peel onions when used as seasoning and cooked in a liquid that will be strained. Leaving the skin on will add a little color to the finished broth.

To chop celery ribs—make 3 or 4 cuts down the entire length, leaving the top intact. Holding the rib together, use a heavy French chef's knife to cut across it.

To truss—see directions on page 306.

Add the thyme after skimming so you won't skim it off.

To simmer—cook liquid just below boiling (185°) so that it just shivers.

that rises to the surface. Reduce heat to *simmer* and add the thyme. Cover and cook very slowly until a drumstick is soft when squeezed, and the skin just begins to shrink from the tip of the leg. The length of time will depend on the size of the bird and its age. Count on 1½ hours to 2 hours. Do not overcook. Meat should not fall from the bones.

To reduce—simply boil a liquid over a high heat until the amount left is what the recipe specifies.

Once the chicken has been removed from the broth, place the kettle back over a high heat and *reduce* until there are about 5 to 6 cups of concentrated broth left. Strain. Any you are not using immediately should be refrigerated in pint jars or frozen for future use.

If the chicken is not to be used at once, refrigerate immediately in the broth, uncovered. Give broth an occasional stir to help cool it off as quickly as possible so it won't turn sour. Cover when stone cold.

To present poached chicken: Lift from the broth by sticking a long wooden spoon into the cavity. Allow any broth to drain back into the kettle. Place on a warm serving platter and spoon some of the Lemon Sauce over it. Tuck a parsley bouquet in the tail.

Carve as you would roast chicken. Serve more Lemon Sauce in a warm sauceboat. Serves 5 to 6.

Another Way: Carve the chicken in the kitchen in rather large pieces. Arrange on a heated serving platter. Spoon Lemon Sauce all over the chicken pieces. Serve any extra sauce in a warm, sauceboat.

LEMON SAUCE

EQUIPMENT:
Double boiler; measuring cups and spoons; strainer, lemon squeezer; French chef's knife; wire whisk; spoon; wooden spatula; Saran.

If you haven't mastered the trick of separating egg yolks from egg whites, see directions on page 305.

Use arrowroot as a thickening agent when you want the finished sauce to be clear and transparent. Do not cook beyond the point indicated or the sauce will "thin out."

Use a peppermill for this. Freshly ground pepper is more vibrant than already-ground pepper. Both black and white peppercorns are available, the former being somewhat lustier.

INGREDIENTS:

3 egg *yolks*

2 teaspoons *arrowroot*

Salt

Freshly ground white pepper

2 cups chicken broth, strained

Juice 1 lemon

8 to 10 parsley sprigs, *minced*

Combine yolks, arrowroot, salt and pepper to *taste* in the top of a double boiler. Whip together with a wire whisk until well combined. Add the chicken broth gradually, whipping constantly. Cook over simmering water, whipping vigorously, until the sauce will coat a spoon. Can be prepared to this point in advance, sealed with Saran and set aside.

Sauce can be heated up over simmering water. Stir constantly with a wooden spatula. It must not be allowed to boil or it will curdle. Just before serving stir in the lemon juice and parsley.

To mince parsley—hold the blade of a heavy French chef's knife and chop with rapid up-and-down motions, pulling the ingredients back into a pile with the knife as you work.

Learn to taste. This makes sense, since one person's salt-and-pepper tolerance can be quite different from another's.

ONIONS IN CASSEROLE

EQUIPMENT:

Measuring cups and spoons; sharp paring knife; peppermill; large, heavy skillet; large ovenproof casserole that is attractive enough to go to the table and large enough to hold the onions in 1 layer; kitchen fork.

To peel, slice, mince, or dice onions, garlic and shallots the easy way—see directions on page 306.

INGREDIENTS:

24 small, uniform white onions, *peeled*

1½ tablespoons butter

1½ tablespoons vegetable oil

½ cup canned condensed beef broth

Salt

Freshly ground pepper

4 stalks parsley

½ bay leaf

Good pinch dried thyme

Use a peppermill for this. Freshly ground pepper is more vibrant than already-ground pepper. Both black and white peppercorns are available, the former being somewhat lustier.

Preheat the oven to 350° (or moderate) for 15 minutes before baking the onions.

To sauté—cook or brown food in a very small amount of very hot fat.

Heat the butter and oil in the skillet until bubbling. Add the onions and *sauté* over moderate heat for 10 minutes, shaking the pan to roll them around so they will brown as evenly as possible.

Add the broth, salt and pepper to *taste*, parsley, bay leaf and thyme, then pour into casserole.

Learn to taste. This makes sense, since one person's salt-and-pepper tolerance can be quite different from another's.

Bake, uncovered, in the preheated oven for 40 to 50 minutes or until onions are tender when pierced with the point of a small sharp knife, but still shapely. Turn them over once or twice to brown them. Remove the parsley and the bay leaf.

The onions can be cooked hours ahead, then reheated in a low (140°) oven. Serves about 6.

CUCUMBER SALAD, SWEDISH STYLE

EQUIPMENT:
Measuring cups and spoons; fork; French chef's knife; wooden spatula; mixing bowl; Saran.

INGREDIENTS:

2 large firm cucumbers	6 tablespoons sugar
2 teaspoons salt	⅔ cup white or cider vinegar

Wipe the cucumbers with a fresh, damp cloth. Then *score* the skin. Slice the cucumbers very, very thin. Place in the bowl and sprinkle with salt and sugar. Add the vinegar. Then, using the back of a wooden spatula, press the slices until the salad becomes quite juicy. Refrigerate. A sort of uncooked pickle—cool, crisp, and delicious—that will keep extremely well in a covered jar, refrigerated. Serves 5 to 6.

To score—pull the tines of a sharp fork down the length of the cucumber all around. Not essential, but decorative.

APPLE PING

EQUIPMENT:

Measuring cups and spoons; flour sifter; 1-quart casserole or deep baking dish; vegetable peeler; apple corer; medium mixing bowl; rotary or electric beater; wooden spatula.

INGREDIENTS:

To measure sifted flour properly, spoon it—after sifting—into dry measuring cup (or spoon) well above the top, then level or cut off with the edge—not the flat surface—of the metal spatula or knife. Do not shake flour down.

Always pack down brown sugar when measuring cup quantities.

1 cup *sifted* all-purpose flour
½ teaspoon baking powder
⅛ teaspoon salt
4 tablespoons (½ stick) butter
1 cup brown sugar, firmly *packed*

5 firm cooking apples
1 egg
1 cup granulated sugar
¼ cup boiling water
1 teaspoon vanilla

Preheat the oven to 375° (or moderate) for 15 minutes before baking the Ping.

Sift the flour, baking powder, and salt together. Set aside.

Combine the butter and brown sugar in the casserole. Place in preheated oven just long enough for the butter to melt.

Peel and core the apples. Cut in half, then into eighths. Take the casserole out of the oven, but leave the heat on. Mix the apple slices thoroughly into the butter-sugar mixture. Set aside.

In the mixing bowl, beat the egg with a rotary or electric beater until light in color, gradually beating in the granulated sugar. Add the boiling water and vanilla. Then thoroughly stir in the flour mixture, using the wooden spatula. Pour the batter over the apples, place in the oven and bake 45 to 60 minutes or until the hard crust "pings" when tapped with your fingernail.

Serve warm or at room temperature with heavy cream.

CURRIED CHICKEN WITH CONDIMENTS

Boiled Rice, the Chinese Way

Cold Beer or Chilled Alsatian Wine

Oranges in Syrup   *Coffee*

YOUR COOKING SCHEDULE: On the assumption that the chicken is already poached, this is not a difficult menu. The Curry Sauce can be prepared in advance, even a day ahead, and the chicken can be added at the time the sauce is reheated. With the exception of the bacon and scallions, the condiments come in cans or jars. The rice can be cooked in advance. If more than a day or so, it can be frozen. The oranges, however, must be prepared the day they are to be served because they don't "stand" well overnight. Obviously, the beer or wine should have time enough in the refrigerator to be properly chilled.

CURRIED CHICKEN WITH CONDIMENTS

EQUIPMENT:
Measuring cups and spoons; sharp paring knife; apple corer; vegetable peeler; lemon squeezer; heavy French chef's knife; peppermill; small sauce-

pan; large, heavy enameled saucepan; wooden spatula; kitchen scissors; Saran.

Curried chicken makes a splendid buffet supper because it can be prepared ahead and reheated. Further, since it is not necessary to use knives, it can be eaten "on the lap" as it were. Lamb, veal, chicken, turkey, shellfish, eggs and some vegetables lend themselves to being curried.

INGREDIENTS:

The meat (approximately 4 cups) from a Poached Chicken (page 22) cut into large bite-size pieces

2 large onions, *peeled* and chopped fine

2 large apples, cored, and chopped fine

2 to 3 tablespoons good curry

½ cup all-purpose flour

4 cups chicken broth, strained and heated

1 cup heavy cream

Salt

Freshly ground pepper

Lemon juice

To peel, slice, mince, or dice onions, garlic, and shallots the easy way—see directions on page 306. Cored apples can be chopped as you would onions.

Use a peppermill for this. Freshly ground pepper is more vibrant than already-ground pepper. Both black and white peppercorns are available, the former being somewhat lustier.

Melt the butter in the large saucepan. Add the onions, apples and 1½ cups water. Cook over moderate heat until all the water has boiled away and both onions and apples are soft. If necessary, add more water. Stir in the curry, using a wooden spatula, and cook for about 2 minutes. Taste here to see how strong a curry flavor you want. Next, stir in the flour until smooth and cook another 3 to 4 minutes. Then stir in the hot broth and *simmer* for 10 to 15 minutes, giving mixture an occasional stir. Finally, add the cream, salt, pepper, and lemon juice to *taste*. Add the chicken meat and bring up to a boil.

To simmer—cook liquid just below boiling (185°) so that it just shivers.

Learn to taste. This makes sense, since one person's salt-and-pepper tolerance can be quite different from another's.

Since our assumption is that you are using a poached chicken, you will, therefore, have both chicken meat and broth to work with. Lacking your own broth, canned condensed chicken broth can be used equally well. For a smaller quantity of meat (about 2 cups which might be left over from a roast chicken) simply cut the sauce recipe in half.

If the curry is not to be served at once, seal with Saran. Keep hot over simmering water taking care not to cook further. Pour into a deep, warm serving dish and serve with several condiments. Serves 6 to 8.

Condiments: Unlike India, where the curry business all started, it is customary in this country to serve curry with a battery of condiments: such things as flaked *coconut,* crisp *bacon pieces,* peanuts or chopped almonds, chopped chives or scallions, raisins soaked in cognac and always chutney. Place each in a separate serving bowl so that each person can help himself.

Use commercial coconut which is readily available. Fresh coconut can be used, of course, but it's quite a production to open and grate it.

To fry bacon in pieces— take it straight from the refrigerator. Don't separate it. Cut, with a pair of kitchen scissors, into ½-inch pieces. Drop into a cold frying pan, turn heat to moderate and cook until crisp. The pieces will separate as they warm up. Drain on paper towels.

BOILED RICE, THE CHINESE WAY

EQUIPMENT:
Medium kitchen bowl; colander; 1½-quart saucepan with cover; kitchen fork; heavy French chef's knife.

Long-grain white rice should be used whenever rice plays an important role in a recipe or menu.

To cook *long-grain rice* the Chinese way, wash in a bowl of cold water, rubbing the grains between your palms. Rinse until the water is clear. Drain in colander.

To simmer—cook liquid just below boiling (185°) so that it just shivers.

Pour 2 cups washed rice into the *saucepan;* add 3 cups cold water. Bring to a boil. Lower heat to *simmer,* cover and cook 15 to 20 minutes or until all the water has been absorbed. Fluff the rice with a fork. Pour into a warm serving dish. If not to be served immediately, cover lightly with a fresh dish towel and keep warm over hot water.

Be sure to use a 1½-quart saucepan. If too small a pan is used, the rice will boil over when covered, and it is essential to cover it.

Parsleyed Rice: Just before serving, stir about ½ cup of parsley sprigs, minced, into the rice. Serves 6 to 8.

ORANGES IN SYRUP

EQUIPMENT:
French chef's knife; vegetable peeler; small, sharp knife; heavy saucepan; large kitchen bowl.

INGREDIENTS:
6 navel oranges
1 cup sugar
Grand Marnier

To cut thin pieces of peel from citrus fruit—use a vegetable peeler.

Using a vegetable *peeler*, cut the rind off two of the oranges in long, very thin pieces, taking care not to pick up any of the white skin. With the small knife, cut the rind into long slivers. Combine in the saucepan with the sugar and ½ cup water. Bring to a boil slowly. Cook over moderate heat for about 8 minutes or until the syrup is about as thick as corn syrup. Remove from the heat.

To peel and section citrus fruit—see directions on page 307.

Meanwhile, *section* the oranges and place in the bowl. Pour the hot syrup over the oranges and refrigerate. Just before serving, stir in about 2 tablespoons of Grand Marnier (or to taste).

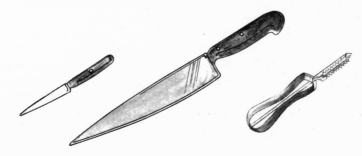

Hot Consommé with Sherry

CHICKEN SOUFFLÉ

Olive and Mushroom Sauce

French Bread   *Belgian Endive*

Rich Strawberry Shortcake   *Coffee*

YOUR COOKING SCHEDULE: The base for the Chicken Soufflé, as the recipe indicates, can be prepared early in the morning. You can also make the Olive and Mushroom Sauce as well as the shortcake. A total of an hour, at the most, in the kitchen should clear up this much of the cooking. This soufflé is an excellent way to use up bits and pieces left from a roast or poached chicken (pages 4 and 22) that are not handsome enough to appear some other way.

The strawberries should be washed, then hulled, sometime before they are used in order to dry and, for good flavor, kept at room temperature. Once dry, they can be mashed and set aside. As for the endive, remove any withered leaves, split each endive in half or quarters lengthwise, place in a polyethylene bag and refrigerate. Shortly before dinner arrange on individual plates and dress with Sauce Vinaigrette (page 44). The shortcake must be finished just before going to the dinner table if you would serve it at its most delicious best.

Finally, heat canned condensed consommé to the boiling point, without diluting. Spoon a tablespoon of dry sherry into each soup cup, then add the boiling bouillon. Serve at once.

CHICKEN SOUFFLÉ

EQUIPMENT:

Measuring cups and spoons; flat grater; can opener; peppermill; nutmeg grater; 1-quart soufflé dish; heavy saucepan; wooden spatula; electric blender; wire whisk; Saran; rotary or electric beater; rubber spatula.

Anyone with her wits about her can make a soufflé, for it is nothing more than a thick sauce into which, first, egg *yolks*, then beaten egg *whites* are incorporated. The beaten whites are the secret ingredient; the air in them, in the form of little bubbles, expands as the soufflé cooks and pushes it into its magnificent puff. The flavoring element can be almost anything—cheese, chocolate, lemon, orange, chicken, oysters, corn, and so on. Once you've mastered one soufflé, you've mastered them all.

If you haven't mastered the trick of separating egg yolks from egg whites, see directions on page 305.

INGREDIENTS:

3 tablespoons butter	Salt
6 tablespoons *freshly grated* Parmesan cheese	Freshly ground white pepper
2 tablespoons flour	*Freshly grated* nutmeg
1 cup chicken broth (your own or canned condensed), heated	4 whole eggs, separated
	2 or 3 extra egg whites
	1½ cups finely *diced* chicken meat

Cut Parmesan cheese into relatively small chunks and grate in the blender or on a flat grater. The ready-grated, available in jars, does not have the vibrant quality of freshly grated.

For this, you need a small nutmeg grater and, of course, whole nutmegs. Like cheese and pepper, freshly grated nutmeg makes all the difference in the finished dish because the flavor is so delicious.

To dice—cut into fairly small, even pieces.

Preheat the oven to 375° (or moderate) for 15 minutes before the soufflé goes in the oven.

To coat—spoon the grated cheese into the buttered soufflé dish. Then, holding the dish in your hands, roll it around and around so that the cheese covers sides and bottom evenly but lightly. Turn upside down and give it a good bang to get rid of any surplus. Best done over the sink.

Beat egg whites only to the stiff, shiny stage. If beaten longer, they become granular.

For exact folding technique —see directions on page 305.

Butter the soufflé dish heavily, making sure you cover the curve at the bottom of the dish. *Coat* with 2 tablespoons of the cheese. Refrigerate.

Melt the remaining butter in the saucepan, and with a wooden spatula stir in the flour until smooth. Cook over moderate heat for 2 or 3 minutes, stirring constantly. Do not allow this mixture, the roux, to brown. Add the hot broth, then cook, whipping constantly with a wire whisk, until the sauce (correctly called Velouté) has thickened. Season to *taste* with salt, pepper, and nutmeg. Stir in 2 tablespoons of the cheese. Cool slightly. Add the egg yolks, one at a time, beating hard with a wire whisk after each addition. The sauce can be prepared in advance to this point, sealed with Saran, and set aside.

Beat the egg whites with a rotary or electric beater until they hold stiff, shiny peaks when the beater is held up straight. Whip about a third of the beaten whites into the sauce vigorously with the wire whisk. Mix in the chicken, using a rubber spatula, then *fold* in the remainder of the whites.

Spoon into the prepared soufflé dish, sprinkle with the remaining cheese, and bake in the preheated oven for 25 to 30 minutes. Serve at once with Olive and Mushroom Sauce. Serves 4.

To serve, place the soufflé dish on a tray with a folded linen napkin underneath. This keeps the dish from sliding around when you plunge into it. Also, it looks attractive.

Learn to taste. This makes sense, since one person's salt-and-pepper tolerance can be quite different from another's.

OLIVE AND MUSHROOM SAUCE

EQUIPMENT:
Measuring cups and spoons; French chef's knife; paring knife; can opener; peppermill; heavy saucepan with a cover; wooden spatula; fine sieve; medium saucepan; Saran.

INGREDIENTS:

2 tablespoons (¼ stick) butter
1 carrot, coarsely chopped
1 medium onion, coarsely *chopped*
1 garlic clove, coarsely *chopped*
3 tablespoons flour
2 cups chicken broth (your own or canned condensed)
1 can (8-ounce size) tomato sauce

¼ teaspoon dried thyme
1 bay leaf
Salt to taste
Freshly ground white pepper
½ cup pitted green olives
1 can (4-ounce size) mushroom caps, drained

To peel, slice, mince, chop or dice onions, garlic and shallots the easy way—see directions on page 306.

Use a peppermill for this. Freshly ground pepper is more vibrant than already-ground pepper. Both black and white peppercorns are available, the former being somewhat lustier.

Melt the butter in the heavy saucepan, add the carrot, onion, and garlic. Cook over a very low heat, stirring occasionally with a wooden spatula, until almost tender but not browned. Stir in the flour until smooth, then add all remaining ingredients except the olives and mushrooms. Bring to a boil, reduce heat to *simmer*, cover, and cook for 30 minutes. *Taste* for seasoning. Strain through a fine sieve into a clean medium saucepan. Add the olives and mushrooms. Place back over the heat just long enough to heat through. The sauce can be prepared ahead, sealed with Saran, then reheated at serving time. Caution: Reheat to boiling point only. Makes about 3 cups.

To simmer—cook liquid just below boiling (185°) so that it just shivers.

Learn to taste. This makes sense, since one person's salt-and-pepper tolerance can be quite different from another's.

BELGIAN ENDIVE SALAD

EQUIPMENT:
French chef's knife.

To prepare, discard any withered leaves and slice off the tips of the root ends. Split each stalk lengthwise, twice. Arrange in a shallow serving dish or on individual plates and dress with Sauce Vinaigrette (page 44). One stalk is usually sufficient for one person.

RICH STRAWBERRY SHORTCAKE

EQUIPMENT:

Measuring cups and spoons; colander; flour sifter; nutmeg grater; 8-inch round cake pan; mixing bowl; pastry blender; wire whisk; wooden spatula; metal spatula; toothpicks; cake rack; kitchen fork; rotary or electric blender.

To far too many Americans strawberry shortcake is sponge cake soaked with strawberry juice and served with a blob of whipped cream. A far cry from a rich cake such as this, which puts Strawberry Shortcake in the same league as such lovely French desserts as Vacherin aux Fraises (meringues with strawberries and cream).

INGREDIENTS:

½ cup (1 stick) butter (cold)
2 cups (1 pint) fresh strawberries
   (about)
2 cups *sifted* all-purpose flour
¼ cup sugar
4 teaspoons *baking powder*

½ teaspoon salt
Few grains freshly grated nutmeg
2 egg *yolks*
⅓ cup milk
1 cup heavy cream

To measure sifted flour properly—spoon it—after sifting—into a dry measuring cup (or spoon) well above the top, then level or cut off with the edge—not the flat surface—of a metal spatula or knife. Do not shake flour down.

Two baking powders are available: regular or double acting. Use regular unless a recipe specifies double acting.

If you haven't mastered the trick of separating egg yolks from egg whites, see directions on page 305.

Preheat the oven to 450° (or very hot) for 15 minutes before baking the shortcake.

Butter cake pan thoroughly, making sure you include the curve at the bottom. Set aside.

Wash the unhulled strawberries, drain in a colander until thoroughly dry.

Meanwhile sift all dry ingredients together into the mixing bowl. Cut the remaining butter into 3 or 4 pieces, then with the pastry blender work it into the dry ingredients until the mixture looks mealy. Beat the egg yolks slightly with a wire whisk. Stir into the flour mixture along with the milk, using the wooden spatula. Stir only until all the flour has disappeared. Don't attempt to beat the batter smooth. Spoon into the prepared pan and smooth the top with a metal spatula dipped in milk. (This helps to prevent batter sticking to the spatula).

Place in the preheated oven and bake for 12 minutes or until a toothpick inserted in the center comes out dry. Turn out on a cake rack to cool.

Back to the strawberries. Hull and set 8 or so of the handsomest aside to decorate the cake. Crush the remainder with a fork and sweeten with superfine sugar to taste.

To finish, cut shortcake in half horizontally to make two layers. Place the bottom layer on a serving plate, cover with the crushed strawberries, top with the second layer. Whip the cream (with a little sugar if you like it sweet), spoon over the top of the cake and arrange the whole strawberries on top. Serve immediately.

CHICKEN SALAD

Fresh Sliced Tomatoes with Basil   *Baked Toast*

Pavé au Chocolat   *Coffee*

YOUR COOKING SCHEDULE: The chicken should be poached a day in advance and cooled in its own broth (see recipe page 22). However, in dire necessity, it could be done the same day if the meal is to be served at night. In which case, the chicken must be removed from the broth immediately after it's cooked, then wrapped securely and cooled quickly in the refrigerator. When cool, not necessarily cold, follow recipe instructions. The Pavé is best done the day it is served and long enough in advance to give it time to mellow. Allow 3 hours, but do not refrigerate because the texture of the frosting changes. The tomatoes should be prepared shortly before serving and the toast can be baked any time you have a free moment. The day before, if you like.

CHICKEN SALAD

EQUIPMENT:
Large mixing bowl; peppermill; lemon squeezer; kitchen spoon.

Once the meat is stripped from the bones of the Poached Chicken and all skin and gristle is removed, cut into nice big pieces. (Don't fall for that snide trick of mincing the meat and mixing it up with a lot of chopped celery to stretch it.) Use both light and dark meat for best flavor. Place in a large bowl, mix in salt and *freshly ground* white pepper to *taste*. Pepper and chicken are singularly sympatico, so be generous here.

Combine with enough Mayonnaise—made with lemon juice in place of vinegar—to coat the meat lightly. Mix with your hands rather than a spoon, so as not to break up the chicken pieces.

Use a peppermill for this. Freshly ground pepper is more vibrant than already-ground pepper. Both black and white peppercorns are available, the former being somewhat lustier.

Learn to taste. This makes sense, since one person's salt-and-pepper tolerance can be quite different from another's.

Lift into a large salad bowl (crystal is pretty) and surround with lettuce, preferably Bibb because the green is so green, tucking the ends under the salad. Spoon a little mayonnaise on top. You can, if you like, add a garnish of capers, well drained. Serve extra mayonnaise in a serving bowl. Serves 5 or 6.

Sometimes it makes a nice change to combine the Mayonnaise with sour cream. Allow about ½ cup to 1¼ cups mayonnaise.

Chicken Salad Variations: Add 1 cup or so of fresh seedless grapes, washed and dried; or add 1 cup of walnuts, coarsely chopped, to the salad before mixing with Mayonnaise.

BLENDER MAYONNAISE

EQUIPMENT:
Electric blender; measuring cup and spoons.

INGREDIENTS:

2 egg yolks

½ teaspoon dry mustard

½ teaspoon salt

2 tablespoons vinegar or lemon juice

1 cup vegetable oil or half vegetable and half olive oil

Place the yolks, mustard, salt, vinegar and ¼ cup of the oil in the container of an electric blender. Cover container and turn motor to high. Immediately remove the cover and quickly add the remaining oil in a steady stream. When all the oil is added, turn off the motor. Makes 1¼ cups.

FRESH SLICED TOMATOES WITH BASIL

EQUIPMENT:
Serrated tomato knife; peppermill.

Slice ripe tomatoes thin and arrange, overlapping slightly but not on top of each other, on a flat serving platter. Sprinkle with olive oil, salt, *freshly ground* pepper and crumbled basil to taste.

Allow about 1 large tomato per person.

Use a peppermill for this. Freshly ground pepper is more vibrant than already-ground pepper. Both black and white peppercorns are available, the former being somewhat lustier.

BAKED TOAST

EQUIPMENT:
Serrated bread knife; butter knife; baking or cookie sheet.

Stack several slices of firm white or protein bread and cut off the crusts all at one time, using a serrated bread knife. Then cut into triangles, either two or four to a slice.

Butter very generously with *softened butter*. Place on a baking sheet and bake in a preheated 300° (or slow) oven for 25 to 30 minutes, or until the toast is crisp and golden.

To soften butter—take it from the refrigerator an hour or so before using.

Baked toast tastes just as good cold as hot and keeps remarkably well in a covered container. Note, it's a practical way to use up bread that is going stale.

PAVÉ AU CHOCOLAT

EQUIPMENT:

Measuring cups and spoons; double boiler; electric beater; wooden or rubber spatula; flat, shallow pan or dish; small metal spatula.

INGREDIENTS:

4 squares (1-ounce size) unsweetened chocolate

½ cup (1 stick) butter

¾ cup sifted confectioners' sugar

4 egg *yolks*

4 tablespoons dark rum or Cognac

2 packages (2½-ounce size) ladyfingers

Candied violets or roses, or pistachio nuts (optional)

If you haven't mastered the trick of separating egg yolks from egg whites, see directions on page 305.

Melt chocolate over hot, not boiling, water because if steam rises, then condenses, the chocolate will tighten and become unmanageable. Should this happen, add 2 tablespoons of vegetable shortening and work into the chocolate until it becomes soft again.

Melt the chocolate in the top of the double boiler over hot, not boiling, water. Work or cream the butter with an electric beater until soft and fluffy, then work in the sugar until smooth. Add the egg yolks, one at a time, and beat thoroughly, after each addition. Mix in the melted chocolate.

Using a wooden or rubber spatula combine the rum or Cognac with ¾ cup water in the shallow pan or dish. It must be flat so the ladyfingers can be dipped in the mixture, then flipped over quickly. The important thing is not to allow them to soak or they will disintegrate.

Take one-third of the fingers and dip them, one by one, into the rum mixture. Arrange in a neat row on an oblong serving platter. Cover the top with a coating of the chocolate frosting, using a small metal spatula. Add a second layer of the fingers, frost, then finish off with the remainder of the fingers. Next frost the sides, then the top of the pavé. Garnish with candied violets or roses, if available, or shower with finely chopped pistachio nuts.

Allow to stand at room temperature at least 3 hours for the pavé to mellow. Very rich, so serve in very thin slices.

COQ AU VIN   (Chicken in Wine)

Boiled Potatoes with Parsley

Green Salad, Vinaigrette

Mousse au Chocolat   *Coffee*

YOUR COOKING SCHEDULE: Prepare the Coq au Vin early in the day or even the day before. If the latter, refrigerate and bring to room temperature before reheating. Wash the salad greens thoroughly under cool, not cold, running water. Wrap in a fresh dish towel to dry, tuck into a polyethylene bag, squeeze out all the air, tie securely and refrigerate. Best done immediately after purchase. When you start the potatoes depends on their size. Small new potatoes will take 12 to 15 minutes; mature potatoes 45 to 50 minutes.

COQ AU VIN

EQUIPMENT:
French chef's knife; measuring cups and spoons; peppermill; corkscrew; can opener; large, heavy saucepan; 2 large, heavy skillets with covers; slotted

spoon; large metal spoon; paper towels; large flameproof casserole attractive enough to go to the table; small saucepan; 2-pronged kitchen fork; wire whisk; Saran.

Essentially a stew, this lovely dish is worthy of your most important dinner parties.

INGREDIENTS:

¼ pound salt pork or unsmoked bacon all in one piece

9 tablespoons (1 stick plus 1 tablespoon) butter

2 2½- to 3-pound ready-to-cook, broiler-fryer chickens, cut up for frying

Salt

Freshly ground pepper

¼ cup Cognac or brandy

1 bottle dry white wine

2 cans (10½-ounce size) condensed chicken broth (about)

2 cloves garlic, *peeled* and *crushed*

4 bay leaves

½ teaspoon dried thyme

4 tablespoons vegetable oil

36 small white onions, *peeled*

½ pound button *mushrooms*

3 tablespoons flour

Use a peppermill for this. Freshly ground pepper is more vibrant than already-ground pepper. Both black and white peppercorns are available, the former being somewhat lustier.

To simmer—cook liquid just below boiling (185°) so that it just shivers.

To crush garlic—give it a good whack with a side of a cleaver, heavy knife or any heavy implement.

To peel, slice, mince, or dice onions, garlic, and shallots the easy way—see directions on page 306.

Button mushrooms, the least expensive, are best in cooked dishes. Mushrooms need not be peeled.

Cut the rind off the pork, then cut into pieces about ¼ × 1 inch (known professionally as lardons).

Simmer in a big saucepan of water for 10 minutes. Rinse in cold water and dry. Heat 2 tablespoons of the butter in a skillet, add the pork or bacon and fry slowly until lightly browned. Lift from the fat with a slotted spoon onto paper towels. Set aside.

Pat the pieces of chicken dry with paper towels and brown on both sides in the hot fat. Sprinkle with salt and pepper. Combine the cooked pork or bacon and the chicken pieces in the casserole. Heat the Cognac in the small saucepan, light with a match, and pour over the chicken. Shake the casserole until the flames die out. Add the wine, stir in enough chicken broth to cover the chicken completely. Add the garlic, bay leaves, and thyme. Bring up to a boil, reduce to simmer, cover, and cook slowly for 25 to 30 minutes or until the chicken is tender when pierced with a fork and the juices run clear yellow. Lift the chicken from the casserole and set both aside.

While the chicken is cooking, peel the onions. Heat 3 tablespoons of the butter and 3 tablespoons of the vegetable oil in a large heavy skillet. When hot, add the peeled onions and *sauté* over a moderate heat just long enough to brown the onions as evenly as possible. Shake the pan for about 10 minutes to keep them rolling over. Add the remaining chicken broth, cover, then simmer until the onions are tender. Approximately 20 minutes. Set aside for the moment.

> To sauté—cook or brown food in a very small amount of very hot fat.

Wipe the mushrooms with a damp cloth, cut off the tips of the stems and slice very thin, stems and all. Heat 2 tablespoons of the butter with 1 tablespoon of the oil in a second large skillet. As soon as the fat is very hot, add the mushrooms. Toss and shake the pan for 4 or 5 minutes. As soon as they have browned lightly, remove from the heat. Set aside.

Place the casserole back on the fire, bring the broth to a boil, then *reduce* rapidly until there are about 3 cups left. Lift out and discard the bay leaves. Skim off any superfluous fat with a large metal spoon.

> To reduce—simply boil liquid over a high heat until the amount left is what the recipe specifies.

Mix the remaining butter with 3 tablespoons of flour to make a beurre manié. Drop by bits into the simmering liquid and cook, whipping constantly with a wire whisk for 2 or 3 minutes or until the sauce has thickened enough to coat a spoon. Add the chicken pieces, onions, and mushrooms. Bring up to a boil. *Taste* for seasoning. The Coq au Vin can be prepared in advance to this point, sealed with Saran, and set aside.

> Learn to taste. This makes sense, since one person's salt-and-pepper tolerance can be quite different from another's.

To reheat, bring slowly to a boil, then simmer just long enough to heat the chicken through. Do not cook further or the chicken will be tough and stringy. Serve straight from the casserole garnished with a nice bouquet of fresh parsley. Serves 6 to 8.

BOILED POTATOES WITH PARSLEY

EQUIPMENT:
Big, heavy saucepan with a cover; sharp paring knife; French chef's knife.

Drop the potatoes, in their jackets, into the saucepan with enough boiling salted water to cover them generously. Allow 3 or 4 small new potatoes per person (cook approximately 12 to 15 minutes) or about 1½ medium-size mature potatoes (cook approximately 30 minutes).

Bring to a boil again, add the lid, and cook over moderate heat, until the potatoes can be pierced easily with the point of a small, sharp knife.

Drain at once. Then, to prevent sogginess, dry quickly by shaking the pan over a high heat.

Peel and place in a heated vegetable dish. Add a few tablespoons of melted butter and a sprinkling of *minced* parsley. Keep warm.

To mince parsley—hold the blade of a heavy French chef's knife at both ends and chop with rapid up-and-down motions, pulling the ingredients back into a pile with a knife as you work.

GREEN SALAD WITH SAUCE VINAIGRETTE

EQUIPMENT:
Salad or kitchen bowl; measuring cups and spoons; peppermill; wire whisk; large salad fork and spoon; lemon squeezer.

In this country we know Sauce Vinaigrette as French Dressing. It is a simple basic sauce made with wine vinegar or lemon juice, oil, salt, pepper, fresh minced herbs (parsley, chives, tarragon, or basil), or a pinch of dried herbs, or dry or prepared mustard. Minced garlic can be added if used with a wise hand.

INGREDIENTS:

Wine vinegar or lemon juice
Salt
Freshly ground pepper

Dry or prepared French mustard
(optional)
Peanut or olive oil or half of each

Use a peppermill for this. Freshly ground pepper is more vibrant than already-ground pepper. Both black and white peppercorns are available, the former being somewhat lustier.

Pour into salad bowl ½ to 2 tablespoons of vinegar or lemon juice (the amount depends on how sharp you like your dressing). Add a dash of salt, pepper, and if you like, ¼ teaspoon dry or prepared mustard. Whip with a wire whisk until the mixture is perfectly smooth. Add 6 tablespoons of oil, by drops, whisking vigorously. If you are using herbs, add them to the dressing at this point (a good pinch of dried or about a tablespoon of fresh, minced). These measurements make about ½ cup. Figure on 1 tablespoon of dressing per person.

Wash all salad greens under cool running water to eliminate the sand, shake to get rid of as much surplus water as possible, roll in a fresh dish towel to dry, and refrigerate in the vegetable container.

Add the *greens*, broken up if necessary, as you are ready to take the bowl to the table. (It is essential for the salad greens to be dry. Otherwise, the sauce will not cling to the leaves.) Then toss with a large fork and spoon.

MOUSSE AU CHOCOLAT

EQUIPMENT:

Double boiler; 2 medium mixing bowls; rotary or electric beater; large serving bowl; rubber spatula; Saran.

INGREDIENTS:

2 bars (4-ounce size) sweet cooking
    chocolate
6 eggs, *separated*

⅛ teaspoon salt
1 cup heavy cream

If you haven't mastered the trick of separating egg yolks from egg whites, see directions on page 305.

Melt chocolate over hot, not boiling, water because if steam rises, then condenses, the chocolate will tighten and become unmanageable. Should this happen, add 2 tablespoons of vegetable shortening and work into the chocolate until it becomes soft again.

Melt the chocolate in the top of a double boiler. Beat the egg yolks with a rotary or electric beater until thick and creamy. Then, with a rubber spatula, stir in the melted chocolate.

Add the salt to the egg whites and *beat* with a rotary or electric beater until they form stiff, shiny peaks when you hold the beater straight up. Scoop all the beaten whites on top of the cooled chocolate mixture. Then *fold* in with a rubber spatula.

Whip the cream until it holds a shape. Then fold it, too, into the mousse. Pour into a large serving bowl, seal with Saran and refrigerate. Serve with or without whipped cream.

Beat egg whites only to the stiff, shiny stage. If beaten longer, they become granular.

For exact folding technique —see directions on page 305.

Fresh Mushroom Soup

CHICKEN BREASTS SAUTÉED IN BUTTER

Green Beans   *Risotto*

Angel Paper   *Coffee*

YOUR COOKING SCHEDULE: The soup can be prepared early in the day, then heated up just before dinner in a double boiler. In which case, cook it initially in the top of the double boiler (this will save you two pots), seal with Saran and refrigerate. The butter can be clarified and the parsley minced whenever you have a minute. Wrap parsley in a fold of waxed paper to keep it from drying, and refrigerate. Both the beans and the risotto (take a look at the recipes) can also be prepared ahead—the beans even a day early if you like. The Angel Paper must be prepared the day before. Actually, the only last-minute cooking is the chicken breasts and they should be started about 25 minutes before dinner is served.

FRESH MUSHROOM SOUP

EQUIPMENT:

French chef's knife; can opener; measuring cups; nutmeg grater; electric blender; Saran; double boiler.

INGREDIENTS:

1 pound fresh, white button *mushrooms*	½ cup heavy cream
	Salt
2 cans (10½-ounce size) condensed chicken broth	*Freshly ground* nutmeg
	Minced parsley

Wipe the caps of the mushrooms with a clean damp cloth and chop coarsely, stems and all. Place a small quantity at a time in the container of the electric blender along with a small amount of the chicken broth. Blend until all the mushrooms have been puréed. Then pour into the top of the double boiler with

Button mushrooms, the least expensive, are best in cooked dishes. Mushrooms need not be peeled.

For this, you need a small nutmeg grater and, of course, whole nutmegs. Like cheese and pepper, freshly grated nutmeg makes all the difference in the finished dish because the flavor is so delicious.

To mince parsley—hold a heavy French chef's knife at both ends and chop with rapid up-and-down motions, pulling the ingredients back into a pile with the knife as you work.

all remaining broth and the heavy cream. Season to taste with salt and nutmeg.

Bring to a boil over a low heat. (If you are preparing the soup in advance, seal with Saran to prevent skin forming, and refrigerate.) When reheating to serve, do not cook further or you'll lose all that lovely woodsy flavor. Serve in heated cups with a sprinkling of parsley. Serves 6.

To serve cold: Chill, covered, in the refrigerator. Garnish with parsley just before serving.

CHICKEN BREASTS SAUTÉED IN BUTTER

EQUIPMENT:
Measuring cups and spoons; peppermill; heavy French chef's knife; saucepan; large, heavy skillet; lemon squeezer.

INGREDIENTS:

6 chicken breasts (boned and skinned)	Flour
Salt	¾ cup (1½ sticks) butter, *clarified*
Several twists of the peppermill (white pepper)	10 to 12 parsley sprigs, *minced*
	1 tablespoon lemon juice

To clarify butter—see directions on page 306.

To mince parsley—hold a heavy French chef's knife at both ends and chop with rapid up-and-down motions, pulling the ingredients back into a pile with the knife as you work.

Sprinkle the breasts with salt and pepper, then roll in flour, shaking off any excess. Set aside for the moment.

Pour enough of the clarified butter into a good-size, heavy skillet to cover the bottom with a good film. Place over a moderate heat. When the butter begins to turn color ever so slightly, add the chicken breasts—only as many as the pan will accommodate without crowding. Allow at least ¼ inch between chicken breasts, otherwise they will steam rather than brown. *Sauté* about 3 minutes. Turn the breasts and sauté the other side for 2 minutes, or until they feel springy to the touch. At that point they should be cooked perfectly. Place on a heated platter and keep warm.

To sauté—cook or brown food in a very small amount of very hot fat.

Add the remaining clarified butter to the skillet and place over a moderately high heat until the butter has turned brown—a minute or two at most. Immediately remove from the heat, stir in the parsley and lemon juice and *taste* for seasonings. Pour over the breasts and serve at once. Serves 6.

Learn to taste. This makes sense, since one person's salt-and-pepper tolerance can be quite different from another's.

GREEN BEANS

EQUIPMENT:
Large kettle; colander; peppermill.

INGREDIENTS:

Choose clean, fresh, firm beans that "snap" when broken.

3 pounds green *beans*	*Freshly ground* pepper
Salt	Butter

Use a peppermill for this. Freshly ground pepper is more vibrant than already-ground pepper. Both black and white peppercorns are available, the former being somewhat lustier.

Wash the beans. If small, leave whole but snip off the ends; if large, slice on the bias about 2½ inches long.

Bring a large kettle of water with salt (allow about 1½ teaspoons per quart) to a rolling boil. Drop the beans, a handful at a time, into the rapidly

Always cook green vegetables uncovered to retain their color.

boiling water. Bring to a boil again as quickly as possible, then reduce heat to moderate. Boil *uncovered* until beans are tender but still with some crispness. Depending on age and size, this will take from 10 to 15 minutes. Take a taste after they've cooked about 8 minutes. When cooked, drain at once. Pour back into the kettle and shake over a high heat until all moisture has evaporated.

Learn to taste. This makes sense, since one person's salt-and-pepper tolerance can be quite different from another's.

If the beans are to be used immediately, season to *taste* with salt and pepper, turn into a heated serving dish and add 3 or 4 good lumps of butter. Serves 6.

If not to be served at once, run the beans under cold water to stop the cooking and retain the color. Then dry thoroughly in a fresh dish towel. Set aside in a colander or refrigerate in a covered bowl. They will keep nicely for about 24 hours.

To reheat: Place the beans in a pan with a couple of tablespoons of hot melted butter. Cover and place over moderate heat just long enough to heat through. Shake the pan occasionally so that the beans become coated with butter.

To serve as a salad—simply toss the cold beans in Sauce Vinaigrette (page 44).

RISOTTO

Use an enameled pan because iron or aluminum will discolor foods containing wine or egg yolks.

EQUIPMENT:

Measuring cups and spoons; French chef's knife; grater; can opener; good-size heavy *enameled* saucepan; wooden spatula; corkscrew.

Riso, in Italian, means "rice," and risotto means "cooked rice." A fine risotto is creamy but, at the same time, chewy. It takes a bit of experimenting to achieve this result, but it's worth the effort. The variations on risotto are almost endless. The basic risotto can be turned into a main dish by the addition of cooked fish, shellfish, chicken, game, meat, or vegetables.

INGREDIENTS:

3 tablespoons butter

1 small onion, *minced*

1 cup *long-grain* rice

⅔ cup dry white wine

4 cups chicken broth (your own) or 3 cans (10½-ounce size) heated

Saffron, about 3 filaments

2 tablespoons *freshly grated* Parmesan cheese

To peel, slice, mince or dice onions, garlic, and shallots the easy way—see directions on page 306.

Long-grain white rice should be used whenever rice plays an important role in a recipe or menu.

Cut Parmesan cheeese into relatively small chunks and grate in the blender. It is available in jars, ready-grated, but does not have the vibrant quality of freshly grated cheese.

Melt 2 tablespoons of butter in saucepan. Add the minced onion and cook over moderate heat, stirring constantly, until the onion has turned pale gold. Do not allow it to brown. Now add the rice, stirring with a wooden spatula, until every grain is completely coated with the butter (about 3 minutes). The rice must remain white.

Add the wine and cook, still over a moderate heat, until the wine has almost all evaporated. Add the saffron filaments to 1 cup of the hot broth and set aside to steep. Add the remainder of the hot broth, about a cup at a time, to the rice. As the broth is absorbed, add more. Finally, strain in the saffron broth.

It will take from 20 to 25 minutes for the rice to absorb all the broth and to finish cooking. When done, it will be tender and creamy, but not sticky. Stir constantly during the last few minutes or rice may stick to the pan.

Just before serving, stir in 1 tablespoon of butter and 2 tablespoons of grated cheese. Serve additional butter and cheese separately. Serves 4 to 6.

ANGEL PAPER

EQUIPMENT:
Six custard cups; waxed paper; measuring cups and spoons; rotary or electric beater; cookie or baking sheet; heavy 8-inch saucepan; bulb baster or large metal spoon.

INGREDIENTS:

Butter	1½ cups sugar
6 egg *yolks*	3 to 4 whole cloves

If you haven't mastered the trick of separating egg yolks from egg whites, see directions on page 305.

To butter—crumple up a little waxed paper, scoop up a bit of butter and coat the bottom and sides of each cup generously.

To simmer—cook liquid just below boiling (185°) so that it just shivers.

Preheat the oven to 375° (or hot) for 15 minutes before baking the yolks.

Butter 6 custard cups well. Beat the egg yolks vigorously with a rotary or electric beater until very thick and creamy. Divide evenly among the cups. Place cups on a cookie sheet and bake in the preheated oven for 10 minutes.

Meanwhile, combine the sugar and 1 cup of water and the cloves in the saucepan. Stir until the sugar is dissolved and the mixture comes to a boil. Reduce heat to *simmer* and cook for 2 to 3 minutes. Turn the cooked yolks into the bubbling syrup, bring the heat up to moderate and cook 2 minutes, *basting* constantly with the syrup, using either a bulb baster or large metal spoon. Refrigerate overnight.

To baste—spray, spoon, or brush a liquid or melted fat over food while it cooks.

To serve, place one of the little "crowns" in each serving dish with a spoonful of the syrup.

A Brazilian delicacy that is unusually interesting and extremely good.

PALETTE KNIFE   MEDIUM METAL SPATULA   LONG METAL SPATULA   RUBBER SPATULA   WOODEN SPATULA   "KITCHEN" CAKE SPATULA

THE SPATULAS

Wooden spatulas (you should have at least two) are better than wooden spoons for stirring because the flat surface is easily scraped off on the side of a pan or bowl; rubber spatulas with wooden handles (have two, at least) are indispensable for stirring, folding, creaming, "smearing" and scraping out bowls or pans; stainless-steel spatulas are necessary for lifting foods, when flexibility is important, and also in frosting; palette knives are especially valuable for frosting small cakes; the "kitchen" cake spatula is useful to lift large foods, such as cakes or fish, onto serving platters.

CORNISH HENS

ROCK CORNISH GAME HENS

Stuffed Mushrooms   *Puréed Celeriac*

Green Onion Salad

Cheesecake   *Coffee*

YOUR COOKING SCHEDULE: Since the cheesecake needs a good long spell in the oven, you might even make it the night before and leave it there all night. Failing that, then up with the birds so your oven will be free when it comes time to roast the hens and bake the mushrooms. Both can go in the oven at approximately the same time. You should probably give yourself about half an hour to stuff the mushrooms and another 20 to 25 minutes to stuff the hens. While you are in the kitchen doing these two jobs, it would be as good a time as any to prepare and cook the onions so they will have sufficient time to chill. Sauce Vinaigrette (p. 44) is, of course, a matter of seconds.

ROCK CORNISH GAME HENS

EQUIPMENT:
Measuring cups and spoons; kitchen string; roasting pan (or pans) with a rack; bulb baster or a large metal spoon.

A special breed, they are a cross between Rock Cornish and White Rock birds. Small, available frozen, each weighs about 1 pound or slightly better. Serve 1 to a person. Thaw in the refrigerator in original wrappings (allow about 24 hours), or place in a polyethylene bag, with all air squeezed out and tied securely, and thaw under running water.

Preheat the oven to 450° (or hot) for 15 minutes before roasting the hens.

Rock Cornish Hens can be roasted with or without stuffing. See stuffing for chicken (page 4).

To roast, cover each breast with a thin slice of salt pork or bacon and tie securely. Add to the pan 1 tablespoon butter for each hen. Place on a rack in a roasting pan and roast, uncovered, in the preheated oven for 5 minutes. Reduce heat to 350° (or moderate) and continue roasting another 15 to 20 minutes, depending on size. Make the doneness test (page 5). *Baste* frequently with pan drippings, using a bulb baster or large metal spoon. Serve with the pan juices.

To baste—spray, spoon, or brush a liquid or melted fat over food while it cooks.

Cold, unstuffed: These little hens are ideal to take on picnics if you belong to the elaborate-picnic school.

STUFFED MUSHROOMS

EQUIPMENT:

Measuring cups and spoons; heavy French chef's knife; peppermill; sharp, paring knife; grater for cheese; large skillet; kitchen tray or cookie sheet; wooden spatula; rotary or electric beater.

INGREDIENTS:

18 big mushrooms
Salt
2 tablespoons (¼ stick) butter
2 tablespoons vegetable oil
1 medium onion, *minced*
Dash dried thyme
Dash *freshly ground* pepper

1 large ripe tomato, *peeled, seeded, and chopped*
3 egg *yolks*
¼ cup *freshly grated* Parmesan cheese
¼ cup freshly grated Swiss cheese

To peel, slice, mince or dice onions, garlic and shallots the easy way—see directions on page 306.

Use a peppermill for this. Freshly ground pepper is more vibrant than already-ground pepper. Both black and white peppercorns are available, the former being somewhat lustier.

Wipe the mushroom caps with a clean damp cloth. Break off the stems and set aside. Place caps, bottom side up, in the skillet. Sprinkle with salt. Melt 1 tablespoon of the butter and mix with 1 tablespoon of the oil. Sprinkle over the mushroom caps. Cover and cook over a low heat for 10 minutes. Lift the caps from the skillet and lay, bottom side up, on a clean tray. Refrigerate until cool.

Preheat the oven to 350° (or moderate) for 15 minutes before baking the mushrooms.

Chop the mushroom stems fine. Put the remaining butter and oil into the

To peel and seed tomatoes —cut out the stem ends, with a small, sharp knife, then cover the tomatoes with boiling water and allow to stand for about 20 seconds. (Unripe tomatoes may take a few seconds longer.) Plunge into cold water. Start peeling at the stem end. To seed: slice the tomato in half crosswise. Squeeze gently to extract seeds.

If you haven't mastered the trick of separating egg yolks from egg whites, see directions on page 305.

Cut Parmesan cheese into relatively small chunks and grate in the blender. It is available ready-grated, in jars, but does not have the vibrant quality of freshly grated cheese.

skillet. Add the chopped stems and minced onion and *sauté* 3 minutes, stirring constantly with a wooden spatula. Stir in the thyme, pepper, and tomato. Bring to a boil, then simmer 12 minutes. Remove from the heat. Cool slightly.

Beat the egg yolks with a rotary or electric beater until very thick, then stir gradually into mushroom mixture. Bring to a boil and cook, stirring constantly, for 1 minute. Remove from the heat and cool.

Fill the mushroom caps, dividing the mixture evenly. Sprinkle with the two cheeses, mixed together. Place on a baking sheet and bake in the preheated oven for 25 to 30 minutes or until lightly brown. Serves 6.

To sauté—cook or brown food in a very small amount of very hot fat.

PURÉED CELERIAC

EQUIPMENT:
Vegetable peeler; 2 heavy saucepans with covers; sharp paring knife; potato ricer; wooden spatula; peppermill; double boiler; Saran.

INGREDIENTS:

4 big celeriac	*Freshly ground* pepper
2 medium potatoes	Heavy cream, about ¼ cup
Salt	

Peel the celeriac and potatoes, using a vegetable peeler; quarter, then drop each into separate saucepans of boiling, salted water. Cover and cook until each is tender when pierced with the point of a paring knife. Approximately 20 minutes. Take care not to overcook.

Push both vegetables through a potato ricer, then mix together thoroughly, using a wooden spatula. Season with salt and pepper to *taste* and stir in enough heavy cream to give the mixture a light consistency. Serve at once or keep warm in a double boiler over *simmering* water; seal with Saran. Serves 6.

Use a peppermill for this. Freshly ground pepper is more vibrant than already-ground pepper. Both black and white peppercorns are available, the former being somewhat lustier.

Learn to taste. It makes sense, since one person's salt-and-pepper tolerance can be quite different from another's.

To simmer—cook liquid just below boiling (185°) so that it just shivers.

GREEN ONION SALAD

EQUIPMENT:
French chef's knife; large skillet; fresh dish towels.

Trim off root ends from 4 bunches (about 30) green onions. Cut off all but about 3 inches of the green tops. Drop into a large skillet of boiling, salted water. After the water comes to a boil again, boil, uncovered, for 5 minutes. Lift from the water and cool quickly under cold running water. Drain thoroughly. Then wrap in a fresh dish towel and refrigerate.

To serve, arrange on a platter and coat lightly with Sauce Vinaigrette (page 44). Serves 6.

CHEESECAKE

EQUIPMENT:
Measuring cups and spoons; flat grater; lemon squeezer; flour sifter; electric blender or rolling pin; 8-inch spring-form pan; sieve; 2 medium-size mixing bowls; electric or rotary beater; wooden spatula; large spoon; rubber spatula.

INGREDIENTS:

Shortening
1 package (6-ounce size) zwieback
½ cup sifted confectioners' sugar
½ cup (1 stick) butter, melted
1 pound large-curd creamed cottage
    cheese
4 eggs

1 cup granulated sugar
¼ teaspoon salt
Grated rind 1 large lemon
Juice of the lemon
½ teaspoon vanilla
1 cup heavy cream
¼ cup *sifted* all-purpose flour

To grate rind of citrus fruit, which must be done before squeezing—work on a flat grater placed on top of a piece of waxed paper.

To measure sifted flour properly, spoon it—after

sifting—into a dry measuring cup (or spoon), well above the top, then level or cut off with the edge —not the flat surface—of a metal spatula or knife. Do not shake flour down.

To grease a pan—crumple up a little waxed paper, scoop up a bit of butter and coat the bottom and sides of the pan generously.

If you haven't mastered the trick of separating egg yolks from egg whites, see directions on page 305.

Beat egg whites only to the stiff, shiny stage. If beaten longer, they become granular.

For exact folding technique —see directions on page 305.

Break up the zwieback and grate in the electric blender or, lacking that, roll into fine crumbs with a rolling pin. Mix with the confectioners' sugar and butter.

Preheat the oven to 250° (or low) for 15 minutes before placing the cake in the oven.

Grease spring-form thoroughly, bottom and sides. Set aside about 3 tablespoons of the crumb mixture, then pat the remainder on the bottom and around the sides of the greased pan. It will hold better than you think.

Work cottage cheese into mixing bowl through a sieve to break up the lumps.

Separate the eggs. Beat the yolks with a rotary or electric beater until very thick. Then gradually beat in ½ cup of the granulated sugar until smooth. Combine with salt, lemon rind and juice, vanilla, heavy cream, flour, and the cheese. Mix very thoroughly.

Beat the egg whites with a rotary or electric beater until they form soft peaks. Gradually add the remaining granulated sugar and continue beating until the resulting meringue holds stiff, shiny peaks. Using a rubber spatula, *fold* into the egg mixture. Spoon into the prepared pan carefully so as not to disturb the crumb coating and sprinkle the reserved crumbs over the top. Bake in the preheated oven for 1¾ hours.

Turn the heat off and leave the cake right in the oven until cool. This will take several hours.

To serve, release and remove the sides of the pan, place the cheesecake on a suitable serving platter. Do not attempt to remove the bottom of the pan.

MEASURING CUPS AND SPOONS

*You need two sets of metal cups for dry measuring in four graduated sizes:
¼-cup, ⅓- ½- and 1-cup measure. You need two sets of metal spoons:
¼- ½- 1-teaspoon, one tablespoon. Use a marked-glass measuring cup;
it is desirable to have both 1-cup and 2-cup sizes.*

DRY MEASURING CUPS   MEASURING SPOONS   LIQUID MEASURING CUP

PASTRY EQUIPMENT

*For rolling out pastry or cookies, there is no equivalent
for the pastry cloth and the knitted sleeve that fits
on the rolling pin. With this combination you can roll
dough to paper-thinness. The pastry blender and
the pastry brush are essential and the pastry wheel
is often useful.*

PASTRY BLENDER

PASTRY BRUSH

WHEEL

ROLLING PIN

CLOTH AND SIEVE   FEATHERED PASTRY BRUSH

TURKEY

Oysters on the Half Shell

ROAST TURKEY
WITH SAUSAGE-CHESTNUT STUFFING

Yellow Turnips Mousseline   *Braised Leeks*

Coffee Mousse   *Coffee*

YOUR COOKING SCHEDULE: Depending on the speed with which you work, you should be able to prepare and stuff the bird in an hour. The stuffing itself can be made the preceding day and refrigerated. Assuming you are having dinner at 7 P.M., the turkey should be stuffed and in the oven about 3:30 P.M. While it is roasting, both the turnips and leeks can be cooked, then reheated during the turkey's "resting" period.

Since the mousse "calls for" at least 3 hours in the refrigerator, it can be done a day ahead. Failing that, it must be done early on the day it is to be served.

Oysters, fresh, are always last minute, and the time it takes to present them depends on whether you open them yourself or buy them already opened. Although a salad is not included in the menu, you can, if you wish, serve a mixture of fresh greens with Sauce Vinaigrette (page 44).

OYSTERS ON THE HALF SHELL

EQUIPMENT:
Oyster knife; peppermill.

As a first course it is customary to serve six oysters on the half shell in a bed of crushed ice with lemon wedges and, if you like, *freshly ground* pepper. There are some—we think unfortunately—who serve oysters with what is known as "cocktail" sauce. All it can do for a delicious oyster is to destroy its delicate flavor.

If you do not open the oysters yourself but, rather, buy them opened from the fish market, then be sure to ask for deep shells on which to serve them.

Use a peppermill for this. Freshly ground pepper is more vibrant than already-ground pepper. Both black and white peppercorns are available, the former being somewhat lustier.

ROAST TURKEY WITH SAUSAGE-CHESTNUT STUFFING

EQUIPMENT:
Measuring cups and spoons; heavy French chef's knife; electric blender; peppermill; can opener; large, heavy skillet; slotted spoon; large mixing bowl; cheesecloth; large roasting pan with rack; bulb baster or large metal spoon; 2-pronged kitchen fork; white string; wooden spatula; strainer; saucepan.

INGREDIENTS:

1 8- to 10-pound ready-to-cook
    turkey
Half a lemon
1½ cups (3 sticks) butter
1 medium onion, *minced*
½ pound pork sausage
Turkey liver and heart, chopped
    fine
2 cups unseasoned *bread crumbs*
½ teaspoon thyme
5 or 6 parsley sprigs, *minced*

Salt
Freshly ground pepper
1 can (11-ounce size) imported
    whole fresh *chestnuts*, drained,
    coarsely chopped
Heavy cream or Cognac
2 medium onions, chopped
2 medium carrots, chopped
2 ribs celery, chopped
2 cups chicken broth, your own or
    canned condensed

To peel, slice, mince or dice onions, garlic and shallots the easy way—see directions on page 306.

Use firm day-old bread for bread crumbs (1 slice makes ¼ cup). Break into pieces and grind crust and all in the electric blender, or crumble by hand until very fine.

To mince parsley—hold the blade of a heavy French chef's knife at both ends and chop with rapid up-and-down motions, pulling the ingredients back into a pile with the knife as you work.

To sauté—cook or brown food in a very small amount of very hot fat.

Use a peppermill for this. Freshly ground pepper is more vibrant than already-ground pepper. Both black and white peppercorns are available, the former being somewhat lustier.

To shell fresh chestnuts is a difficult and messy job. Canned chestnuts (*marrons entier au naturel*) are expensive, but worth the price.

Preheat the oven to 350° (or moderate) for 15 minutes before the turkey goes in.

Rub the inside of the turkey with the cut side of half a lemon, salt, and pepper. Set aside.

Melt 2 tablespoons of the butter in a large, heavy skillet. Add the chopped onion and a ½ cup of water. Bring to a boil and cook over moderate heat until all the water has boiled away and the onions are tender and translucent. If necessary, add a little more water. Scoop out of the pan with a slotted spoon into a large bowl.

Add the sausage to the skillet, breaking it up with a fork as it begins to cook. Brown lightly. Add to the onion. Drain off all fat from the pan.

Melt 2 tablespoons of the butter in the same skillet. When hot, add the liver and heart and *sauté* lightly. Now, in the mixing bowl, combine thoroughly the sautéed onions, sausage, liver and heart, bread crumbs, thyme, parsley, salt, pepper, and chopped chestnuts. If the stuffing seems too dry, add a few tablespoons of cream or Cognac. Stuff the cavity of the turkey and *truss*.

To truss—see directions on page 306.

(Any of the stuffings suggested for chicken (page 4) can be used to stuff turkey. Double the quantities, all except the seasonings, which must be added by taste. You need about 6 cups of stuffing for any 8-pound bird.)

Smooth the skin of the turkey all over, generously, with softened butter (allow about ½ cup—1 stick) and sprinkle with salt and pepper. Soak a double layer of fresh cheesecloth, large enough to drape over the breast, legs and thighs, in ½ cup melted butter.

Scatter the chopped onions, carrots, and celery in the bottom of a large roasting pan. Place the turkey on a rack, above the vegetables.

Roast in the preheated oven for about 3 hours (approximately 25 minutes per pound). *Baste* with the pan drippings, every 20 minutes or so, right through the cheesecloth. Half an hour before the bird has finished cooking, remove the cheesecloth to allow it to brown. Test for doneness; juices should run clear when the drumstick is pierced with a fork in the thickest part. The leg feels soft when squeezed and moves easily in its socket.

Remove the turkey to a heated platter and allow to *"rest"* for 20 to 30 minutes. Meanwhile, make the *sauce* by adding the chicken stock to the roasting pan. Bring to a boil, scraping down with a wooden spatula all the brown particles that adhere to the pan. *Reduce* to 1½ cups. *Taste* here for salt and pepper. Remove from the heat, strain into a saucepan and add a tray of ice cubes. The fat will congeal around the ice, and both can then be discarded. Bring sauce to a boil again and boil another 3 to 5 minutes. Pour into a heated sauceboat.

Unstuffed Roast Turkey: The technique is the same as for stuffed turkey but see Unstuffed Chicken (page 5) for the preparation of the bird. Roast at 350° (or moderate) in a preheated oven, although for a slightly shorter time than for a stuffed turkey (about 20 minutes per pound). The test for doneness (see Roast Stuffed Turkey) is the sure way to know when it is properly

To baste—spray, spoon or brush a liquid or melted fat over food while it cooks.

If you prefer the traditional Giblet Gravy (although with this menu we would not recommend it), see recipe, page 5.

To reduce—simply boil liquid over a high heat until the amount left is what the recipe specifies.

Allow any roasted poultry or meat that is to be carved a "resting" period to give the juices time to settle and to make carving easier.

Learn to taste. This makes sense, since one person's salt-and-pepper tolerance can be quite different from another's.

roasted. Like an overcooked chicken, turkey cooked too long is dry and tasteless.

Cold Roast Turkey follows the hot feast as naturally as night follows day. We suggest for the first course a good soup, perhaps Vichyssoise (page 211). With the bird, Asparagus Hollandaise (page 94), brown-and-serve rolls with sweet butter, and for dessert sliced fresh peaches with a dollop of Kirsch.

To present the turkey, carve in the kitchen, arrange on a platter and garnish with a bouquet of watercress or parsley.

YELLOW TURNIPS MOUSSELINE

EQUIPMENT:
Vegetable peeler or sharp paring knife; French chef's knife; 2 saucepans with covers; sieve; food mill or potato ricer; electric beater or electric mixer; double boiler; Saran.

INGREDIENTS:

3 large yellow turnips	Pepper
3 large potatoes	Butter, softened
1 teaspoon sugar	Heavy cream
Salt	

Peel the turnips and potatoes, using a vegetable peeler, then slice into *cubes*. Cook each separately in boiling salted water, covered, until tender when pierced with the point of a small, sharp knife. Drain extremely well and dry quickly by shaking pans over high heat for a minute or two.

Purée the vegetables by pushing them through a fine sieve, food mill, or

To cube—simply cut into fairly large even pieces. Use same technique as for mincing onions, page 306.

ricer. Combine. Then beat in the sugar, salt, and pepper to *taste*, a big lump of butter, and enough heavy cream to achieve a smooth, creamy, lumpless consistency. An electric beater or an electric mixer makes this easy. Place in the top of a double boiler over simmering water to keep warm. Place a piece of Saran flat on top of the purée to prevent discoloration and drying out.

To serve, spoon into a heated vegetable dish and place a lump of butter on top. Serves 8.

Learn to taste. This makes sense, since one person's salt-and-pepper tolerance can be quite different from another's.

BRAISED LEEKS

EQUIPMENT:
French chef's knife; measuring cups and spoons; shallow baking dish with a cover, attractive enough to go to the table; can opener; heavy saucepan with a cover; sharp paring knife; tongs; foil.

INGREDIENTS:
24 leeks (4 to 5 bunches)
½ cup (1 stick) butter
1½ teaspoons salt

2 cans (10½-ounce size) condensed chicken broth (about)

Trim the roots off the leeks and remove any withered leaves. Slit the green part lengthwise, twice. Wash thoroughly, running cold water down through the stalks to make sure they are well washed. Leeks are very gritty and it is essential to get rid of it all.

Cut off enough of the green tops to leave the leeks approximately 7 inches long all told. Place in a heavy saucepan just large enough to hold them in roughly 3 layers. Add the butter and salt and enough broth to cover. Bring to a boil over a high heat and cook, partially covered, for about 20 minutes or until the leeks are tender when pierced with the point of a paring knife.

Lift from the saucepan carefully with tongs and arrange in a shallow baking dish. Cover with the liquid. (Can be prepared to this point in advance and reheated just before serving.)

To reheat, cover with a lid or foil and place in a preheated 325° (or low) oven for 15 to 20 minutes, or until bubbling hot and just beginning to glaze. Serves 6 to 8.

COFFEE MOUSSE

EQUIPMENT:
Measuring cups and spoons; double boiler; wire whisk; saucepan; rotary or electric beater.

INGREDIENTS:

6 egg *yolks*

1 cup sugar

5 tablespoons *powdered instant* coffee

½ cup (1 stick) butter, softened

2½ cups heavy cream

If you haven't mastered the trick of separating egg yolks from egg whites, see directions on page 305. Do not use freeze-dried coffee; it does not dissolve readily in this mixture.

Combine the yolks, sugar, and coffee in the top of a double boiler. Place over simmering water and cook, beating constantly with a wire whisk for 5 minutes, or until the mixture doubles in volume, has a creamy consistency, and the sugar has dissolved.

Take off the heat, place top of double boiler in a saucepan of cold water, and beat mixture hard with the whisk for 2 to 3 minutes or until the mixture thickens, gets quite pasty, and holds a shape.

Beat in the softened butter, a small amount at a time. Whip the cream until thick, using a rotary or electric beater. *Fold* into the coffee mixture, spoon into a serving dish and refrigerate for 2 to 3 hours.

For exact folding technique —see directions on page 305.

THE GRATERS

There are innumerable types of graters, both domestic and imported, but you can get along just fine with these three, plus a peppermill.

The stainless-steel nutmeg grater is essential when a recipe calls for freshly grated nutmeg.

NUTMEG GRATER

A STANDING
4-SIDED GRATER

You can use a set of three flat stainless-steel graters, each with a different degree of coarseness, or the standing 4-sided grater. Use over wax paper to shred cheese, grate vegetables, rind of citrus fruit, etc.

ITALIAN NUT AND
CHEESE GRATER

SET OF THREE FLAT GRATERS

Nuts can be ground very fine in the electric blender. Certain recipes call for grated nuts, or more precisely, shredded; for this, use a nut grater.

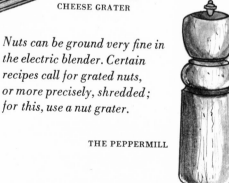

THE PEPPERMILL

Peppermills are available in silver, pewter, wood or porcelain: For the kitchen, 8-inch wooden French peppermills are the most practical: one for black pepper, one for white.

DUCK

ROAST DUCK
WITH MADEIRA SAUCE

Buttered Broccoli   *Shoestring Potatoes*

Orange and Onion Salad
(page 19)

Caramel Custard   *Coffee*

YOUR COOKING SCHEDULE: Obviously, the Caramel Custard should be done in the morning or, if you like, the day before. It will take the duck about 2 hours to roast. Cooking the broccoli is a 10-minute job, but it can be prepared almost at any time, covered with Saran, and set aside. Cooked the last minute. The orange and onions for the salad can be done ahead, but they should not be combined or dressed until shortly before dinner. Protect them meantime with Saran. Shoestring potatoes come in a can and need only to be taken out of the can, placed in a shallow pan, and heated. Tuck them into the oven after the duck comes out.

ROAST DUCK

EQUIPMENT:

Measuring spoons; paring knife or vegetable peeler; peppermill; kitchen fork; French chef's knife; paper towels; shallow roasting pan with a rack; bulb baster or large metal spoon; can opener; wooden spatula; strainer; corkscrew; saucepan.

INGREDIENTS:

To thaw, place in refrigerator in original wrappings for at least 24 hours or, to thaw in a hurry, place in a polyethylene bag, securely tied, under cool running water. Remove and refrigerate giblets immediately.

Use a peppermill for this. Freshly ground pepper is more vibrant than already-ground pepper. Both black and white peppercorns are available, the former being somewhat lustier.

1 ready-to-cook 5½- to 6-pound duck, *thawed*
½ teaspoon salt
⅛ teaspoon *freshly ground* pepper
Pinch thyme
1 medium onion, peeled and quartered

1 medium onion, *peeled* and *sliced*
1 carrot, washed and sliced
1½ cans (10½-ounce size) condensed beef broth
3 or 4 tablespoons Madeira or port wine
Watercress

To peel, slice, mince, or dice onions, garlic and shallots the easy way—see directions on page 306.

Preheat the oven to 450° (or hot) for 15 minutes before putting duck in to roast.

Pull out and discard any lumps of fat from the cavity and around the neck.

Combine the salt, pepper, and thyme and rub the duck's cavity, then tuck in the quartered onion. Prick the skin around the thighs, back and lower breast with a fork, so superfluous fat will run out during roasting. Dry the duck's skin thoroughly with paper towels.

Place breast side up, on a rack, in roasting pan. Add the sliced onion and carrot to the pan. Place in the preheated oven for 20 minutes to brown. Reduce heat to 350° and roast 1 hour and 35 minutes or approximately 20 minutes per pound. Duck does not call for basting since it is so fat, but the fat in the pan should be removed when it has accumulated. Lacking a bulb baster, which does this job the easiest way, tip the pan a little and dip fat out with a large metal spoon. About 15 minutes before the duck is done, sprinkle lightly with salt.

To test for doneness: Prick the fat part of the thigh or drumstick with a fork. If the juices run clear yellow, it is cooked to the well-done stage. If you prefer duck medium-rare, as the French do, roast only until the juices run faintly pink when the leg is pierced. When roasted, place the duck on a heated serving platter and keep warm.

To make the sauce: Pour off all but about 1 tablespoon of the fat from the roasting pan. Add beef broth or 2 cups *duck broth*. Bring up to a high boil and cook, scraping down all the brown crustiness and crushing the vegetables with a wooden spatula. *Reduce* to about half. *Taste* for seasonings. Add Madeira or port wine. Strain.

To serve, spoon a little of the sauce over the duck so it will look shiny and inviting. Pour remainder into a warm sauceboat, tuck a bouquet of fresh watercress into the duck's tail and carry it to the table. Serves 4.

Roast duck may also be served with Orange Sauce (page 78).

To make duck broth, combine the giblets, neck (cut up), and wing tips in a saucepan with 1 onion (quartered), 1 carrot (chopped coarsely), 3 cups water, 2 or 3 stalks of parsley, a small bay leaf and 1/8 teaspoon of thyme. Bring to a boil, reduce heat to simmer and cook, covered, for at least 1 hour but, better, 2 hours. Skim off any scum. Strain and use in place of the canned broth called for.

To reduce—simply boil liquid over a high heat until the amount left is what the recipe specifies.

Learn to taste. This makes sense, since one person's salt-and-pepper tolerance can be quite different from another's.

SAUSAGE AND APPLE STUFFING

EQUIPMENT:

Measuring cups and spoons; large, heavy skillet; kitchen fork; slotted spoon; large kitchen bowl; vegetable peeler; apple corer; colander.

As is true of chicken and turkey, stuffed duck is very good indeed. Follow the instructions for preparing the duck for roasting (above), but do not place onion in cavity of the bird. Season it, however, as directed. Follow same roasting instructions allowing a somewhat longer time—about 15 to 20 minutes—than for unstuffed duck. Make the "doneness" test.

INGREDIENTS:

½ pound pork sausage

4 to 5 firm eating *apples*

1 tablespoon sugar

¼ teaspoon cinnamon

¼ teaspoon salt

¼ teaspoon sage

2 tablespoons brandy (optional)

¼ cup port wine

¼ cup canned condensed beef broth
    or duck broth

Buy apples that are in season, and here it is advisable to depend on the advice of the market.

To sauté—cook or brown food in a very small amount of very hot fat.

Sauté the sausage in a large, heavy skillet, breaking it up with a fork as it cooks. Lift sausage out of the fat into a large bowl, using a slotted spoon. Mash with a fork.

Peel apples with a vegetable peeler; core and slice fairly thick. Add to the hot fat in the skillet and sauté, a few slices at a time, until lightly browned and almost tender, but still shapely. Drain in a colander and discard the fat. Sprinkle the apple slices with the sugar, cinnamon, salt, sage, and brandy. Set aside.

Add the port wine and broth to the skillet, bring to a boil and *reduce* rapidly over a high heat until there are 2 to 3 tablespoons left. Pour over the sausage meat.

To reduce—simply boil liquid over a high heat until the amount left is what the recipe specifies.

Mix the sausage meat and apples together. Best done with your hands so as not to mash the apples. Spoon into the cavity of the duck.

Since ducks have short legs, it isn't necessary to truss as you do chicken and turkey. However, the legs should be tied and the opening should be sewed or skewered so the stuffing won't ooze out.

GARLIC POTATO STUFFING

EQUIPMENT:

Medium saucepan; colander; heavy saucepan; electric blender; wooden spatula; peppermill; kitchen spoon.

Follow directions for Roast Duck, seasoning the cavity as suggested, but do not add the vegetables.

Break *2 large heads of garlic* apart (you'll have approximately 30 cloves). Drop the cloves into boiling salted water and boil 2 minutes. Drain and cool under cold water, then *peel*.

Melt 4 tablespoons (½ stick) butter in a heavy saucepan, add the garlic, and 1 cup of water. Bring to a boil, reduce heat, cover and cook slowly until all the water has evaporated and the garlic is very tender. If the water boils away before the garlic is tender, add a bit more. Combine with a little milk and blend in the electric blender to make a smooth purée.

Prepare the equivalent of four servings of *instant potatoes* according to package directions. Beat in the garlic purée, using a wooden spatula, and adding salt, *freshly ground* white pepper to *taste* and a lump of butter. Spoon the stuffing into the cavity of the duck, sew or skewer the vent and follow roasting directions for Roast Duck. You would not serve potatoes as a vegetable if the duck was stuffed with Garlic Potato Stuffing.

This "stuffing" can also be used as a vegetable, in which case, beat in some heated heavy cream just before serving. Excellent with beef, chicken, and fish.

If this seems like a horrendous amount of garlic, relax; the cooking reduces its potency to a delicious level.

Use a peppermill for this. Freshly ground pepper is more vibrant than already-ground pepper. Both black and white peppercorns are available, the former being somewhat lustier.

Instant potatoes remain one of the best of the instant foods. Since manufacturers' box sizes and instructions vary, you will have to figure out which kind to buy to arrive at the quantity needed.

Learn to taste. This makes sense, since one person's salt-and-pepper tolerance can be quite different from another's.

BUTTERED BROCCOLI

EQUIPMENT:
Peppermill; sharp paring knife; large saucepan; colander.

INGREDIENTS:

1 bunch (2½ pounds) broccoli   *Freshly ground* pepper
Salt   Butter

Use a peppermill for this. Freshly ground pepper is more vibrant than already-ground pepper. Both black and white peppercorns are available, the former being somewhat lustier.

Wash and drain. Then cut off the tops and divide into flowerets about 3 inches long. With a paring knife peel the thin green skin off the stalks, right down to the white flesh, then cut into short lengths. If the stalks are not all of a size, split them so they will be the same thickness.

Always cook green vegetables uncovered to retain the color.

Bring a good, big pot of salted water to a rolling boil. Add the stalks and boil, *uncovered*, about 5 minutes, then add the flowerets. Boil another 5 minutes or until the point of a knife will pierce the stalks easily. Drain very thoroughly in colander.

Place in a serving dish. Season with salt and pepper and dress with melted butter. This amount will serve 4.

CARAMEL CUSTARD

EQUIPMENT:
Measuring cups and spoons; 1-quart soufflé dish, or baking dish; 1 small saucepan; medium saucepan; large kitchen bowl; rotary or electric beater; roasting pan; kitchen knife; metal spatula.

INGREDIENTS:

1 cup sugar

2½ cups milk

1 vanilla bean, *split,* or 1 teaspoon
     vanilla

3 whole eggs

3 egg *yolks*

Split the bean before adding to syrup to get more flavor. When a vanilla bean has been used to flavor milk, as here, it can be washed, dried, stored, and reused.

If you haven't mastered the trick of separating egg yolks from egg whites, see directions on page 305.

Preheat the oven to 350° (or moderate) for 15 minutes before baking the custard.

Set the soufflé dish or baking dish in a saucepan of hot water to warm. Set aside.

Combine ½ cup of the sugar with 2 tablespoons of water in a small saucepan and cook over moderate heat, shaking the pan frequently, until the syrup caramelizes (in other words, turns brown). Pour into the warm soufflé dish, tipping it back and forth so the caramelized syrup covers the bottom. When it is no longer running, turn the dish upside down over waxed paper. It will set very hard.

Pour the milk into medium saucepan, add the vanilla bean and bring to a boil slowly. When a film shines over the surface, remove from the heat, cover, and allow the vanilla bean to *steep* while you continue with the custard.

Combine the eggs and yolks in a large bowl. Beat with a rotary or electric beater until well mixed. Gradually beat in the remaining sugar.

Remove the vanilla bean from the milk and gradually add the hot milk to the egg mixture, in a thin, steady stream, beating constantly.

Pour into the prepared dish, place in a roasting pan and *add enough boiling water* to the pan to reach to half the depth of the dish. Place in the bottom third of the preheated oven. Reduce heat immediately to 325° (or slow) and bake for 40 minutes or until *done.* Refrigerate to chill.

To unmold, run a metal spatula around the edge of the dish, place a serving

Test by the standard method for baked custards. If the custard is to be served cold, insert the blade of a knife 1 inch from the outside edge; if it is to be served hot, insert the knife blade 1 inch from the center. With both tests the knife blade should come out clean; that is, without any mixture clinging to it.

To steep—extract the essence from an ingredient by soaking in a hot liquid (as tea, for example).

Place the roasting pan with the soufflé dish on a rack in the oven before adding the boiling water.

dish upside down over the baking dish and reverse the two. Lift off the baking dish.

BROILED DUCKLING WITH ORANGE SAUCE

Steamed Brown Rice   *Artichokes, Sauce Ravigote*

Sour Cream Torte   *Coffee*

YOUR COOKING SCHEDULE: The duck should be in the marinade overnight, or at least 3 hours before it is to be broiled. In this instance the artichokes are served cold, so must be cooked at least 3 or 4 hours before they are to be served to give them time to cool. It might make sense to do this little job at the same time you prepare the duck marinade. The same situation exists with the cake.

Actually, these three jobs could well be done a day ahead, leaving you pretty much free until broiling time the day the dinner will be served.

NOTE: The rice takes about the same time to cook as the duck takes to broil. This makes it easy, since you'll be in the kitchen anyway. The ravigote is the last little chore and simplicity itself.

BROILED DUCKLING WITH ORANGE SAUCE

EQUIPMENT:

Measuring cups and spoons; heavy French chef's knife; lemon squeezer; polyethylene bags; mixing bowl or flat pan; paper towels; broiling pan; bulb baster or large metal spoon; 2-pronged fork or tongs.

INGREDIENTS:

1 4- to 5-pound duck, ready-to-cook,
thawed and cut up for broiling

To thaw, place in refrigerator in original wrappings for at least 24 hours or, to thaw in a hurry, place in a polyethylene bag, securely tied, under cool running water. Remove and refrigerate giblets immediately.

To peel, slice, mince or dice onions, garlic, and shallots the easy way—see directions on page 306.

MARINADE:

1 teaspoon salt

1 teaspoon powdered ginger

3 bay leaves, crumbled

1 medium onion, *peeled* and coarsely chopped

2 cloves garlic, *crushed*

Juice 1 orange, strained

Juice 1 lemon, strained

To crush garlic—give it a good whack with the side of a cleaver, heavy knife, or any flat implement. No need to peel.

Mix all marinade ingredients together thoroughly. Place the *duck pieces* in a large polyethylene bag, add the marinade, squeeze out all air, and tie securely. Place in a bowl or pan (in case there is any leakage) and allow to marinate for several hours (if overnight, refrigerate), turning occasionally so the duck meat is well saturated.

While the duck is marinating, make the Orange Sauce.

If the butcher thaws the duck for you, have him split it, remove the back bone and wing tips, then cut into quarters. You can do the same thing at home, using a big, sharp, French chef's knife or poultry shears. Whatever, cut off any surplus fat and skin.

ORANGE SAUCE

EQUIPMENT:

Mixing cups and spoons; flat grater; waxed paper; can opener; kitchen bowl; medium saucepan; wire whisk; Saran.

INGREDIENTS:

2 navel oranges

3 tablespoons sugar

¼ cup red wine vinegar

2 cups chicken broth, your own or
    canned condensed, or duck broth
    (page 71) heated

¾ cup port or Madeira

2 tablespoons *arrowroot*

Use arrowroot as a thickening agent when you want the finished sauce to be clear and transparent. Do not cook beyond the point indicated or the sauce will "thin out."

To grate rind of citrus fruit—which must be done before squeezing—work on a flat grater placed on top of a piece of waxed paper.

Grate the rind off the oranges and set aside. Then, *section* the oranges over a bowl and set them aside too.

Combine the sugar and wine vinegar in a saucepan and boil over a moderately high heat for 5 to 6 minutes or until the mixture caramelizes into a dark brown syrup. Add the chicken broth and stir until the syrup has dissolved. Remove from the heat.

Mix 3 tablespoons of the wine into the arrowroot until smooth. Whip into the sauce with a wire whisk. Put back over a low heat and *simmer* until the sauce is clear and slightly thickened. Set aside. Can be done to this point early in the day. If so, seal with Saran to prevent a skin forming on top.

Preheat the *broiler* for 15 minutes prior to broiling.

Remove the duck from the marinade and strain the marinade into the sauce. Pat the duck pieces dry with paper towels, then rub with softened butter. Takes about 4 tablespoons (½ stick.)

Place on the cold broiling pan, skin side down, 4 to 5 inches from the heat in

To peel or section citrus fruits (oranges, lemons, grapefruits)—see directions on page 307.

To simmer—cook liquid just below boiling (185°) so that it just shivers.

Remove broiling pan before lighting oven, or the duck pieces will stick.

the preheated broiler. Broil for 25 minutes, *basting* occasionally with pan drippings, using a bulb baster or large metal spoon. Turn with a 2-pronged fork or tongs, and broil, skin side up for another 20 minutes, or until the skin is brown and crisp.

To baste—spray, spoon, or brush a liquid or melted fat over food while it cooks.

To finish the sauce, add the remaining wine, the orange rind, and any juice from the orange bowl. Bring up to a boil only.

Arrange the duck on a hot serving platter and garnish with the orange sections. Spoon a little sauce over each piece of duck and pour the remainder into a heated sauce dish. Add a bouquet of watercress to the platter. Serve at once to 4.

STEAMED BROWN RICE

EQUIPMENT:
Measuring cups and spoons; kitchen bowl; colander; waxed paper; large heavy saucepan with a cover; kitchen fork.

INGREDIENTS:

1 cup brown rice
Butter
½ teaspoon salt

3 cups or 2 cans (10½-ounce size) canned condensed chicken or beef broth

To get rid of excess starch, wash the rice thoroughly in a bowl of cool water, rubbing it between the palms of your hands. Give it 3 or 4 washings, until the water is clear. Drain.

To butter—crumple up a little waxed paper, scoop up a bit of butter and coat the bottom and sides of the pan generously.

Butter the saucepan lightly. Add the rice, salt, and broth. Bring to a boil rapidly over a high heat. Lower the heat, cover, and cook slowly until all the liquid has been absorbed and rice is tender to the bite. This will take about 30 to 40 minutes. Fluff with a fork. Serves 4.

Rice can be kept warm over hot water, covered lightly with a fresh dish towel.

ARTICHOKES RAVIGOTE

EQUIPMENT:

Heavy French chef's knife; kitchen scissors; kitchen string; enamelware kettle (not aluminum or cast iron; they turn artichokes grayish) large enough to accommodate all the artichokes comfortably; cheesecloth.

Allow 1 artichoke per person. Cut off the stems; then, using the chef's knife, trim the base. Break off all small leaves. Lay the artichoke on its side and slice about ¾ inch off the top. Trim the points off the remaining leaves with a pair of scissors. Tie a thick slice of fresh lemon on the bottom of each artichoke. (This helps to keep the heart white.)

Have ready a big kettle of boiling, salted water. Add the artichokes and bring to a rolling boil. Cover the tops with a double layer of cheesecloth to keep them moist. *Do not cover* with a lid. Reduce heat and boil slowly for 40 to 50 minutes or until a leaf will pull out easily. Lift out of the kettle and turn upside down to drain.

Serve hot or warm with melted butter, lemon butter (this is nothing more than melted butter combined with lemon juice to taste) or Hollandaise (page 94).

Serve cold with Sauce Ravigote (page 162). Place each artichoke on a side plate, large enough to accommodate the leaves discarded as the *artichoke* is eaten. Serve about 2 tablespoons of the Sauce Ravigote in small individual bowls at the side.

Always cook green vegetables uncovered to retain their color.

For further information on serving artichokes— see page 305.

SOUR CREAM TORTE

EQUIPMENT:

Measuring cups and spoons; flour sifter; large mixing bowl; pastry blender; small kitchen bowl; wire whisk; 3-tined fork; several round 9-inch cake pans; paring knife; broad metal spatula; cake racks; rolling pin.

INGREDIENTS:

3 cups *sifted* all-purpose flour	1 cup (2 sticks) butter, cold
¾ cup sugar	1 egg
Pinch salt	

To measure sifted flour properly—spoon it into a dry measuring cup (or spoon) well above the top, then level or cut off with the edge—not flat surface —of a metal spatula or knife. Do not shake flour down.

Preheat the oven to 350° (or moderate) for 15 minutes before baking the torte.

Combine the flour, sugar, and salt and sift into a large mixing bowl. Cut the butter up coarsely, then work into the flour mixture with a pastry blender until the mixture looks mealy.

Beat the egg slightly in a small bowl, using a wire whisk. Stir into the flour mixture with a fork. Now, with clean hands, work the dough until it holds together. Shape into an oblong and slice into 7 equal parts.

To coat—add a couple of tablespoons of flour to the buttered pan. Then, holding it over the sink, tip the pan back and forth so the flour clings to the buttered bottom. Turn upside down and give it a good thump to knock off any excess.

Take as many 9-inch cake pans as you have. Turn upside down, *butter* the bottoms, and *coat* lightly with flour.

To butter—crumple up a small piece of waxed paper, scoop up as much butter as needed and rub onto bottom of pan.

Roll each piece of dough with a lightly floured rolling pin on a prepared pan. Cut off with a sharp paring knife any dough that hangs over the edge. Keep dough refrigerated until needed. If you don't have seven pans, clean each pan after baking, butter and flour again.

Bake in the preheated oven for 10 minutes or until lightly browned. Place two—or no more than three—pans in the oven at a time, with at least two inches between pans and oven walls. Immediately on removing from the oven, carefully slide a broad metal spatula under the thin pastry to loosen it. Place a cake rack on top and reverse the rack and the pan. Cool each layer completely. They are extremely fragile so must always be moved with a metal spatula.

FILLING

EQUIPMENT:
Can opener; electric blender; mixing bowl; metal spatula.

INGREDIENTS:

3 cups or 3 cans (4-ounce size) walnuts

2 cups commercial or 1 carton (16-ounce size) sour cream

2¼ cups sifted confectioners' sugar

1 teaspoon vanilla

Grind the walnuts in the electric blender until very fine. Mix with all remaining ingredients thoroughly.

Lift the first layer of the pastry onto a flat serving platter, then spread a thin layer of the filling on top, using a metal spatula. Continue, layer after layer, with the filling between, leaving the top plain. To finish, sift a film of confectioners' sugar over the top. Refrigerate until serving time.

MEAT

BEEF

STANDING RIBS OF BEEF

Yellow Turnips Mousseline   *Yorkshire Pudding*
(page 65)

Gravy

Artichokes Vinaigrette
(page 80)   (page 44)

Cream Puffs   *Coffee*

YOUR COOKING SCHEDULE: Since the artichokes are served cold, and the Cream Puffs must be cooked and cooled before filling, both can be done early in the day or, if more convenient, the day before. However, the puffs should be filled shortly before serving. Assuming the roast weighs about 7 or 8 pounds, it should go into the oven approximately 2 hours before dinner is to be served. The turnips can be cooked and finished during the time the beef is roasting. The Sauce Vinaigrette can be made at this time, too. As the recipes make clear, both the Yorkshire Pudding and the gravy must be made during the roast's "resting" period, but neither is much of a chore.

STANDING RIBS OF BEEF

EQUIPMENT:

Roasting pan with a rack; peppermill; meat thermometer; platter; measuring cups.

The larger the roast the better, but do not buy less than three ribs, remembering that if there is any left over, cold roast beef is delicious. Figure on approximately 1 pound of beef, bone in, per person, or ½ to ¾ of a pound if the ribs have been boned and rolled.

Have the butcher cut off the short ribs (they can be used for another dinner, page 102) and remove the chine (back) bone to facilitate carving. He should also attach a piece of suet where the chine bone has been removed and tie the roast properly for the oven.

NOTE WELL: If the roast has been refrigerated, it should be brought to room temperature—allow three hours, depending on size—before roasting, or the timing will be off.

Use a peppermill for this. Freshly ground pepper is more vibrant than already-ground pepper. Both black and white peppercorns are available; the former are somewhat lustier.

Rub the meat well with salt and *freshly ground* black pepper. Place on a rack, rib side down, in a roasting pan. If you do not have a pan with its own rack or a separate meat rack, use your broiler pan.

Preheat the oven to 325° (or slow) 15 minutes before putting in the meat. Roast 13 to 15 minutes per pound or until a meat thermometer registers 120° to 125° for rare; 18 to 20 minutes per pound (130° on meat thermometer) for medium rare. (So-called well done roast beef is really ruined roast beef and should never be done.) Do not cover; do not add water to the pan; do not baste.

Once the roast has come from the oven, it should "rest" on a heated platter for 20 to 30 minutes to allow the juices to settle and to make carving easier. All meat continues to cook after it is taken from the oven. Pour the pan drippings into a measuring cup and set aside.

To serve, garnish with a bouquet of watercress just before the roast goes to the table.

COLD ROAST BEEF

Sliced very thin, this is delicious served with canned stewed tomatoes (heated), followed by Green Beans (page 49) dressed with Sauce Vinaigrette (page 44), and a nice easy dessert such as cream cheese, ginger marmalade, and saltines.

ROLLED ROAST OF BEEF

A rolled roast is nothing more than a rib roast from which the butcher has removed the ribs, then rolled and tied the meat. Meat with the bone in takes somewhat less time to cook than meat with the bone out. Here, as always, rely on a meat thermometer, but make sure to get the weight of the roast from the butcher to guide your timing. Follow same menu as for Standing Ribs of Beef.

YORKSHIRE PUDDING

EQUIPMENT:

Measuring cups and spoons; 8 × 3 10-inch shallow earthenware baking dish attractive enough to go to the table; rotary or electric beater.

INGREDIENTS:

3 eggs

1⅓ cups milk

1¼ cups all-purpose flour, scant

½ teaspoon salt

¼ cup beef drippings

Preheat the oven to 450° (or hot) for 15 minutes before baking the pudding.

In the oven, heat the baking dish. Add all but 2 tablespoons of the beef drippings. Beat the eggs with a rotary or electric beater until light and fluffy. Add the milk, then gradually beat in the flour and the 2 tablespoons of reserved beef drippings. Continue beating until the batter is absolutely smooth. Pour into the prepared dish and bake in the preheated oven for 10 minutes. Reduce heat to 350° and bake 10 to 15 minutes longer, or until the pudding is puffed and lightly browned. To serve, cut into squares. Serves 5 or 6.

BEEF GRAVY

EQUIPMENT:

Can opener; measuring cups and spoons; wooden spatula.

The lovely juices that come from the beef as it is carved make the best of all sauces, but the quantity is obviously limited. With this particular menu, a gravy or sauce seems called for.

To make the gravy: Pour off and discard remaining fat from the roasting pan. Add ½ cup canned brown gravy and ½ cup dry white wine or dry vermouth to the pan. Place over a high heat (a large pan will cover 2 burners or electric units) and cook, scraping up all the coagulated juices and encrustations with a wooden spatula. Continue boiling until the sauce has *reduced* by about one third. Take off the heat and stir in 2 or 3 tablespoons (¼ stick) of softened butter. This will thicken the gravy slightly. Pour into a warm sauceboat. Taste for seasoning.

To reduce—simply boil liquid over a high heat until the amount left is what the recipe specifies.

CREAM PUFFS

EQUIPMENT:
Measuring cups and spoons; flour sifter; heavy saucepan; wooden spatula; large metal tablespoon; baking or cookie sheet; cake racks; small sharp knife.

INGREDIENTS:

Shortening	1 cup *sifted* all-purpose flour
½ cup (1 stick) sweet butter	4 whole eggs
⅛ teaspoon salt	1 recipe Crème Patissiére

To measure sifted flour properly, spoon it—after sifting—into a dry measuring cup or spoon well above the top, then level or cut off with the edge—not the flat surface—of a metal spatula or knife. Do not shake flour down.

Preheat the oven to 375° (or hot) for 15 minutes before baking the puffs. *Grease* a cookie or baking sheet with shortening.

To grease: use a small piece of crumpled-up waxed paper and as much butter or vegetable shortening as needed.

Combine butter, salt, and 1 cup of water in the saucepan. Bring to a boil. Take off the heat and stir in the flour all at once with a wooden spatula. Place the saucepan back over a very low heat and beat vigorously until the dough leaves the sides of the pan and forms a ball. Take off the heat at once and beat in the eggs, one at a time, beating hard and briskly after each addition until the dough is smooth. Drop by rounded tablespoons onto prepared baking sheet, leaving about 2 inches between the puffs to allow for spreading. Place in the preheated oven and bake for 30 minutes. When the puffs are cooked perfectly, no bubbles of fat will show on the surface and the sides will feel rigid when touched. Cool on wire cake racks.

To fill Cream Puffs: With a small, sharp knife, split each puff almost, but not quite, all around and, using a spoon, fill with Crème Patissiére or sweetened whipped cream. Once filled, puffs should be refrigerated unless served immediately.

CRÈME PÂTISSIÈRE

EQUIPMENT:
Measuring cups and spoons; medium heavy saucepans; large mixing bowl; rotary or electric beater; wooden spatula; wire whisk; Saran.

INGREDIENTS:

2 cups milk

4 egg *yolks*

¾ cup sugar

1 teaspoon vanilla

¼ cup flour

Scald the milk in a saucepan. Set aside. Combine the yolks, sugar, and vanilla in bowl and beat with a rotary or electric beater until the mixture "makes ribbons" (about 3 or 4 minutes). Now mix in the flour until smooth, using the wooden spatula. Gradually add the hot milk, whipping constantly with a wire whisk. Pour into a clean saucepan, bring to a boil over moderate heat, whipping constantly. Boil, over low heat, still whipping for 5 to 6 minutes. Remove from the heat and seal with Saran so a skin won't form on top. Refrigerate until you are ready to fill puffs. Makes 3 cups.

If you haven't mastered the trick of separating egg yolks from egg whites, see directions on page 305.

To scald milk or cream —heat to the boiling point, when it will wrinkle on top.

BROILED STEAK

Baked Bananas   *Horseradish Sauce*

Asparagus Hollandaise

Iced Coffee Soufflé   *Coffee*

YOUR COOKING SCHEDULE: Working backward, the soufflé, since it is served cold, can be prepared early in the day or, even better, the day before; the Horseradish Sauce (if you make your own) can be whipped up anytime you have a spare moment. As for the asparagus, it, too, can be made ready anytime. If early, remember to wrap it securely in Saran or foil. Refrigerate, and bring to room temperature a half hour before cooking. Hollandaise can always be made in advance, sealed with Saran so a skin won't form on the surface, then heated at serving time over lukewarm water. If you have only one oven, the bananas can be baked while the steak is broiling, placed, of course, on the rack below the broiler pan, so it bakes rather than broils. Both bananas and steak take about the same length of time. You'll have just enough time to cook the asparagus after you turn the steak.

BROILED STEAK

EQUIPMENT:

Broiling pan; peppermill; 2-pronged fork; boning knife; carving knife.

Sirloin is a good cut when there are several people to eat it and the T-bone a sensible choice for 2 or 3. Have the butcher grind the tail of the T-bone and tie it into the center of the steak.

Preheat broiler at highest temperature.

Allow ½ pound per person, cut at least 1½ inches thick. Meat should be at room temperature before broiling. If refrigerated, this takes at least an hour. Slash the fat in several places to keep the meat from curling. Place on the *cold broiling pan* in the preheated broiler about 4 to 5 inches from the source of heat. Reduce the heat to a little better than medium. To broil the steak rare, allow 4 to 5 minutes on the first side, then turn and broil 5 to 6 on the second side; for medium rare, broil a few minutes longer on the first side. To test for doneness, cut near the bone with a sharp knife to determine if the meat is done to your taste.

Remove the steak to a hot platter, season with salt and *freshly ground* black pepper and coat the meat generously with softened butter. Garnish with a bouquet of parsley or watercress.

To carve: Steadying the steak with a 2-pronged fork, cut down and around the bone with a small, sharp boning knife. Remove and discard the bone. Then carve the steak on the diagonal in fairly thick slices.

Remove broiling pan before preheating the broiler, or the meat will stick.

Use a peppermill for this. Freshly ground pepper is more vibrant than already-ground pepper. Both black and white peppercorns are available, the former being somewhat lustier.

BAKED BANANAS

EQUIPMENT:
Fireproof baking dish suitable for serving; lemon squeezer; sharp paring knife; vegetable peeler; electric blender; rubber spatula.

INGREDIENTS:

Butter	Sugar
Firm but ripe bananas	Lemon juice

To butter a pan—crumple up a little waxed paper, scoop up a bit of butter and coat the bottom and sides of the pan generously.

Preheat the oven to 450° (or hot) for 15 minutes before baking the bananas. *Butter* the baking dish. Allow 1 banana per person. Peel the bananas; place in the prepared dish. Sprinkle lightly with sugar and lemon juice. Dot generously with butter.

Bake for about 10 minutes, or until bananas are tender when pierced with the point of a small sharp knife. *Baste* once during the baking period and again just before broiling. Slide under the broiler for about 1 minute, just long enough to fleck the bananas with gold. Don't close the door.

To baste—spray or brush a liquid or melted fat over food while it cooks.

FRESH HORSERADISH SAUCE

You can, of course, use commercial sauce, but if you like to make your own, here's how: Grate enough peeled horseradish root to make about 1½ tablespoons. Mix together well with 1 tablespoon wine vinegar, a few drops of lemon juice, ½ teaspoon dry mustard, a few grains of salt and *freshly ground pepper* and sugar to taste. Then *fold* mixture into ½ cup heavy cream, whipped with a rubber spatula. Taste for seasoning.

For exact folding technique —see page 305.

Use a peppermill for this. Freshly ground pepper is more vibrant than already-ground pepper.

ASPARAGUS HOLLANDAISE

EQUIPMENT:

Swivel-bladed vegetable knife; vegetable peeler; soft white string; large, heavy skillet or saucepan; sharp paring knife; paper towels; linen napkin.

To prepare the asparagus the way the French do—the best way—slice off all the tough root ends with a big knife in one fell swoop. Using a vegetable peeler, peel from the tips down, rolling the stalk around as you work. Peel, the stalks until they are all approximately the same thickness and, except for the tips, all of a color. Allow about 5 spears per person. Line up the stalks, tips all at one end, and tie in small bundles with soft string, for easy, quick removal from the pan when cooked.

Lay the bundles in rapidly boiling, well-salted water in a skillet with enough water to cover completely. Bring water to the boil again and cook asparagus *uncovered* at a moderate boil until barely tender. Test a few stem ends with the point of a small, sharp knife. Cook *only 2 or 3 minutes* after the water comes to a boil the second time. Lift from the water onto paper towels for a minute or two to drain. Then arrange (tips facing in the same direction) in a serving dish lined with a fresh linen napkin to absorb any additional liquid. Cut off the string. Wrap the napkin around the spears to keep them warm.

Cold asparagus is delicious served with Sauce Vinaigrette (page 44) or Mayonnaise (page 38).

Always cook green vegetables uncovered to retain their color.

To serve cooked asparagus cold run immediately under cold water. Drain thoroughly, wrap in a fresh dish towel, then in a polyethylene bag, and refrigerate.

Do not boil asparagus to death. Once you've enjoyed it the French way, you will never again follow any other method.

BLENDER HOLLANDAISE SAUCE

EQUIPMENT:

Measuring cups and spoons; electric blender; small saucepan.

INGREDIENTS:

If you haven't mastered the trick of separating egg yolks from egg whites, see directions on page 305.

3 egg *yolks*
2 tablespoons lemon juice
¼ teaspoon salt

Pinch cayenne
½ cup (1 stick) butter

Combine the yolks, lemon juice, salt, and cayenne in the container of the blender. Heat the butter in the saucepan until it bubbles. Do not allow it to brown. Cover container, turn motor to high and—immediately—remove cover and add the butter quickly in a steady stream. When all the butter is in, turn off motor at once. Serve in a warm (the chill off only) serving dish or keep warm by placing the container of the blender in a saucepan with about 2 inches of warm, not boiling, water.

Never heat Hollandaise over direct heat or it will curdle.

If Hollandaise *curdles*, rinse a mixing bowl with hot water and dry. Place a teaspoon of lemon juice and a tablespoon of the curdled sauce in the bowl. Whip with a wire whisk until the sauce thickens and gets creamy. Beat in the rest of the sauce, a tablespoon at a time, beating hard after each addition until the sauce thickens.

ICED COFFEE SOUFFLÉ

EQUIPMENT:
Measuring cups and spoons; double boiler; wooden spatula or wire whisk; rotary or electric beater; rubber spatula; 1-quart soufflé dish.

INGREDIENTS:

Do not use freeze-dried coffee. It will not dissolve in this mixture.

1 envelope unflavored gelatin
2 tablespoons *powdered instant* coffee
4 eggs, *separated*

1 cup sugar
½ teaspoon salt
1 teaspoon vanilla
1 cup heavy cream

If you haven't mastered the trick of separating egg yolks from egg whites, see directions on page 305.

Sprinkle the gelatin over ½ cup cold water to soften; dissolve the instant coffee in ½ cup cold water.

Combine the egg yolks, liquid coffee, ½ cup of the sugar, and the salt in the top of a double boiler. Place over simmering water and cook, stirring constantly with a wooden spatula or a wire whisk, until the mixture has thickened and coats a spoon. Remove from heat and stir in the softened gelatin until dissolved. Add vanilla. Set aside to cool.

For exact folding technique —see page 305.

Beat the egg whites with a rotary or electric beater until they hold shape. Add the remaining sugar gradually, and continue beating until the whites form firm, shiny peaks when the beater is held straight up. Whip the heavy cream until it, too, holds shape, then *fold* into beaten whites, using a rubber spatula. Finally fold in the coffee mixture. Pour into soufflé dish and refrigerate until firm.

BOEUF À LA BOURGUIGNONNE

Boiled Potatoes
(page 44)

Mixed Green Salad Vinaigrette
(page 44)

Burgundy   **Charlotte Malakoff**   **Coffee**

YOUR COOKING SCHEDULE: This is an all-French dinner that is not too arduous to prepare and is perfectly delicious. The charlotte needs a good six hours in the refrigerator, so make it a day ahead. With that out of the way, the only major cooking is the stew, and you should be able to complete all the preliminaries in an hour or a little better. We are not, however, of the school that believes this, or any stew for that matter, is improved by being cooked a day or so in advance. The salad greens might as well be washed and got out of the way while you're in the kitchen, thus giving them sufficient time to dry. Then all that remains to be done is to boil the potatoes and heat up the stew in time to meet your dinner hour. It's such a good dinner, why don't you invite someone to share it?

BOEUF À LA BOURGUIGNONNE

EQUIPMENT:
French chef's knife; measuring cups and spoons; peppermill; can opener; paring knife; kitchen scissors; large skillet with a cover; slotted spoon; paper towels; enameled flameproof casserole with a cover; wooden spatula; 2-pronged kitchen fork; large strainer; wire whisk.

The best cuts of beef to buy for stew are round, rump or chuck.

As is true of many great dishes, the variations on this famous French beef stew are endless. Carefully made and seasoned, it is perfectly delicious and worthy of your most important dinner parties.

INGREDIENTS:

6 strips bacon

3 pounds stewing beef, cut into
    2-inch cubes

1 carrot, peeled and coarsely
    chopped

1 onion, peeled and coarsely
    chopped

1 tablespoon salt

Several twists of the peppermill

3 tablespoons flour

2 cups dry red wine

2 cans (10½-ounce size) condensed
    beef broth

2 cloves garlic, *peeled* and *crushed*

½ teaspoon dried thyme

1 bay leaf, crumbled

1 pound fresh *button* mushrooms

6 tablespoons butter

4 tablespoons salad oil

24 small white onions, peeled

Minced parsley

To peel, mince or slice onions, garlic and shallots the easy way—see directions on page 306.

To crush garlic—give it a good whack with the side of a cleaver, heavy knife, or any flat implement.

Button mushrooms, the least expensive, are best in cooked dishes. Mushrooms need not be peeled. Wipe with a clean, damp cloth, and snip off the tip of the stems.

To mince parsley—hold a large French chef's knife at both ends and chop with rapid up-and-down motions, pulling the ingredients back into a pile with the knife as you work.

Preheat oven to 325° (or slow) for 15 minutes.

Take the bundle of bacon strips from the refrigerator and cut into ½-inch pieces with scissors. Drop into a large, heavy, cold skillet. Place over moderate heat, separating the pieces as they get warm; cook until crisp. Lift bacon out of the fat with a slotted spoon and drain on paper towels.

Dry the pieces of beef thoroughly with paper towels. Add to hot bacon fat, a few at a time and *sauté* until lightly brown all over. Lift meat from the pan with a slotted spoon and set aside. Add the carrot and chopped onion to the same hot fat and cook until nicely browned.

Lift the vegetables from the fat to a heavy, enameled, flameproof casserole. Add the beef and bacon. Sprinkle with salt, pepper, and flour. Stir with a wooden spatula to coat the meat with the flour and seasonings. Add the wine, 2 cups of the beef broth (undiluted), garlic, thyme, and bay leaf. Heat to the boiling point. Cover tightly and place in the preheated oven. Cook for 1½ to 2 hours or until the meat is very tender when pierced with a fork.

Meanwhile, heat 3 tablespoons of the butter and 2 tablespoons of the oil in a

Be sure the meat is perfectly dry and do not crowd the pan.

To sauté—cook, or brown meat in a small amount of very hot fat.

large, heavy skillet. When the butter is hot, add the *mushrooms* (do not crowd the pan). Sauté about 5 minutes tossing and shaking the pan. Lift from the fat and set aside.

To sauté mushrooms perfectly, be sure they are completely dry. At first, the mushrooms absorb the fat, but in 2 or 3 minutes the fat will reappear on their surface and the mushrooms will begin to brown.

Heat remaining butter and oil in same skillet. Add the small white onions and cook over a moderate heat for 10 minutes, shaking the pan occasionally so onions turn over and brown evenly. Add the remaining beef broth, bring to a boil, then *simmer*, covered, until the onions are tender (but still shapely) when pierced with the point of a small, sharp knife. Do not overcook. Set aside.

To simmer—cook liquid just below boiling (185°) so that it just shivers.

When the meat is tender, strain the pot liquid through a large sieve into a saucepan. Rinse out the casserole and return to it the beef and bacon, cooked onions and mushrooms. To the strained broth add a tray or more of ice cubes, so the fat will congeal around the ice and can be discarded. Place the saucepan over a good heat and bring to a boil. Boil for 2 minutes. If the sauce is not thick enough to coat a spoon (that is, to make a film that clings to the spoon), thicken with a beurre manié: knead 1 tablespoon of butter into 2 tablespoons of flour. Roll into tiny balls, drop into the sauce and cook, whipping constantly with a wire whisk, until the sauce has thickened slightly. Pour over the meat and vegetables, bring to a boil, and simmer just long enough to heat through, 2 to 3 minutes.

Serve from the casserole or pour the stew into a deep, warmed platter; surround with the freshly boiled, peeled potatoes, and garnish with a sprinkling of minced parsley. Serves 6.

CHARLOTTE MALAKOFF

EQUIPMENT:
Measuring cups and spoons; pastry feather, or small clean paintbrush, or Kleenex; 4-cup charlotte mold, or straight-sided porcelain or Pyrex mold;

waxed paper; electric blender; rotary or electric beater; wooden or rubber spatula; sharp paring knife.

INGREDIENTS:

Vegetable *oil*	2½ cups heavy cream
1 package (3-ounce size) ladyfingers	4 tablespoons kirsch or light rum
½ cup *blanched* almonds	1 tablespoon sifted confectioners'
½ cup (1 stick) butter, softened	sugar
½ cup superfine sugar	*Candied violets*, if available
1½ teaspoons vanilla	

Use any vegetable oil except those with definite flavors, such as olive or walnut.

To blanch—drop shelled almonds into boiling water and boil 1 minute. Drain. Squeeze each nut between thumb and forefinger and it will slip out of its skin.

To oil—use a pastry brush, feather brush, or even a small, clean paintbrush. Lacking a brush, use soft paper such as Kleenex.

Buy candied violets, imported from France and used extensively by French chefs. They are usually available in stores specializing in fine imported foods.

To line—place the mold on a piece of waxed paper. Outline the shape with a pencil, then cut out with scissors, and place in bottom of the mold.

Lightly *oil* a 4-cup charlotte mold and *line* the bottom. Split the ladyfingers and arrange vertically around the sides of the mold. Set aside.

Grind the almonds in the electric blender until as fine as possible. Cream the butter with your hands or an electric beater until very soft and light. Gradually work in the superfine sugar, beating until mixture is very fluffy. Stir in the almonds and vanilla thoroughly. Whip 2 cups of the cream with a rotary or electric beater until just frothy. Then mix about 4 tablespoons of this cream into the butter mixture, using a wooden or rubber spatula. Continue whipping the remaining cream just to the point where the beater drawn across the surface of the cream leaves light marks. Do not beat further. Stir in the kirsch or rum. Then combine the whipped cream with the butter mixture.

Spoon carefully into the prepared mold. With a small, sharp knife, trim off ladyfingers that extend above the cream, and press the trimmed bits into the top of the cream. Cover with waxed paper, place a plate or saucer on top and a heavy weight on top of that. (If the butter in the cream is not firm, the charlotte will collapse when unmolded.) Refrigerate at least six hours.

To unmold, lift off the top waxed paper. Run a metal spatula around the inside of the mold and invert the charlotte on a chilled serving platter. Peel off the bottom waxed paper with care. Whip the remaining half cup of cream with the confectioners' sugar. Frost the top of the charlotte with the cream, then garnish with candied violets. Refrigerate again until serving time.

— ◆ —

BARBECUED SHORT RIBS

Barley Casserole   *Cold Beets in Sour Cream*

Sliced Oranges with Grand Marnier

Coffee

YOUR COOKING SCHEDULE: If the ribs are frozen, bring to room temperature. Allow a couple of hours. Assuming dinner is to be served at 7 o'clock, the ribs should be started no later than 5 o'clock. Slice the beets and allow them to marinate while the ribs are cooking. Drain and dress just before serving. At this time, the casserole can be prepared up to the point where you add the broth, then placed in the oven about 45 minutes before the ribs have finished cooking. While the casserole bakes, slice the oranges and arrange on individual plates.

BARBECUED SHORT RIBS

EQUIPMENT:

Measuring cups and spoons; French chef's knife; large, heavy, deep casserole with cover; paper towels; sharp paring knife.

Short ribs are the aftermath of a good rib roast. Properly wrapped and sealed, they can always be frozen on the day of purchase against future use. A 3-rib roast of beef will yield about 2½ pounds of short ribs, which will serve 2 to 3, depending on appetites. If the dinner is planned for more people, buy another couple of pounds. You will still be ahead of the game on a cost basis.

INGREDIENTS:

5 to 6 pounds short ribs, cut into 2-inch pieces

4 tablespoons (½ stick) butter

2 small cloves garlic, *peeled* and *minced*

1 large onion, peeled and minced

2 ribs celery, cut into small *cubes*

2 tablespoons all-purpose flour

1 can (8-ounce size) tomato sauce

2 teaspoons salt

¼ teaspoon *freshly ground* pepper

¼ teaspoon allspice

1½ tablespoons prepared mustard

1½ tablespoons cider vinegar

To peel, mince, or slice onions, garlic, and shallots the easy way—see directions on page 306.

To cube celery ribs—make 3 or 4 cuts down the entire length, leaving the top intact. Then holding the rib together with your hands, cut across the rib to the size you want.

To simmer—cook liquid just below boiling (185°) so that it just shivers.

Use a peppermill for this. Freshly ground pepper is more vibrant than already-ground pepper. Both black and white peppercorns are available, the former being somewhat lustier.

To sauté—cook or brown food in a very small amount of very hot fat.

Melt the butter in the large casserole. When hot, brown the short ribs, a few at a time. Lift from the pan as they cook, and drain on paper towel. Add the garlic, onion, and celery and *sauté* over a high heat for about 2 minutes, stirring constantly with a wooden spatula. Stir in the flour until smooth. Stir in all remaining ingredients. Return the ribs to the pan and add 1 cup of water. Bring up to a boil, then *simmer*, covered, for 1½ to 2 hours or until the meat is very tender when pierced with a fork. If the meat leaves the bones, remove the loose bones before serving. Serves 4.

BARLEY CASSEROLE

EQUIPMENT:

Measuring cups and spoons; French chef's knife; can opener; 1-quart oven-proof casserole attractive enough to go to the table; large skillet; slotted spoon; wooden spatula.

INGREDIENTS:

¼ cup (½ stick) butter
½ pound button mushrooms
1 large onion, peeled and diced

1 cup pearl barley
2 cups condensed chicken or beef broth

To butter—crumple up a small piece of waxed paper, scoop up a bit of butter, and coat the bottom and sides of the casserole generously.

Preheat the oven to 325° (or slow) for 15 minutes before baking the casserole. *Butter* a 1-quart casserole generously. Set aside. Wipe the mushrooms with a damp cloth, snip off the ends of the stems, then slice thin. Melt the butter in a skillet. When very hot, add the mushrooms, a few at a time. *Sauté* 4 to 5 minutes, shaking the pan to toss them about. As soon as they have browned lightly, lift out of the pan with a slotted spoon onto paper towels. When all the mushrooms are cooked, add the onion. Sauté, stirring constantly with a wooden spatula, until lightly brown. Remove onion. Finally add the barley and brown it lightly. Combine the barley, onion, and mushrooms in the prepared casserole. Add the broth, cover and bake for about 45 to 60 minutes or until all the liquid has been absorbed and the barley is tender. Serves 4.

To sauté—cook or brown food in a very small amount of very hot fat.

COLD BEETS IN SOUR CREAM

EQUIPMENT:
Can opener; polyethylene bag; bowl; strainer.

INGREDIENTS:
1 can (8-ounce size) beets
½ cup Sauce Vinaigrette (page 44)
Sour Cream

Drain the beets thoroughly, then slice very thin. Place in a polyethylene bag, add the Sauce Vinaigrette, squeeze out all air and tie securely. Set in a bowl in case of leakage and allow to marinate for at least 2 hours, turning frequently so the slices will be well bathed. An hour or so before serving, drain the beets, arrange on individual salad plates. Immediately before serving, dress lightly with sour cream. Serves 4.

SLICED ORANGES WITH GRAND MARNIER

EQUIPMENT:
Medium sharp knife, such as a boning knife.

To peel and section oranges —see directions on page 307.

Peel large navel oranges, allowing 1 per person. Slice the oranges, on the bias, at about a 45° angle. This greatly minimizes the membrane and the slices look more attractive. If there are any seeds, pick them out. Arrange the slices on individual plates, sprinkle lightly with sugar if it seems necessary, and with about a tablespoon of Grand Marnier for each plate.

LONDON BROIL ORIENTALE

Boiled Rice, the Chinese Way
(page 29)
Sautéed Green Pepper Rings

Hearts of Lettuce with Roquefort Cream Dressing

Greek Cake   *Coffee*

YOUR COOKING SCHEDULE: This menu has both Chinese and Greek overtones. It would be sensible to make the cake a day before you plan to use it. The meat benefits by a long soaking in the marinade, so it might be a good idea to start that a day ahead, too. About 20 minutes before serving time, cook both rice and peppers. While that's going on, you can make the Roquefort Cream Dressing. Broiling the meat is a 6-minute job and should be done at the last minute.

LONDON BROIL ORIENTALE

EQUIPMENT:
Measuring cups and spoons; French chef's knife; sharp paring knife; polyethylene bag; pan; bulb baster or large metal spoon; sharp carving knife.

INGREDIENTS:

1 3-pound flank steak
½ cup soy sauce
¾ cup dry vermouth or dry sherry
½ teaspoon tabasco

3 cloves garlic, *minced*
1 piece *fresh ginger root* (about 1 inch), grated
½ cup parsley sprigs, *minced*

If you cannot find fresh ginger root (usually procurable in Chinese stores), use Jamaica ginger (whole dried ginger) which is readily available.

Place the steak in a large polyethylene bag. Mix together all remaining ingredients, pour over the steak and tie securely. Place in a pan, in case there is some leakage, and refrigerate. Allow to marinate for several hours, or even overnight, turning the bag when you think of it so the meat will be well saturated with the marinade.

Remove broiling pan before preheating the broiler, or the meat will stick.

If you don't like rare steak, don't buy this cut.

Remove broiler pan and then turn the broiler to high. Heat for 15 minutes prior to broiling the steak.

Place the steak on the cold broiling pan and *broil*, about 3 inches from the source of heat, for 3 minutes on each side for *rare, basting* it once during the broiling with a bulb baster or large metal spoon. Because of the highly seasoned marinade, you do not season the steak after broiling as is customary with steaks that have not been marinated.

Unlike other steaks, flank is carved very thin. Use a very sharp knife, held almost flat to the top of the meat, and slice diagonally, cutting across the tough fibers of the flank. This gives you wide, diagonal slices. Arrange the slices, overlapping, on a heated platter. Heat some of the marinade and strain over the slices. Garnish with minced parsley. Serves 4 to 6.

To peel, mince, or slice onions, garlic, and shallots the easy way—see directions on page 306.

To mince parsley—hold the blade of a large French chef's knife at both ends and chop with rapid up-and-down motions, pulling the ingredients back into a pile with the knife as you work.

Always broil flank steak, sometimes called London Broil, cold from the refrigerator.

To baste—spray or brush a liquid or melted fat over food while it cooks.

PLAIN LONDON BROIL

The broiling and carving instructions remain the same. The meat, however, should be seasoned with salt and freshly ground pepper after it is cooked. Plain London Broil tastes very good served on hot buttered toast, accompanied by French-fried Onion Rings (page 226) and a green salad.

SAUTÉED PEPPER RINGS

EQUIPMENT:
French chef's knife; sharp paring knife; large, heavy skillet; peppermill.

This is an especially delightful way to enjoy sweet green peppers and you can, if you like, use a mixture of red, green, and yellow. Allow about 1½ peppers per person.

Wash the peppers, cut off the tops, and cut out the white membrane and the core. Brush out the seeds. Slice into rings about ¼ inch wide.

Heat a film of olive oil in a large, heavy skillet. Add the pepper rings, lower the heat to moderate, and cook, stirring occasionally, for 10 to 12 minutes, or until peppers are tender but still somewhat crisp to the tongue. Take care not to let them burn or they will turn bitter.

Spoon into a serving dish and season with salt and freshly ground pepper.

With garlic: Peppers are delicious when cooked with garlic. In this instance, however, the use of garlic would not be wise, since the marinade for the steak is heavily seasoned with garlic. Just add a clove or two, minced, to the pan while the peppers are sautéeing.

HEARTS OF LETTUCE WITH ROQUEFORT CREAM DRESSING

EQUIPMENT:
Measuring cups and spoons; rotary or electric beater; rubber spatula.

Cut chilled iceberg lettuce into wedges, place on individual serving plates and dress with Roquefort Cream Dressing.

To make Roquefort Cream Dressing: Whip ½ cup heavy cream until stiff. Fold into 1 cup thick Mayonnaise (page 38). Crumble about 2 tablespoons Roquefort cheese (or blue cheese) and fold into the dressing. Serves 4 to 6.

GREEK CAKE

EQUIPMENT:
Measuring cups and spoons; flat grater; electric mixer; wooden spatula; flour sifter; rotary or electric beater; wire whisk; rubber spatula; 10-inch tube pan; toothpicks; metal spatula; cake rack.

INGREDIENTS:

1 cup butter, softened, cut in pieces	3 cups *sifted* all-purpose flour
2 cups sugar	4 teaspoons baking powder
4 large eggs, *separated*	½ teaspoon salt
1 carton (8-ounce size) plain yogurt	Rind of 2 lemons, *grated*

If you haven't mastered the trick of separating egg yolks from egg whites, see directions on page 305.

Preheat oven to 350° (or moderate) for 15 minutes before baking the cake.

Place the butter in the bowl of the electric mixer and start at low speed; then, as butter softens, increase to moderate speed and beat until fluffy. Increase speed to high. Gradually add the sugar and continue beating until the

To measure sifted flour properly, spoon it—after sifting—into a dry measuring cup (or spoon) well above the top, then level or cut off with the edge —not the flat surface—of a metal spatula or knife. Do not shake flour down.

To grate rind of citrus fruit, which must be done before squeezing, work on a flat grater placed on top of a piece of waxed paper.

mixture is very creamy and smooth. Add the yolks, one at a time, and continue beating until batter makes "ribbons" and falls back on itself. Mix in the yogurt, using a wooden spatula.

Place flour, salt, and baking powder in the sifter and sift into the batter, a small amount at a time, mixing with a spatula until very smooth. Finally, stir in the lemon rind.

Beat the egg whites with a rotary or electric beater until they form stiff, shiny peaks when the beater is held straight up. Whip about a third into the yogurt mixture thoroughly with a wire whisk. Then *fold* in the remainder with a rubber spatula. Pour into tube pan and bake for 60 minutes or until a toothpick inserted in the center comes out dry.

Cool on a cake rack for 15 minutes. Then run a metal spatula around the pan, turn the cake out on the cake rack and allow to cool completely.

Beat egg whites to the stiff, shiny stage only. If beaten longer, they become granular.

For exact folding technique —see page 305.

VEGETABLE POT ROAST

Buttered Noodles with Poppy Seeds   Dill Pickles

Avocado and Orange Salad Vinaigrette

Jelly Roll   Coffee

YOUR COOKING SCHEDULE: The Jelly Roll must be baked and finished a good bit ahead of time, if not in the morning then, certainly, early in the afternoon.

As for the Pot Roast, it must be in the oven at least 2 hours before dinnertime, so you should be in the kitchen preparing the vegetables 30 to 40 minutes prior to that. The salad is more or less last minute, and the noodles definitely last minute.

VEGETABLE POT ROAST

EQUIPMENT:

French chef's knife; heavy, ovenproof casserole, large enough to accommodate meat comfortably, and with a tight-fitting lid; 2-pronged kitchen fork; 1 medium saucepan; electric blender; slicing knife.

INGREDIENTS:

To peel, slice, mince, or dice onions, garlic, and shallots the easy way—see directions on page 306.

To dice the carrots—follow the same techniques as for onions, omitting the horizontal slicing.

To cut celery ribs—slice from one end up to, but not through, the top. Then cut down the length of the ribs into cubes.

1 4- to 5-pound rump, chuck or round, rolled and tied
2 medium onions, *peeled*, diced fine
1 clove garlic, *peeled*, *minced*
2 small white turnips, peeled and diced fine
2 carrots, *diced* fine
2 ribs celery, *diced* fine

1 green pepper, *diced* fine
Few parsley sprigs, *minced*
2 tablespoons (¼ stick) butter, vegetable oil, or bacon fat
2 tablespoons salt
Several twists of the peppermill
Good dash of cayenne

To prepare the green pepper, cut off the top, cut in half, cut out the ribs and brush away the seeds. Make narrow vertical slices from top to bottom, then bundle up the strips and cut into small cubes.

To mince parsley—hold the blade of a heavy French chef's knife at both ends and chop with rapid up-and-down motions, pulling the ingredients back into a pile with the knife as you work.

The success of this unusually good pot roast lies in the quantity and variety of the vegetables which flavor the meat and, in themselves, turn into a delicious sauce. The vegetables must be chopped into the finest possible pieces.

Preheat the oven to 325° (or slow) for 15 minutes before the pot roast goes in. Heat the fat in the ovenproof casserole. When the fat is hot, add the meat and brown quickly on all sides. Take off the heat, sprinkle with salt, pepper, and cayenne. Add the chopped vegetables, cover, place in the oven and cook for 2 hours, or until the meat is very tender when pierced with a fork. Lift from the casserole and set aside for the moment.

Pour the vegetable sauce from the casserole into the container of the electric blender and blend to a smooth purée. If the blender won't hold it all at once, purée a small quantity at a time. Pour into a saucepan to reheat and *taste* for seasoning.

To serve, *slice* the meat very thin and arrange slices overlapping on a heated platter. Spoon a little of the hot sauce over the sliced meat and pour the remainder into a warm sauceboat. Serves about 6 to 8.

Cold Pot Roast is marvelous the second day accompanied by Sautéed Green Peppers (page 107), Fried Potato Cake (page 135), and perhaps Hot Gingerbread (page 199) for dessert.

To carve rolled pot roast (sometimes a problem because of the string)—place the roast on its side on a warm platter. Steadying it with a fork, slice down vertically in even slices, removing the string as you go along. Then turn roast, cut side up, so meat won't lose its juices.

Learn to taste. It makes sense, since one person's salt-and-pepper tolerance can be quite different from another's.

BUTTERED NOODLES WITH POPPY SEEDS

EQUIPMENT:
Large (6-quart) kettle; colander; kitchen knife; measuring cups and spoons; serving dish.

INGREDIENTS:
1 package (8-ounce size) noodles
Butter
Poppy Seeds

Bring about 3 quarts of salted water to a rolling boil in the kettle. Add the pasta gradually so water will not stop boiling. Boil briskly, uncovered, for 4 minutes. At this point taste. Noodles should be al dente or firm to the bite. Continue taste-testing until the noodles are only very slightly resistant. Drain immediately through a colander. Pour the noodles into the heated serving dish, add about ¼ cup (½ stick) butter cut into pieces, and a tablespoon or so of poppy seeds. Toss until the noodles are well buttered. Serve immediately. Serves 6.

AVOCADO AND ORANGE SALAD VINAIGRETTE

EQUIPMENT:
French chef's knife; lemon squeezer; kitchen bowl; measuring cups and spoons.

INGREDIENTS:

Fresh crisp *salad greens*
2 avocados
Juice 1 lemon

2 navel oranges
Sauce Vinaigrette (page 44) made
   with lemon juice

Wash all salad greens under cool running water to eliminate any sand, shake to get rid of as much surplus water as possible, roll in a fresh dish towel to dry and refrigerate in the vegetable container.

To peel the orange, see page 307.

Cut the avocados in half, remove the *seed*, peel, then slice thin. Arrange on top of greens on individual plates and sprinkle with the lemon juice.

Peel the orange and slice very thin. Add any juice to salad dressing. Arrange orange slices on top of the avocado. Spoon a tablespoon or so of the Sauce Vinaigrette over each serving. Serves 6.

To extricate the seed—cut the avocado lengthwise, twisting gently to separate the halves. Then whack a heavy, sharp knife directly into the seed and twist to lift out.

JELLY ROLL

EQUIPMENT:

Measuring cups and spoons; flour sifter; 15 × 10 × 1-inch jelly-roll pan; waxed paper; rotary or electric beater; 2 generous mixing bowls; rubber spatula; paring knife; clean dish towels; metal spatula.

INGREDIENTS:

Vegetable shortening	½ cup tart currant jelly
½ cup sifted cake flour	½ cup granulated sugar
⅛ teaspoon salt	½ teaspoon vanilla
3 eggs, *separated*	Sifted confectioners' sugar

If you haven't mastered the trick of separating egg yolks from egg whites, see page 305.

To grease—crumple up a little waxed paper, scoop up a bit of the fat and coat pan.

Preheat oven to 400° (or hot) for 15 minutes before baking the Jelly Roll.

Grease jelly-roll pan. *Line* with waxed paper, then grease the paper. Set aside. Sift the flour and salt together. Set it aside, too.

To line—place the pan on a piece of waxed paper. Outline the shape with a pencil, then cut out with scissors and place in bottom of the pan.

Beat the egg yolks with a rotary or electric beater for approximately 5 minutes. Next, beat the egg whites until they begin to hold a soft shape. Add the granulated sugar very gradually, beating constantly, until the meringue holds firm, shiny peaks when the beater is held straight up. Pour the beaten yolks over the beaten whites. Add the vanilla, then *fold* in carefully, but thoroughly with a rubber spatula. Sift the flour mixture over the top. Fold that in, too, with care.

For exact folding technique —see page 305.

Pour batter into the prepared pan and bake in the preheated oven for 13 to 15 minutes or until the cake pulls away from the sides of the pan.

Loosen the edges of the cake with a knife as soon as it comes from the oven. Turn the pan upside down onto a clean towel that has been *dusted* with sifted confectioners' sugar. Peel off the waxed paper gently. With a sharp knife trim

To dust—sift a light film of confectioners' sugar over the cloth.

off any crusty edges. While still warm, roll up the cake, starting with the narrow end. Cake rolls more easily if you push or urge it along with the towel. Wrap the roll in waxed paper and cool. When completely cold, unroll and spread with the jelly, using a metal spatula. Roll again and place on a suitable serving dish. Finish the top with a sprinkling of sifted confectioners' sugar. Slice to serve.

PAN-FRIED HAMBURGERS

French Bread or Fresh Soft Toast   *Coleslaw*

Quick Baba au Rhum   *Coffee*

YOUR COOKING SCHEDULE: Both the coleslaw and the Baba au Rhum (except for the whipped cream, which is added just before serving) can be made early in the day. The coleslaw, in fact, would benefit by a few hours of mellowing. If toast, rather than French bread, is used, it should be made more or less at the last minute, otherwise it will dry out, and one of its purposes is to mop up the good juices. The hamburgers must be cooked just before serving, but you can mince the parsley ahead, wrap in foil or Saran and refrigerate.

PAN-FRIED HAMBURGERS

EQUIPMENT:

French chef's knife; heavy skillet; peppermill; paper towels; measuring spoons.

The quality of a cooked hamburger depends on the *quality of the meat* and the amount of handling. Shape into patties gently, never pound into shape. Pan-frying hamburgers is far superior to broiling.

INGREDIENTS:

2 pounds ground chuck	*Freshly ground* pepper
½ cup (1 stick) butter (about)	8 to 10 sprigs parsley, *minced*
Salt	Dry vermouth or dry red wine

Have a platter warming in a 140° (very low) oven before you start the hamburgers.

Shape the meat into 8 patties, about ½ to 1 inch thick. Melt 2 to 3 tablespoons butter in skillet to make a good film on the pan. When piping hot, add as many patties as the pan will accommodate without crowding. Move them around so they get buttered, then turn and move again to butter the other side. This helps to keep them from sticking. *Sauté*, over a high heat, 3 minutes on one side and 2 minutes on the second side for rare (the only way to serve a good hamburger).

Immediately lift onto the heated platter. Add more butter to the skillet as it is needed. Sauté the remaining hamburgers the same way. Sprinkle with salt and pepper to *taste* and keep warm.

Cool the pan a bit, then wipe out with paper towel. Add about 3 or 4 tablespoons (½ stick) fresh butter. When this is hot and melted, but not browned,

Use a peppermill for this. Freshly ground pepper is more vibrant than already-ground pepper. Both black and white peppercorns are available, the former being somewhat lustier.

To sauté—cook, or brown meat in a small amount of very hot fat.

Learn to taste. It makes sense, since one person's salt-and-pepper tolerance can be quite different from another's.

If you are in an extravagant mood, buy ground sirloin. It makes a "King" of a hamburger. Otherwise we recommend ground chuck because it has just the right proportions of fat to meat (15% meat to 20% fat). Whatever the meat, look for the bluish-red color that indicates freshly ground. Note: ground meat does not freeze well; always use on the day of purchase or at least within 24 hours.

To mince parsley—hold the blade of a large French chef's knife at both ends and chop with rapid up-and-down motions, pulling the ingredients back into a pile with the knife as you work.

add about 6 tablespoons of wine and the parsley. Bring to a boil, then pour over the cooked hamburgers. Serves 4.

COLESLAW

EQUIPMENT:

Serrated bread knife; measuring cups and spoons; double boiler; wire whisk; medium-size mixing bowl; colander; Saran.

INGREDIENTS:

1 2-pound head *cabbage*	6 tablespoons sugar
¼ cup (½ stick) butter	1 teaspoon dry mustard
1 tablespoon flour	1 teaspoon salt
½ cup milk, heated	½ cup vinegar
2 eggs	1 teaspoon caraway seeds

Choose cabbages that feel heavy for their size, that are firm, free from worm injury, decay, yellow leaves, and burst heads. Any type of cabbage can be used for coleslaw.

To shred—remove any wilted or damaged outside leaves. Cut cabbage in two. Place cut side down. Then, with a long, sharp knife —a serrated bread knife is good—slice cabbage very thin, skipping the core.

Shred the cabbage very fine. Cover with cold, salted water and allow to stand for 1 hour.

Melt the butter in the top of the double boiler, then stir in the flour until smooth. Gradually add the milk, whipping with a wire whisk until smooth.

Place the eggs, sugar, mustard, and salt in the mixing bowl and whip together, using a wire whisk. Dribble in the hot milk slowly, whipping constantly. Pour back into the top of the boiler and place over *simmering* water and cook, whipping constantly, just until the sauce thickens and coats a spoon. Cooked longer it will curdle.

To simmer—cook liquid just below boiling (185°) so that it just shivers.

Take off the heat at once and gradually stir in the vinegar and caraway seeds. Cool.

Drain the cabbage in a colander, pressing out any remaining water. When thoroughly drained place in a suitable serving dish and add the cooked dressing. Toss lightly. Seal with Saran until serving time. Serves 4 to 6.

QUICK BABA AU RHUM

EQUIPMENT:
Measuring cups and spoons; waxed paper; 8-inch ring-mold pan; small saucepan; wooden spatula; metal spatula; bulb baster.

INGREDIENTS:

Butter
1 box yellow cake mix
½ cup sugar
½ cup dark rum

1 cup heavy cream, whipped
Candied violets or rose petals (optional)

Preheat oven to 350° (or moderate) for 15 minutes before baking the Baba.

Butter ring-mold pan very thoroughly. Set aside. Mix up the yellow cake mix according to package directions. Pour enough of the *batter* into the prepared mold to reach to almost half the depth of the mold. Bake for 25 minutes or until a toothpick inserted in the cake comes out with no batter clinging to it. Allow to stand on a rack for 10 minutes before turning out.

While the cake is baking, combine the sugar with ½ cup of water in a small saucepan and stir with a wooden spatula, over low heat, until the sugar has dissolved. Take off the heat and stir in the rum.

Run a metal spatula around the edge of the pan, then invert the cake on a suitable serving platter and lift off the mold. While the cake is still hot, pour the rum syrup over the entire surface. It will soak in immediately. If any of the syrup remains on the plate, suck it up with a bulb baster and spray over the cake, or use a spoon.

To serve, fill the center of the ring with whipped cream and, if you like, garnish with candied violets or rose petals (if you happen to have some).

To butter—crumple up a small piece of waxed paper, scoop up a bit of butter, and coat the bottom and sides of the mold generously.

Bake any remaining batter in greased custard cups or muffin tins, according to package directions.

—◆◆—

ITALIAN MEAT LOAF WITH TOMATO SAUCE

Buttered Baby New Potatoes   *Sautéed Eggplant*

Mixed Green Salad, Vinaigrette
(page 44)

Spiked Squash Pie   *Coffee*

YOUR COOKING SCHEDULE: Salad greens, as always, should be washed, wrapped in a fresh dish towel to dry, and refrigerated several hours before serving time. A mixed green salad is nothing more than a combination of two or more greens. Here, we suggest curly endive and Boston lettuce, the endive adding a bright "bite." If you like your Squash Pie at room temperature, it should go into the oven about 3 o'clock if dinner is to be at 7:00. But if you like it warm, it should go in the oven around 5:00. The meat loaf should take no more than 20 minutes to prepare, and it should be baking at approximately 6 o'clock. During this brief interlude, the eggplant can be sautéed. Cook and dress the potatoes during the last 20 minutes the meat loaf bakes.

ITALIAN MEAT LOAF WITH TOMATO SAUCE

EQUIPMENT:
Measuring cups and spoons; peppermill; can opener; French chef's knife; 8 × 10-inch shallow baking dish, attractive enough to go to the table; flat grater; 2 mixing bowls.

INGREDIENTS:

1 pound ground beef

2 tablespoons (¼ stick) butter

2 slices rye bread or about 8 slices cocktail rye

2 slices firm white bread

1 cup milk

1 medium onion, *minced*

5 to 6 sprigs parsley, *minced*

3 tablespoons *freshly grated* Parmesan cheese

1 egg

1 teaspoon salt

Several twists of the peppermill

1 can (8-ounce size) tomato sauce

1 teaspoon oregano

To peel, mince, or slice onions, garlic, shallots the easy way—see directions on page 306.

To mince parsley—hold the blade of a large French chef's knife at both ends and chop with rapid up-and-down motions, pulling the ingredients back into a pile with the knife as you work.

Cut Parmesan cheese into relatively small chunks and grate in the blender. It is available in jars, ready-grated, but does not have the vibrant quality of freshly grated cheese.

To butter—crumple up a little waxed paper, scoop up a bit of butter and coat the bottom and sides of the baking dish generously.

Preheat the oven to 375° (or moderate) for 15 minutes.

Butter the baking dish and set aside.

Break up both breads into relatively small pieces, place in a bowl with the milk and allow it to soak.

Combine thoroughly the meat, onion, parsley, cheese, egg, salt and pepper. Best done with clean hands. Drain off any surplus milk from the bread, then work the bread into the meat mixture, making sure it is well distributed. Place in the prepared pan and shape into a neat loaf. Dot with the remaining butter and bake in the preheated oven for 30 minutes. At this point, pour the tomato sauce over the loaf, sprinkle with the oregano, and bake 20 minutes longer.

This is one of those rare things, a meat loaf that tastes equally good cold. Serves 4 to 6, depending on appetites.

BUTTERED BABY NEW POTATOES

EQUIPMENT:
Heavy saucepan with a cover; sharp paring knife; peppermill; French chef's knife.

Scrub the potatoes (allow about 3 to 4 per person) depending on size. Place, skin on, in a saucepan, add a tablespoon of salt and enough *boiling water* to cover. Put lid on the pan and cook over moderate heat for about 20 minutes, or until potatoes are just tender when pierced with the point of a small sharp knife. If water boils away, add more boiling water to cover. Drain thoroughly, then shake over a high heat or out the window to dry quickly. Do not peel. Sprinkle with salt and freshly ground pepper. Add about ¼ cup (½ stick) butter, melted, and roll the potatoes around so they are lightly coated. Pour into a heated serving dish.

Always start potatoes cooking in boiling, salted water.

Another way, with chives: Just before serving sprinkle generously with finely *minced* chives, or parsley, or a combination of both.

To mince parsley or chives —hold the blade of a heavy French chef's knife at both ends and chop with rapid up-and-down motions, pulling the ingredients back into a pile with a knife as you work.

SAUTÉED EGGPLANT

EQUIPMENT:
Peppermill; paring knife; French chef's knife; measuring cups and spoons; clean paper bag such as a garbage bag; large, heavy skillet; paper towels; cookie or baking sheet; lemon squeezer.

INGREDIENTS:

1½- to 2-pound eggplant	6 tablespoons (¾ stick) butter
Flour	2 tablespoons olive oil
Salt	Lemon juice
Freshly ground pepper	

Use a peppermill for this. Freshly ground pepper is more vibrant than already-ground pepper. Both black and white peppercorns are available, the former being somewhat lustier.

Peel the eggplant and cut into slices about ½ inch thick. Season a few table-spoons of flour with salt and pepper and place in any clean paper bag. Drop the slices, a few at a time, into the bag and shake gently to coat. Shake off any excess. In a heavy skillet heat enough butter and oil to reach to a depth of about ¼ inch. Add the eggplant slices, a few at a time, and cook until browned on both sides. As they finish cooking, place on several layers of paper toweling on a baking sheet and keep warm in a low, 140° oven. Serve with a good squeeze of lemon juice. Serves 4 to 6.

SPIKED SQUASH PIE

EQUIPMENT:

Measuring cups and spoons; nutmeg grater; foil or freezer bag; 9-inch pie plate; sharp knife or kitchen scissors; medium-size mixing bowl; rotary beater; rubber or wooden spatula.

INGREDIENTS:

Basic pastry (recipe page 288)	1 cup sugar
1 package (10½-ounce size) frozen Hubbard squash, thawed	1 teaspoon cinnamon
	1 teaspoon freshly grated nutmeg
3 eggs	½ teaspoon ground ginger
1 cup heavy cream	¼ teaspoon ground mace
¼ cup brandy or Cognac	½ teaspoon salt

Preheat oven to 450° (or very hot) for 15 minutes before baking the pie.

Make up half the pastry as directed, following directions for a one-crust pie. Refrigerate while you make the filling.

Beat eggs slightly with a rotary beater in a medium-size mixing bowl. Stir in thawed squash, cream, and brandy with a rubber or wooden spatula. Mix in all remaining ingredients until smooth. Pour into unbaked pie shell and bake in the preheated oven for 10 minutes.

Reduce oven heat to 300° (or slow) and bake for another 45 to 50 minutes or until the tip of a knife inserted one inch from the outside edge comes out clean. Cool.

Serve plain, with Cheddar cheese, or with whipped cream mixed with ginger (½ cup heavy cream, whipped, combined with 2 tablespoons finely chopped crystallized ginger.)

SWEDISH MEAT BALLS

Baked Potatoes, Swedish Style   *Boiled Onions*

Lingonberries   *Cucumber Salad, Swedish Style*
(page 25)

Dacquoise   *Coffee*

YOUR COOKING SCHEDULE: This is one of those lovely meals that can be almost finished early in the day. Except for the final cooking, the meatballs can be completely prepared and "shaped" whenever you have the time; the Dacquoise should be made and frosted several hours before it is to be served; the Cucumber Salad will be improved by a chilling period in the refrigerator; the onions can be cooked hours ahead and reheated just before serving. If you do this, do not drain them until after reheating. To reheat, simply bring to a boil. Do not cook further. Then drain. If you do all these jobs in one fell swoop, you will have nothing to think about until about an hour before dinnertime when the potatoes must go in the oven.

SWEDISH MEAT BALLS

EQUIPMENT:
Measuring cups and spoons; French chef's knife; electric blender (desirable); peppermill; large heavy skillet; wire whisk; tablespoon; Saran; heavy saucepan; paper towels; slotted spoon.

INGREDIENTS:

½ pound finely ground beef

½ pound finely ground lean pork

¼ cup (½ stick) butter

½ small onion, *minced*

2 slices firm bread, *crumbled* fine

1¼ cups milk

1 egg

2 tablespoons cornstarch

1½ teaspoon salt

A few twists of the peppermill

1 tablespoon flour

1 cup (about) light cream

To peel, mince or slice onions, garlic, shallots the easy way—see directions on page 306.

Use firm day-old bread for bread crumbs (1 slice makes ¼ cup). Break into pieces and grind, crust and all, in the electric blender, or crumple by hand until very fine.

Melt 1 tablespoon of the butter in a large, heavy skillet. Add the onion and ½ cup water. Bring to a boil and cook until all the water has evaporated and the onion is very tender and transparent. Add more water if necessary. Combine the bread and milk; beat the egg slightly with a wire whisk. When the bread is soft, mix thoroughly together with all remaining ingredients except the remaining butter, flour and cream.

Dip the spoon in cold water to forestall the mixture sticking to the bowl of the spoon.

Using a tablespoon, *shape* the mixture into balls about the size of a walnut. (Can be prepared in advance to this point, sealed with Saran until time to cook).

Melt 2 tablespoons of the butter in the same skillet. When foaming, place as many meatballs in the pan as it will take comfortably, without crowding. *Sauté* over a good heat, shaking the pan constantly to keep the balls turning over, and shapely. As you finish each batch of the meatballs, pour into a clean saucepan, juices and all. Wipe out the skillet with a paper towel before adding remaining butter and more meatballs. When all have been sautéed, place the saucepan over a moderate heat for 2 or 3 minutes or just long enough to heat through. Lift the meatballs with a slotted spoon to a hot serving dish.

To sauté—cook or brown food in a very small amount of very hot fat.

Learn to taste. It makes sense, since one person's salt-and-pepper tolerance can be quite different from another's.

Mix the flour into the cream until perfectly smooth. Stir into the drippings in the saucepan. Bring to a boil, reduce heat to *simmer* and cook for 5 minutes. *Taste* for seasonings. If sauce seems too thick, add a bit more cream. Pour over the meatballs to serve. Serves about 4, accompanied by the traditional lingonberries, available in jars in fancy groceries, or you can substitute cranberry sauce.

To simmer—cook liquid just below boiling (185°) so that it just shivers.

BAKED POTATOES, SWEDISH STYLE

EQUIPMENT:
Measuring cups and spoons; vegetable peeler; sharp knife; heavy, shallow, earthenware baking dish; bulb baster or metal spoon.

INGREDIENTS:

8 medium-size, mature potatoes
1/4 cup (1/2 stick) butter
Salt

1/4 cup *freshly grated* Parmesan or
    Swiss cheese
2 tablespoons fine bread crumbs

Cut Parmesan cheese into relatively small chunks and grate in the blender. It is available in jars, ready-grated, but does not have the vibrant quality of freshly grated cheese.

Preheat the oven to 500° (or very hot) for 15 minutes before baking the potatoes.

Peel the potatoes, using a vegetable peeler. Wash and dry thoroughly. Then, with a sharp knife, slice each potato in parallel slices, fairly thin, almost all the way through. They will now look like miniature accordions.

Melt 2 tablespoons of the butter in earthenware dish just large enough to accommodate the potatoes easily. Add the potatoes and roll them around in the butter until they are lightly coated. Sprinkle with salt and dot with remaining butter. Place in the preheated oven for 20 minutes. *Baste* a couple of times with the melted butter, using a bulb baster or metal spoon. Then sprinkle with the cheese and bread crumbs and continue baking, without basting, another 25 minutes, or until the potatoes are tender when pierced with the point of a small, sharp knife. Approximately 45 minutes all told. Serve piping hot to 4 or 6.

To baste—spray or brush a liquid or melted fat over food while it cooks.

BOILED ONIONS

EQUIPMENT:

Can opener; measuring cups and spoons; peppermill; large saucepan or skillet with a cover; cheesecloth; sharp paring knife; colander; French chef's knife.

INGREDIENTS:

24 small, white onions, about 1 inch in diameter
½ cup chicken broth, your own or canned condensed
¼ cup (½ stick) butter
Salt

Freshly ground pepper
2 stalks parsley
½ teaspoon thyme
Small piece of bayleaf
Minced parsley

To make bouquet garni, combine parsley, thyme, and bay leaf in a little cheesecloth or bag to make it easy to remove. (Even if other seasonings are added, it is still called a bouquet garni.)

Peel the onions. Place in a heavy, enameled saucepan just large enough to accommodate all the onions flat. You may find a large skillet is better. Add the broth, 2 tablespoons of butter, salt and pepper to taste, and the *bouquet garni*. Bring to a boil, reduce heat to *simmer*, cover and cook 30 to 40 minutes or until tender when pierced with the point of a small, sharp knife. If the liquid boils away before they are cooked, add a bit more. Do not overcook. They should be shapely. Drain and turn into a warm serving dish. Add the remaining butter, softened, and a sprinkling of minced parsley. Serves 4 to 6.

Use a peppermill for this. Freshly ground pepper is more vibrant than already-ground pepper. Both black and white peppercorns are available, the former being somewhat lustier.

To mince parsley—hold the blade of a heavy French chef's knife at both ends and chop with rapid up-and-down motions, pulling the ingredients back into a pile with the knife as you work.

To simmer—cook liquid just below boiling (185°) so that it just shivers.

DACQUOISE

EQUIPMENT:

Electric blender; measuring cups and spoons; large mixing bowl; three 8-inch cake pans; waxed paper; rotary or electric beater or electric mixer; rubber and wooden spatula; small metal spatula; flour sifter.

INGREDIENTS:

1 cup almonds or filberts, skin on
7 or 8 slices zwieback
6 egg *whites*
½ teaspoon salt
1½ cups sugar

Grated rind ½ lemon
2 tablespoons flour
2 tablespoons cornstarch
2 drops vanilla extract

If you haven't mastered the trick of separating egg yolks from egg whites, see page 305.

To grate rind of citrus fruit, which must be done before squeezing—work on a flat grater placed on top of a piece of waxed paper.

Preheat the oven to 250° (or very low) for 15 minutes before baking the layers for the Dacquoise.

Grind the nuts in the electric blender until very fine; then grind the zwieback. Set both aside.

To coat—spoon the flour onto the buttered bottom of a pan. Holding the pan in your hands, tip back and forth so bottom is evenly but lightly coated. Give pan a good whack to knock off any excess.

Take three 8-inch cake pans. Turn upside down and *butter* the bottoms generously, then *coat* with flour. Place egg whites in a very large bowl with the salt. Beat with a rotary or electric beater or in an electric mixer until they begin to take a shape. Gradually add half the sugar, beating constantly and continuously until the meringue is very stiff and shiny. *Fold* in remaining sugar with a rubber spatula. Then fold in all (except 2 tablespoons) of the nuts, the zwieback, and all remaining ingredients. Spread 1/3 of the meringue mixture on the underside of each of the prepared pans, leaving about 1/2 inch all around the edge to allow for spreading. Place in the preheated oven and bake for 45 minutes or until light brown and crisp, but not dry. With a metal spatula carefully lift the layers off the pans onto cake racks and cool. When cold, frost with:

To butter—crumple up a small piece of waxed paper and use as much butter as needed.

For exact folding technique —see directions on page 305.

COFFEE BUTTER CREAM

INGREDIENTS:

1/2 cup (1 stick) butter

2 teaspooons *powdered instant* coffee

2 teaspoons dark rum

1 1/2 cups sifted confectioners' sugar

4 egg yolks

Do not use freeze-dried coffee. It will not dissolve in this mixture.

Cream or work the butter with your hands or in an electric beater until very soft and light. Then stir in the coffee and rum thoroughly. Gradually work in the sugar, using your hands or a wooden spatula, until mixture is very smooth. Add the egg yolks, one at a time, beating hard with the spatula after each addition. With a small metal spatula, spread the *frosting* between the layers, next around the sides, then over the top. Sprinkle with reserved ground nuts.

In frosting cakes—always finish the sides first, then the top.

———————◆◆———————

SMOKED BEEF TONGUE

Mustard Cream Sauce with Capers

Boiled Potatoes   *Harvard Beets*
(page 44)
Spinach Salad with Tarragon Vinaigrette

Fresh Pears with Cheese   *Coffee*

YOUR COOKING SCHEDULE: The tongue ought to be in its kettle and on the stove a good 3 hours before dinner; but once there, it can be left quite alone until it is cooked. Meanwhile, the spinach should be washed and, like all salad greens, dried completely. Hence, the need to do it far enough in advance to give it time to dry. The sauce for the tongue is very quick to do and can be done ahead nicely, then heated up over simmering water. The beets can be completely prepared ahead and reheated over hot water. As is apparent, the dessert calls for no work whatsoever.

SMOKED BEEF TONGUE

EQUIPMENT:
French chef's knife; large kettle with a cover; sharp paring knife; carving knife.

INGREDIENTS:

1 3- to 4-pound smoked beef tongue
1 onion, skin on, stuck with 2 whole
   cloves
1 carrot, coarsely chopped
1 or 2 ribs celery, coarsely chopped

1 bay leaf
A few peppercorns
2 cloves garlic, *crushed*
Several stalks parsley

To crush garlic—give it a good whack with the side of a cleaver, heavy knife, or any heavy flat implement. No need to peel.

To simmer—cook liquid just below boiling (185°) so that it just shivers.

Place the tongue in a large kettle, cover with cold water and bring to a boil. Boil for about 5 minutes, skimming off with a large metal spoon any scum that rises to the surface. Drain off the water, wash the tongue under cold running water, and rinse out the kettle. Return the tongue to the kettle with all remaining ingredients and enough cold water to cover. Bring to a boil, reduce heat, cover, and *simmer* until tongue is very tender when pierced with a fork. Approximately 50 minutes per pound.

Lift the meat from the broth and peel off the skin, using a small sharp paring knife where needed. Trim the tongue neatly, removing any root bones. Return to the broth to keep warm.

In the kitchen carve, against the grain—that is, cutting straight down—in very, very thin slices and arrange on a warm serving platter. Serve with Mustard Cream Sauce with Capers. Serves about 6.

Cold Smoked Tongue, sliced thin, is delicious with Coleslaw (page 116), accompanied by Baked Toast (page 39), or a sturdy bread with sweet butter, mustard pickles, and a plain dessert.

MUSTARD CREAM SAUCE WITH CAPERS

EQUIPMENT:
Measuring cups and spoons; peppermill; double boiler; wooden spatula; wire whisk.

INGREDIENTS:

2 tablespoons (¼ stick) butter
2 tablespoons flour
1 cup half and half or light cream, heated
Salt

Freshly ground white pepper
1 tablespoon Dijon mustard
1 teaspoon dry mustard
2 tablespoons capers, well drained

Use a peppermill for this. Freshly ground pepper is more vibrant than already-ground pepper. Both black and white peppercorns are available, the former being somewhat lustier.

Melt the butter in the top of a double boiler, then mix in the flour with a wooden spatula until you have a smooth paste. Cook, over moderate heat, stirring constantly, for 2 to 3 minutes. Take off the heat, stir in the hot half and half until smooth. Then cook over *simmering* water, whipping constantly with a wire whisk, until the sauce has thickened. Take off the heat and whip in the pepper and two mustards until smooth. Finally, stir in the capers. Place over simmering water to keep warm.

To simmer—cook liquid just below boiling (185°) so that it just shivers.

HARVARD BEETS

EQUIPMENT:
Can opener; measuring cups and spoons; double boiler; colander.

INGREDIENTS:

1 can (1-pound size) baby beets
¼ cup sugar
½ teaspoon salt
½ tablespoon cornstarch

¼ cup cider vinegar
1½ tablespoons ginger marmalade
2 tablespoons (¼ stick) butter

Drain beets thoroughly in a colander and set aside. Combine sugar, salt, cornstarch, and vinegar in the top of a double boiler. Cook over direct heat, stirring constantly with a wire whisk, until mixture is smooth and comes to a boil. Stir in the beets, marmalade, and butter. Place over *simmering* water for 30 minutes, giving it an occasional stir. Serves 4.

To simmer—cook liquid just below boiling (185°) so that it just shivers.

SPINACH SALAD WITH TARRAGON

INGREDIENTS:

2 pounds young raw spinach
Sauce Vinaigrette (page 44)

½ teaspoon dried tarragon

Wash and dry the spinach thoroughly. If really young, simply cut off the stem at the base of each leaf; if somewhat older, in one hand fold each leaf vertically, the underside up. With the other hand rip the stem off toward the tip of the leaf. Tear the leaves apart.

Pour the dressing into a salad bowl and stir in the tarragon. Just before serving, add the spinach leaves and toss at the dinner table. Serves about 4.

FRESH PEARS WITH CHEESE

Except for perhaps the month of May, fresh pears of one variety or another are available all year. With a blue cheese—Roquefort, if you feel expansive— or a Camembert (our domestic is excellent), or perhaps cream cheese, pears make a refreshing climax to a sturdy dinner. The French, of course, would have some crusty bread. You can, too.

Celeriac Rémoulade

BRAISED FRESH TONGUE

Fried Potato Cake   *Baby Lima Beans*

Indian Pudding   *Coffee*

YOUR COOKING SCHEDULE: Since the tongue is partially cooked, then marinated for several hours, it must be started the day before it is to be served. The Celeriac Rémoulade can also be made the day before, since it improves with mellowing. On the assumption dinner will be served at 7 P.M., the final cooking —the braising, to be more precise—should begin no later than 4:30 in the afternoon. The limas can be cooked at this time and reheated just prior to dinner. The potatoes, however, should be fried just before serving so they'll be at their crisp best. Preliminaries for the pudding should be started at the same time you start braising the tongue (4:30), since the pudding bakes 2 hours and is served hot. Place in the oven, right along with the tongue, at 5 o'clock.

CELERIAC RÉMOULADE

EQUIPMENT:
Sharp knife or vegetable peeler; measuring cups and spoons; rubber spatula.

Peel 3 medium celeriac, using a sharp knife or vegetable peeler. Then cut into slices about $\frac{1}{16}$ inch thick. Next cut the slices into strips about as thin as a toothpick. Combine one cup good Mayonnaise, made with lemon juice (page 38), with 1 tablespoon Dijon mustard or to taste. Mix in the celeriac thoroughly, using a rubber spatula, and refrigerate until serving time. Properly covered and refrigerated, the hors d'oeuvre keeps well. Serves 4 to 6.

BRAISED FRESH TONGUE

EQUIPMENT:
French chef's knife; measuring cups and spoons; can opener; heavy kettle with cover; sharp paring knife; polyethylene bag; mixing bowl or pan; large heavy enameled ovenproof casserole with a cover; 2-pronged kitchen fork; strainer; wire whisk.

There are few meats as delectable as fresh beef tongue when properly cooked. Unlike smoked tongue which is generally available in most markets, chances are you will have to shop around for the fresh or even order it from your market, but you'll find it's worth the effort.

INGREDIENTS:

1 3½- to 4-pound fresh beef tongue
3 or 4 carrots, coarsely chopped
2 small or 1 large onion, coarsely chopped
3 ribs celery, coarsely chopped
1 large clove garlic, split
2 bay leaves
4 or 5 stalks parsley
2 or 3 whole cloves

1 bottle dry red wine
⅓ cup Cognac
½ tablespoon salt
6 to 8 whole peppercorns
2 cans (10½-ounce size) condensed beef broth
1 tablespoon of *arrowroot* (optional)

Use arrowroot as a thickening agent when you want the finished sauce to be clear and transparent. Do not cook beyond the point indicated in recipe or the sauce will "thin out."

To simmer—cook in liquid just below boiling (185°) so that the liquid just shivers.

To boil: Place the tongue in a heavy kettle, cover with cold water, and bring up to a boil. Boil for about 5 minutes, skimming off, with a large metal spoon, any scum that rises to the surface. Reduce heat, cover, and *simmer* for 2 hours. Drain and cover with cold water. When the tongue is cool enough to handle, pull off the skin. Where it is reluctant, run a small sharp knife between the meat and skin. Trim off the root end and pull out any bones. Combine all the remaining ingredients except the beef broth and arrowroot in a large polyethylene bag. Add the tongue. Tie securely, squeezing out all air. Place in a bowl or pan in case of leakage and *marinate* for several hours (a minimum of 6), turning occasionally so the meat is well soaked. If overnight, refrigerate.

To marinate—soak or steep meat or other foods in a marinade (seasoned liquid) to impart flavor and, in some instances, to tenderize.

To braise: Preheat the oven to 325° (or slow) for 15 minutes. Place the tongue with the marinade and beef broth in a large, heavy, enameled overproof casserole. Bring up to a boil over a high heat. Cover tightly, then bake in the preheated oven for 2 hours or until very tender when pierced with a fork. Turn the tongue after the first hour. Lift the meat from the liquid onto a warm platter and keep warm. Place the casserole over a high heat and *reduce* the liquid to about half. *Taste* here for seasonings. Strain. If the sauce seems too thin, mix 1 tablespoon of arrowroot with 2 tablespoons of wine until smooth. Add to the sauce and cook over a low heat, whipping constantly with a wire whip, until slightly thickened.

To serve, slice the tongue and arrange, overlapping, on a large warm platter. Spoon some of the sauce over the meat, and pour remainder into a warm sauceboat. Serves about 6.

Learn to taste. It makes sense, since one person's salt-and-pepper tolerance can be quite different from another's.

To reduce—simply boil a liquid over a high heat until the amount left is what the recipe specifies.

FRIED POTATO CAKE

EQUIPMENT:
Heavy saucepan with a cover; paring knife; heavy 10-inch iron skillet; metal spatula; bulb baster; large kitchen plate.

INGREDIENTS:

4 medium-size mature potatoes	1 tablespoon butter
4 tablespoons vegetable shortening	Salt

Drop the potatoes in their jackets in enough boiling, salted water to cover. Add the lid and cook for 15 minutes. At this point they will be only partially cooked. Drain, cool and chill in their skins for several hours or even overnight in the refrigerator. Peel, then cut into fine *julienne*. Heat the shortening and butter in a heavy 10-inch pan. Sprinkle (don't dump) the shredded potatoes into the pan, then salt lightly. Press the potatoes down with a metal spatula and cook, over medium heat, until the underside is well browned and crusty. To turn, place a plate on top and flip over. Then slide the potato cake back into the pan and brown the other side. Suck off any fat with a bulb baster and ease onto a heated serving platter. Serves 5 or 6.

To julienne any food—simply cut it into thin fine strips.

BABY LIMA BEANS

EQUIPMENT:
Saucepan; peppermill.

Always buy baby limas in the pod and shell just before cooking, as shelled beans turn tough very fast. Available frozen, too.

Shell the *beans* just before cooking (allow about 2 pounds for 4 to 5 people). Cook in just enough boiling salted water to cover, *without the lid*, for 15 to 20 minutes or until the largest beans taste tender. Drain, pour into a heated serving dish and dress with salt, *freshly ground* pepper and melted butter.

Always cook green vegetables uncovered to retain their color.

Use a peppermill for this. Freshly ground pepper is more vibrant than already-ground pepper. Both black and white peppercorns are available, the former being somewhat lustier.

INDIAN PUDDING

EQUIPMENT:
Measuring cups and spoons; double boiler; wooden spatula; 1-quart baking dish.

INGREDIENTS:

5 cups milk
1/3 cup cornmeal
2 tablespoons (1/4 stick) butter
1/4 cup molasses

1/4 cup brown sugar, firmly packed
1/2 teaspoon salt
1/2 teaspoon cinnamon
1/2 teaspoon ground ginger

Preheat the oven to 325° (or slow) for 15 minutes before baking the pudding.

Pour the milk into the top of the double boiler and heat over boiling water. When hot, stir in the cornmeal. Cook, over *simmering* water, stirring frequently with a wooden spatula, for 10 minutes. Stir in all remaining ingredients and continue cooking, with an occasional stir, 10 minutes longer. Pour into a 1-quart baking dish and bake 2 hours in the preheated oven.

Serve hot with heavy cream or vanilla ice cream.

To simmer—cook liquid just below boiling (185°) so that it just shivers.

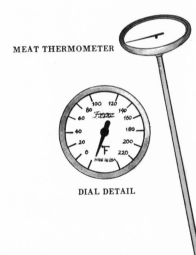

MEAT THERMOMETER

DIAL DETAIL

THE THERMOMETERS

The ideal meat thermometer, which registers from 0° to 220°, is so sensitive you can even use it to test steak for doneness. Every cook worthy of the name should roast meats "by the thermometer." For frosting, syrups of all kinds, candy, deep-fat frying, etc., there is no substitute for a good candy thermometer.

CANDY THERMOMETER

VEAL

VEAL SCALOPPINE

Sautéed Cherry Tomatoes   *French Bread*

Salade à la Crème

Sicilian Cheese Cake   *Coffee*

YOUR COOKING SCHEDULE: Since the Sicilian Cake needs several hours in the refrigerator, it must be made early in the day or, if you like, the day before. As always, salad greens need washing in plenty of time to allow them to dry. Other than that, the entire meal is pretty much last minute, but quick last minute. Both the meat and the tomatoes take about the same amount of time to cook—a matter of minutes—so it really doesn't matter which one you do first. And the salad dressing is next best to instant.

VEAL SCALOPPINE

EQUIPMENT:

Measuring cups and spoons; peppermill; French chef's knife; paper towels; large heavy skillet; lemon squeezer; rubber spatula.

INGREDIENTS:

1½ pounds scaloppine

Butter

Vegetable oil

Salt

Freshly ground pepper

Juice of 1 lemon

Minced parsley

To mince parsley—hold the blade of a heavy French chef's knife at both ends and chop with rapid up-and-down motions, pulling the ingredients back into a pile with the knife as you work.

Use a peppermill for this. Freshly ground pepper is more vibrant than already-ground pepper. Both black and white peppercorns are available, the former being somewhat lustier.

To sauté—cook or brown food in a very small amount of very hot fat.

Dry the meat thoroughly between paper towels, but do not allow it to stand any length of time or the paper will cling tenaciously to it. Before *sautéeing* the veal, have ready, warming in the oven, a platter on which to place the meat as it is cooked. Heat 2 tablespoons of butter and 1 tablespoon of oil in a large, heavy skillet until hot.

As you put each piece of meat in the pan, turn it over immediately with your fingers so it is "buttered" on both sides and won't stick to the pan. Add only as many pieces as the pan will hold comfortably without crowding. Cook for about 1 minute on each side. Then lift from the pan to the heated platter. Add more butter and oil, in the same proportions, as needed. When all the scaloppine is cooked, sprinkle with salt and pepper, and keep warm.

Wipe out the pan with paper towels, add a lump of fresh butter—about 4 tablespoons (½ stick). When melted and barely hot, stir in the lemon juice, stirring constantly with a rubber spatula. The minute the lemon juice and butter meet, the mixture will begin to thicken and turn into a sauce. At this point pour over the scaloppine. Garnish with minced parsley. Serves 4.

French bread or any other sturdy white bread is essential for mopping up the good juices.

SAUTÉED CHERRY TOMATOES

EQUIPMENT:

Large heavy skillet; French chef's knife; peppermill.

INGREDIENTS:

2 boxes ripe cherry tomatoes	Salt
Olive oil	*Freshly ground* pepper
2 cloves garlic (about), *peeled, minced*	Pinch of sugar
	Minced parsley

To peel, slice, mince, or dice onions, garlic, and shallots the easy way—see directions on page 306.

Pull the stems off the tomatoes. Heat enough good olive oil in the skillet to make a generous film over the bottom. Add the tomatoes and the garlic and cook, over a high heat, shaking the pan constantly until a few of the tomatoes just begin to burst—a matter of minutes. Take off the heat, sprinkle with salt, pepper and the sugar. Just before serving stir in minced parsley. Serves 4.

Use a peppermill for this. Freshly ground pepper is more vibrant than already-ground pepper. Both black and white peppercorns are available, the former being somewhat lustier.

To mince parsley—hold the blade of a heavy French chef's knife at both ends and chop with rapid up-and-down motions, pulling the ingredients back into a pile with the knife as you work.

SALADE À LA CRÈME

EQUIPMENT:

Lemon squeezer; measuring spoons; peppermill; wire whisk.

This is simply fresh salad greens such as Boston or Bibb tossed in a cream dressing made in these proportions: 2 teaspoons lemon juice to 3 tablespoons

Learn to taste. This makes sense, since one person's salt-and-pepper tolerance can be quite different from another's.

commercial sour cream or heavy cream, seasoned with salt and *freshly ground* white pepper to *taste*.

To make: Mix the lemon juice with salt and pepper in the salad bowl, then whip in the sour cream with a wire whisk. If heavy cream is used, add another teaspoon of lemon juice. Add the salad greens just before serving. Toss at the table. Figure on about 1 tablespoon of sauce per person.

Use a peppermill for this. Freshly ground pepper is more vibrant than already-ground pepper. Both black and white peppercorns are available, the former being somewhat lustier.

SICILIAN CHEESECAKE

EQUIPMENT:
Measuring cups and spoons; French chef's knife; table fork; wooden spatula; small metal spatula.

INGREDIENTS:

1 commercial sponge cake
6 tablespoons dark rum
1½ pounds cottage or ricotta cheese
½ cup superfine sugar

¼ cup semisweet chocolate pieces, chopped
¼ cup toasted almonds, chopped
½ teaspoon cinnamon

Slice the sponge cake into three thin layers. Sprinkle each layer with 2 tablespoons of the rum. Set aside.

Mash the cheese with a fork until smooth. Then gradually work in the superfine sugar. Best done with your hands. When smooth, stir in all remaining ingredients, using a wooden spatula. Spread mixture between the three layers of cake with a metal spatula, dividing it evenly.

FROSTING

EQUIPMENT:

Measuring cups and spoons; flour sifter; rotary or electric beater; rubber spatula; metal spatula.

INGREDIENTS:

¼ cup (½ stick) butter

2½ cups sifted confectioners' sugar

2 egg *whites*

1 teaspoon almond extract

Work the butter with an electric beater until very soft. Gradually work in 1 cup of the sugar until very smooth.

Beat egg whites with a rotary or electric beater until they just begin to hold shape. Gradually add the remaining sugar, beating constantly until the mixture stands in firm, shiny peaks. *Fold* into the butter mixture with a rubber spatula. Finally, stir in the almond extract.

Frost the sides first, using a metal spatula, and then the top of the cake. Refrigerate for several hours.

Beat egg whites only to the stiff, shiny stage. If beaten longer, they become granular.

If you haven't mastered the trick of separating egg yolks from egg whites, see directions on page 305.

For exact folding technique —see directions on page 305.

BLANQUETTE DE VEAU

Boiled Rice, the Chinese Way
(page 29)

Bibb Salad with Grapes,
Garlic Dressing
(page 12)

Lemon Soufflé   Coffee

YOUR COOKING SCHEDULE: You should allow yourself a good hour in the kitchen to prepare the blanquette. Up to, but not including, the last step—the sauce, which will take you no more than 5 minutes—initial preparations can be made early in the day. While the meat is cooking, you can wash the grapes, make the garlic dressing, boil the rice, and prepare the soufflé, all except the egg whites. A half hour before dinner, reheat the rice in a double boiler over simmering water; make the liaison, the mixture of eggs and cream, and add to the stew. Heat the stew through over a very low fire, remembering it must not boil. As you are about to go to the table, beat the egg whites and combine with the soufflé base. Pour into the prepared mold and bake it while you enjoy your dinner.

BLANQUETTE DE VEAU

EQUIPMENT:

Measuring cups and spoons; French chef's knife; can opener; peppermill; lemon squeezer; heavy kettle with a cover; cheesecloth; 2-pronged fork; large metal spoon; sieve; 2 kitchen bowls; flameproof casserole with a cover (also to be used for serving); large heavy saucepan; paring knife; second large saucepan; wooden spatula; wire whisk; Saran.

This flawless and famous French dish makes an elegant presentation, which in turn makes it a marvelous dish for a big party. However, that doesn't preclude your serving it to your family.

INGREDIENTS:

3 pounds shoulder or breast of veal, cut into 2-inch pieces
6 cups your own chicken broth or 4 cans (10½-ounce size) condensed chicken broth
1 large onion, skin on, stuck with 2 cloves
1 carrot, coarsely chopped
2 ribs celery, coarsely chopped
8 to 10 stalks parsley
½ bay leaf
½ teaspoon dried thyme

Salt
18 to 24 small white onions
½ cup (1 stick) butter
4 tablespoons flour
3½ cups of veal broth
1 pound *button mushrooms*
Freshly ground white pepper
Juice 1 lemon
3 egg *yolks*
½ cup heavy cream
Minced parsley

Button mushrooms, the least expensive, are best in cooked dishes. Mushrooms need not be peeled.

Use a peppermill for this. Both black and white peppercorns are available, the former being somewhat lustier.

If you haven't mastered the trick of separating egg yolks from egg whites, see directions on page 305.

To mince parsley—hold the blade of a heavy French chef's knife at both ends and chop with rapid up-and-down motions, pulling the ingredients back into a pile with the knife as you work.

Place the veal in the kettle, cover with cold water, and bring to a boil. Reduce

To simmer—cook liquid just below boiling (185°) so that it just shivers.

heat and *simmer* for 4 to 5 minutes. Drain, then wash quickly under cold water to remove all traces of scum. Rinse out the kettle and return the meat, adding enough chicken broth to cover. If 6 cups are not sufficient to cover the meat, add enough water to make up the difference. Bring to a boil slowly, skimming off with a large metal spoon any scum that comes to the surface. Tie the large onion, carrot, celery, parsley, bay leaf and thyme in a cheesecloth bag and add to the kettle with 2 teaspoons of salt.

Reduce heat to simmer, cover, and cook for about 1¼ hours or until the veal is tender when pierced with a fork. Take care not to overcook it or the meat will be stringy and tasteless. When tender, drain through a sieve into a bowl, reserving the broth. Discard the cheesecloth bag with vegetables. Turn meat into a flameproof casserole from which you intend to serve it.

To peel, slice, mince, or dice onions, garlic, and shallots the easy way—see directions on page 306.

Meanwhile, *peel* the small onions. Place in a heavy saucepan. Add 3 tablespoons of the butter, a good pinch of salt, several twists of the peppermill and 1 cup of the reserved broth. Cover and cook, over moderate heat, until onions are tender when pierced with the point of a small sharp paring knife, but still shapely. Approximately 20 minutes. Drain and combine with the meat.

Wipe the mushroom caps with a clean damp cloth and break off the stems. (They can be used to make soup.) Melt the remaining butter in a large saucepan. Stir in the flour and cook, stirring with a wooden spatula, for 2 to 3 minutes. Do not brown. Stir in 3½ cups of the veal broth. Bring up to a boil, whipping constantly with a wire whisk. Reduce heat and simmer for 10 minutes. Skim off any scum that rises to the surface. Add the mushroom caps and cook 10 minutes longer. Add salt and pepper to *taste* and the lemon juice. Set aside 1 cup sauce, without mushrooms. Pour remainder over veal and onions. The Blanquette can be prepared in advance to this point, sealed with Saran, and finished later.

Learn to taste. It makes sense, since one person's salt-and-pepper tolerance can be quite different from another's.

Beat the egg yolks and the cream with a wire whisk until well mixed. Then gradually beat in the reserved cup of *hot sauce*. Add to the veal, stirring it in with a wooden spatula, taking care not to break the meat or vegetables. Place over a moderate heat just long enough to heat through, but do not allow it to boil or the sauce will curdle.

Sprinkle generously with minced parsley just before serving. Serve straight from the casserole to 6 or 8.

Blanquette of Lamb is made exactly the same way; simply substitute the same amount of lamb for veal.

Stir 2 or 3 tablespoons of the hot sauce into the beaten eggs to warm them a bit, then gradually combine the two, to avoid "scrambling" the eggs.

LEMON SOUFFLÉ

EQUIPMENT:

Measuring cups; grater; lemon squeezer; 2-quart soufflé dish; waxed paper; double boiler; wire whisk; Saran; large mixing bowl; electric mixer; rotary or electric beater; rubber spatula.

INGREDIENTS:

¾ cup (1½ sticks) butter, cut into pieces	3 extra egg whites
¾ cup sugar	Juice 1½ lemons
9 eggs, *separated*	*Grated* rind 1½ lemons
	Pinch of salt

If you haven't mastered the trick of separating egg yolks from egg whites, see directions on page 305.

To butter—crumple up a little waxed paper, scoop up a bit of butter and coat the bottom and sides of the dish generously.

Butter soufflé dish thoroughly, making sure the bottom and curves are well buttered. To coat, add a few tablespoons of sugar to the buttered mold. Then, holding it over the sink, tip the mold back and forth so the sugar coats the bottom and sides. Turn upside down and give it a good thump to knock out any excess. Refrigerate.

To grate rind of citrus fruit, which must be done before squeezing—work on a flat grater placed on top of a piece of waxed paper.

Combine remaining butter, sugar, egg yolks, and lemon juice in the top of a double boiler. Cook over simmering water, stirring constantly with a wooden spatula until mixture thickens. Take off the heat, and stir in the lemon rind. The soufflé can be prepared in advance to this point, then sealed with Saran.

Before baking the soufflé preheat the oven to 325° (or slow) for 15 minutes.

Place the egg whites in a very large bowl with a dash of salt. The electric mixer is ideal when you have a quantity as large as this.) Lacking a mixer, *beat* with a rotary or electric beater until the whites stand in firm, shiny peaks when the beater is held straight up. Beat about a third of the whites into the lemon mixture vigorously with a wire whisk. Then *fold* in remaining whites with a rubber spatula. Don't worry if there are a few small patches of whites. Better that than a "flat" soufflé.

Pour into the prepared soufflé dish and bake in the preheated oven for 40 minutes. If you like a firm-in-the-center soufflé, bake another 5 minutes or so. Place the soufflé dish on a tray with a folded napkin underneath. This keeps the dish from sliding around when you plunge into the soufflé. Serve at once.

Beat egg whites to the stiff, shiny stage only. If beaten longer, they become granular.

For exact folding technique —see directions on page 305.

VITELLO TONNATO   (Veal with Tuna)

Cold Parsleyed Rice   *Sliced Tomatoes with Basil*

Baked Toast
(page 39)
Fresh Strawberries with Raspberry Sauce

Sugar Cookies   *Coffee*
(page 245)

YOUR COOKING SCHEDULE: This is a two-stage cooking spree with the veal cooked one day and served the next. However, the sauce, a most important ingredient, must be cold when used to dress the veal. That means the broth should be boiled down early in the day it is to be used to give it time to cool off. Once the broth is cold, the sauce can be finished, but the veal should not be dressed until shortly before serving. Seal the sauce with Saran to prevent a skin forming on top. Cook the rice while the broth is cooking down and you might as well bake the toast at the same time, followed by the cookies.

The strawberries can be hulled any time you find a free moment. Do not refrigerate, since they are so much more flavorful at room temperature. Arrange them, however, in a suitable bowl and add superfine sugar, if needed.

A half hour before the meal, take these final steps: Mince the parsley and mix with the cold rice; arrange rice and meat on platter; dress with the sauce; slice and dress the tomatoes; add the raspberry sauce to the strawberries; whip the cream.

VITELLO TONNATO

EQUIPMENT:
French chef's knife; can opener; measuring cups and spoons; large heavy kettle (not aluminum or iron) with a cover; waxed paper; 2-pronged kitchen fork; foil; strainer or sieve; generous mixing bowl; wire whisk; lemon squeezer; carving knife.

INGREDIENTS:

3½ pounds veal, cut off the leg, rolled and tied

1 large onion, skin on, sliced

2 ribs celery, tops on, coarsely chopped

2 cloves garlic, skin on, split

1 carrot, washed and coarsely chopped

1 can (7-ounce size) tuna packed in oil

2 cups dry white wine

½ teaspoon thyme

Few stalks parsley

1 can (2-ounce size) anchovy fillets

½ large sour pickle

6 or 8 peppercorns

8 cups chicken broth or 6 cans (10½-ounce size) condensed

1 pint commercial mayonnaise or about 1½ to 2 cups of your own (page 38), very thick

Juice 1 lemon

Capers, well drained

DO NOT ADD SALT

To simmer—cook liquid just below boiling (185°) so that it just shivers.

Use waxed paper to keep the top of the meat from drying out.

To reduce—simply boil liquid over a high heat until the amount left is what the recipe specifies.

Learn to taste. This makes sense, since one person's salt-and-pepper tolerance can be quite different from another's.

Place the meat in the kettle with enough cold water to cover. Bring to a boil, then *simmer* for 2 or 3 minutes. Take off the heat, drain and wash thoroughly under cold water. Rinse out the kettle, return the meat with all ingredients except the mayonnaise, lemon juice, and capers. Be sure there is enough chicken broth to cover the meat. Bring up to a boil, reduce heat to simmer, cover the top of the kettle with a round of *waxed paper*, add the lid, and simmer until the meat can be pierced easily with a fork. Approximately 1¼ hours. Place the kettle, with the cooked meat and broth, in the *refrigerator* immediately to cool overnight.

The following day, remove the meat from the broth, wrap securely in foil and refrigerate. It should be very cold when served.

Place the broth back over a high heat, bring to a rolling boil, and *reduce* to 3 or 4 cups. Strain. Discard all the vegetables. Refrigerate. When cold, skim off any fat that has risen to the surface.

To make the sauce: Place 1½ cups of mayonnaise in a generous bowl. Gradually, using a wire whisk, beat in enough of the *cooled*, strained broth to make a smooth sauce somewhat thicker than heavy cream. Add more mayonnaise or more broth, if necessary, to bring it to the right consistency. Stir in the lemon juice and *taste* for seasoning. At this point you may find the sauce needs salt.

To serve, mound cold, cooked rice, mixed with *minced* parsley, on a large, handsome platter. Slice the meat very, very thin and arrange, overlapping, down the center of the mound leaving a ring of the parsleyed rice all around. Spoon the sauce over the meat only (it should be heavy enough to cling to the meat but not make a firm mask). Sprinkle with the well-drained capers. Serve remaining sauce on the side with additional capers. Serves 12 to 15 generously.

It is essential to refrigerate the meat and broth immediately to forestall their turning sour. Since the broth cools from the outside in, give it a stir when you think of it to speed the cooling process. Do not cover the kettle until broth is cold.

If the broth has congealed —and it probably has— place over a very low heat just long enough to melt it down. Do not heat.

To mince parsley—hold the blade of a heavy French chef's knife at both ends and chop with rapid up-and-down motions, pulling the ingredients back into a pile with the knife as you work.

COLD PARSLEYED RICE

Cook rice the Chinese way (page 29). Cool. When cold, mix with plenty of minced parsley sprigs. Best done with your hands.

SLICED TOMATOES WITH BASIL

EQUIPMENT:
Serrated knife (best for slicing tomatoes) or other sharp knife; peppermill.

Slice firm, ripe tomatoes very thin and arrange on a serving platter, slightly overlapping. Sprinkle with salt, *freshly ground* pepper, a mere whisper of granulated sugar and basil (if fresh, minced very fine; if dried, crumbled). The amount of the herb depends on the number of tomatoes and your taste buds. Allow 3 or 4 slices per person.

Use a peppermill for this. Freshly ground pepper is more vibrant than already-ground pepper. Both black and white peppercorns are available, the former being somewhat lustier.

FRESH STRAWBERRIES WITH RASPBERRY SAUCE

EQUIPMENT:
Colander; paring knife; electric blender; rotary or electric beater.

Place the unhulled strawberries in a colander and wash under a cool stream of running water. Drain thoroughly and allow to dry. Then hull with a paring

Add the purée at the last minute. If combined with strawberries earlier, it tends to soften them.

knife. Place in a crystal bowl and sprinkle lightly with *superfine sugar*.

Thaw 1 package of frozen raspberries, then purée them in the electric blender. Chill. Just before serving pour the raspberry *purée* over the strawberries. Serve with whipped cream, garnished with candied violets, on the side, if available.

One box (1 pint) will serve 3 to 4 people. For that quantity, you need 1 package frozen raspberries and about ½ cup heavy cream.

Use superfine sugar; especially desirable for fruit because it dissolves instantly.

─────── ◆ ◆ ───────

CALF'S LIVER WITH LEMON BUTTER

Creamed Potatoes   *Baked Stuffed Tomatoes*

Romaine and Chicory Salad, Vinaigrette

Orange Fluff   *Coffee*

YOUR COOKING SCHEDULE: Although there is some last-minute cooking to be done, a great deal can be accomplished ahead of time. The salad greens must be washed in time to allow them to dry thoroughly, and the Orange Fluff needs at least two hours in the refrigerator to chill. The potatoes can be boiled, but not peeled, and the tomatoes stuffed and in their baking dish, sealed with Saran, anytime you feel like it.

About thirty minutes before you will serve dinner, peel, cube and cream the potatoes; bring the liver from the refrigerator and dry according to directions; make the Lemon Butter. Fifteen minutes before dinner, place the tomatoes in a preheated oven; then whip up the Sauce Vinaigrette. Five minutes before dinner, start cooking the liver.

CALF'S LIVER WITH LEMON BUTTER

EQUIPMENT:

Measuring cups and spoons; peppermill; French chef's knife; paper towels; large, heavy skillet; 2-pronged fork.

INGREDIENTS:

1½ pounds calf's liver, sliced very thin

4 tablespoons (½ stick) butter (about)

1 tablespoon vegetable oil (about)

Salt

Freshly ground pepper

Minced parsley

To mince parsley—hold the blade of a heavy French chef's knife at both ends and chop with rapid up-and-down motions, pulling the ingredients back into a pile with the knife as you work.

Use butter and oil combination because it will burn less readily than plain butter. Clarified butter (page 306) can be used as an alternative.

Calf's liver, at its best, is so soft you can almost push your finger through it—like bread. It should not only be sliced very thin but must be absolutely dry, otherwise it will not sauté nicely.

To dry, pat between paper towels, but do not leave it for any length of time or the paper will adhere to the meat. Have a platter warming in the oven before you start to cook the liver.

Heat the *butter* and *oil* in the skillet until the fat is hot but not smoking. As you place each piece of liver in the pan, lift it up with your fingers and turn it over to coat both sides with the butter. Add only as many pieces as the pan will hold without crowding. *Sauté* over a high heat for 1 minute on each side or until the juices run pale pink when meat is pricked with a fork. Lift from the pan to the warm platter. Add more butter and oil as it is needed. When all the liver is cooked, sprinkle with salt and pepper. To serve, spoon Lemon Butter on the hot liver and garnish with a sprinkling of minced parsley. Serves 4.

Use a peppermill for this. Freshly ground pepper is more vibrant than already-ground pepper. Both black and white peppercorns are available, the former being somewhat lustier.

To sauté—cook or brown food in a very small amount of very hot fat.

LEMON BUTTER

EQUIPMENT:
Lemon squeezer; peppermill; small saucepan; wire whisk.

INGREDIENTS:
Juice 1 lemon
Big pinch salt

About 2 twists of the peppermill
½ cup (1 stick) butter

To reduce—simply boil liquid over a high heat until the amount left is what the recipe specifies.

Combine the lemon juice, salt, and pepper in saucepan. Bring to a boil, then *reduce* to 1 tablespoon. Add one quarter of the butter, turn heat to low, and beat with a wire whisk until creamy. Add the remaining butter, a piece at a time, whipping constantly.

CREAMED POTATOES

EQUIPMENT:
Heavy saucepan with a cover; paring knife; peppermill; wooden spatula.

Use a peppermill for this. Freshly ground pepper is more vibrant than already-ground pepper. Both black and white peppercorns are available, the former being somewhat lustier.

Drop potatoes, skins on, into saucepan with enough boiling, salted water to cover generously (allow about 1½ medium-size mature potatoes per person), add the lid, and cook over moderate heat until tender when pierced with the point of a small, sharp knife. Drain and shake dry quickly over a high heat or out the window. Peel with a paring knife. Cut the potatoes into cubes. Return to the saucepan, add heavy cream (allow about 1 cup of cream to 2 cups of potatoes). Season with salt and *freshly ground* white pepper to *taste*. Cook, over moderate heat, stirring constantly with a wooden spatula, until sauce thickens and turns a light gold. Serve immediately.

Learn to taste. This makes sense, since one person's salt-and-pepper tolerance can be quite different from another's.

BAKED STUFFED TOMATOES

EQUIPMENT:

Baking or cookie sheet; French chef's knife; small sharp paring knife; electric blender; 2-pronged fork.

Preheat the oven to 450° (or very hot) 15 minutes before placing the tomatoes in the oven.

Allow 1 whole, ripe tomato per person. Cut out the stem end, then cut the tomatoes in half, crosswise.

Score. Sprinkle with salt, turn upside down and allow to drain for an hour or so. Squeeze the halves gently to extract the seeds.

For 4 tomatoes, combine in the container of the electric blender 2 slices day-old break, broken up, and a big handful of fresh dry parsley sprigs. Blend until very fine. *Mince* 1 clove garlic. Combine with crumbs, enough olive oil to dampen them, salt and pepper to *taste*. Sprinkle a little olive oil over each tomato half. Pack the crumb-parsley mixture into the halves. Add another light sprinkling of oil.

To score—make shallow cuts or slashes. In this instance use a small, sharp paring knife to crosshatch the surface.

To peel, slice, mince, or dice onions, garlic, and shallots the easy way—see directions on page 306.

Learn to taste. This makes sense, since one person's salt-and-pepper tolerance can be quite different from another's.

Place on a cookie sheet in the preheated oven and bake for about 10 minutes or until tomatoes are lightly browned and tender when pierced with a fork.

Served cold, they make a delicious first course.

ORANGE FLUFF

EQUIPMENT:

Measuring cups and spoons; double boiler; large kitchen bowl; rotary or electric beater; rubber spatula; lemon squeezer.

INGREDIENTS:

3 eggs

½ cup sugar

2 tablespoons cornstarch

1 tablespoon dark rum

Grated rind of 1 orange

2 cups fresh, strained or pasteurized orange juice

To grate rind of citrus fruit, which must be done before squeezing—work on a flat grater placed on top of a piece of waxed paper.

If you haven't mastered the trick of separating egg yolks from egg whites, see directions on page 305.

Separate eggs, placing yolks in the top of a double boiler and the whites in a large bowl. Set whites aside.

Beat yolks with a rotary or electric beater until very thick and light in color. Gradually add the sugar and continue beating until the mixture makes ribbons. Mix in all remaining ingredients until smooth.

To simmer—cook liquid just below boiling (185°) so that it just shivers.

Place over *simmering* water and cook, stirring frequently with a wooden spatula, until the mixture is as thick as mayonnaise. Take off the heat. *Beat* the egg whites with a rotary or electric beater until they hold stiff, shiny peaks when the beater is held straight up. Pour the orange mixture over the whites, then *fold* in with a rubber spatula. Pour into a handsome bowl and refrigerate until very cold.

Beat egg whites only to the stiff, shiny stage. If beaten longer, they become granular.

For the exact folding technique—see directions on page 305.

———◆··◆———

VEAL AND LEMON CASSEROLE

Garlic Potatoes   *Carrots with Marsala*

Artichokes   *Sauce Ravigote*
(page 80)

Fresh Strawberries   *Coffee*
in Ice Cream Sauce

YOUR COOKING SCHEDULE: Dishes that can be prepared well ahead—garlic potatoes, artichokes, Sauce Ravigote—can all be got out of the way in the morning. At the same time, take the ice cream from the freezer and place in the refrigerator to allow it to melt. The Veal and Lemon Casserole must go in the oven 2 hours before dinner. With that done, wash, dry, then hull the strawberries, and cook the carrots. Reheat the carrots at the same time you are reheating the potatoes. Allow 20 to 30 minutes.

VEAL AND LEMON CASSEROLE

EQUIPMENT:

Measuring spoons; casserole with tight-fitting cover; foil; kitchen fork; metal spatula; wire whisk; strainer; peppermill.

INGREDIENTS:

2 pounds veal scaloppine (about 10 pieces), ¼ inch thick, not pounded

4 tablespoons olive oil

Salt

Freshly ground pepper

Juice 1 lemon

1 whole lemon, sliced thin

1 teaspoon *arrowroot*, about

Lemon wedges

Parsley bouquet

Use a peppermill for this. Freshly ground pepper is more vibrant than already-ground pepper. Both black and white peppercorns are available, the former being somewhat lustier.

Use arrowroot as a thickening agent when you want the finished sauce to be clear and transparent. Do not cook beyond the point indicated or the sauce will "thin out."

Preheat the oven to 300° (or slow) for 15 minutes before cooking the veal.

The essential here is an ovenproof casserole with a tight-fitting lid just large enough to accommodate the veal in layers. Sprinkle the bottom with 1 tablespoon of the oil. Cover with a layer of the meat, season with salt and pepper, then sprinkle with 1 tablespoon of the oil, 1 of lemon juice and add a couple of lemon slices. Repeat until you have used all the ingredients. Seal with double-duty foil, then cover tightly. Cook in the preheated oven until the meat is very tender when tested with a fork. About 2 hours.

To serve, carefully lift the slices of veal with a metal serving spatula onto a heated platter and arrange overlapping the length of the platter. Discard lemon slices. Keep warm.

Place the casserole back over a high heat and reduce the liquid to about ¾ cup. Mix the arrowroot with enough cold water to make a smooth paste. Add to the casserole and cook over low heat, beating constantly with a wire whisk, until the sauce has thickened lightly. Strain and spoon over the meat. Garnish the platter with lemon wedges and the parsley bouquet. Serves 4 to 6.

GARLIC POTATOES

EQUIPMENT:

Measuring cups and spoons; peppermill; small saucepan; 2 heavy saucepans with covers; electric blender; Saran; double boiler; vegetable peeler; paring knife; potato ricer; wooden spatula; kitchen spoon.

INGREDIENTS:

4 or 5 medium potatoes (about 2½ pounds)
1 head or about 10 cloves garlic
4 tablespoons (½ stick) butter
¼ cup milk

¼ teaspoon salt
Freshly ground white pepper
Heavy cream
Minced parsley

To mince parsley—hold the blade of a heavy French chef's knife at both ends and chop with rapid up-and-down motions, pulling the ingredients back into a pile with the knife as you work.

Use a peppermill for this. Freshly ground pepper is more vibrant than already-ground pepper. Both black and white peppercorns are available, the former being somewhat lustier.

Separate the garlic cloves. Drop into the small saucepan of bubbling boiling water and boil for 5 seconds. Drain, cool under cold water, then slip off the skins.

Melt the butter in a heavy saucepan. When hot, add the garlic and 1 cup water. Cover and cook over moderate heat until the garlic is tender and all the water has boiled away. If necessary, add more water. The garlic must not brown. When cooked combine with the milk in the container of the electric blender and blend to make as smooth a purée as possible. Can be made in advance to this point, sealed with Saran to prevent a skin forming and discoloration. Reheat in a double boiler over *simmering* water.

Peel the potatoes with a vegetable peeler or paring knife, then cut into quarters. Drop into enough boiling, salted water to cover. Add the lid, reduce heat

To simmer—cook liquid just below boiling (185°) so that it just shivers.

to moderate, and boil until tender when pierced with the point of a sharp paring knife.

Drain immediately. Then dry quickly by shaking the pan over a high heat or out the window. Push through a potato ricer. With a wooden spatula, beat in the hot garlic purée, salt and pepper to *taste*, and enough heavy cream (about 3 to 4 tablespoons) to make a smooth light texture. Spoon into a heated vegetable dish and serve at once garnished with a sprinkling of minced parsley. Serves 4 to 6.

Learn to taste. This makes sense, since one person's salt-and-pepper tolerance can be quite different from another's.

CARROTS WITH MARSALA

EQUIPMENT:
Measuring cups and spoons; vegetable peeler; French chef's knife; heavy medium saucepan with a cover; paring knife.

If the carrots are large and old, prepare as recipe indicates; then cut out the woody sections in the centers.

Use a peppermill for this. Freshly ground pepper is more vibrant than already-ground pepper. Both black and white peppercorns are available, the former being somewhat lustier.

INGREDIENTS:
1½ pounds (about 10) *carrots*
2 tablespoons (¼ stick) butter
Salt
Freshly ground white pepper

Sprinkling of sugar
½ cup Marsala wine
Minced parsley

Trim off the root and the stem ends of the carrots with a paring knife. Peel with a vegetable peeler. Cut in half lengthwise, then cut in half across. Now, slice the top halves in two, lengthwise.

Melt the butter in the saucepan. Add the carrots and turn over and over so they are well coated with the butter. Sprinkle lightly with salt, pepper, and a

To mince parsley—hold the blade of a heavy French chef's knife at both ends and chop with rapid up-and-down motions, pulling the ingredients back into a pile with the knife as you work.

little sugar. Add the wine. Bring up to a boil, reduce heat to *simmer*, then cover, and cook 5 minutes. At this point, add enough boiling water to barely cover the carrots. Bring to a boil again, reduce heat to simmer, cover, and cook until the carrots are almost tender when pierced with the point of a small, sharp knife. About 20 minutes. Bring up the heat again and boil rapidly until almost all the liquid has evaporated, leaving the carrots shiny, tender, with a little syrupy sauce. Pour into a heated serving dish and garnish with minced parsley. Serves 4 to 6.

> To simmer—cook liquid just below boiling (185°) so that it just shivers.

SAUCE RAVIGOTE

EQUIPMENT:

Measuring cups and spoons; French chef's knife; mixing bowl; paring knife; wire whisk.

INGREDIENTS:

¼ cup wine vinegar
1 teaspoon salt
Freshly ground pepper
¾ cup vegetable oil
1 teaspoon finely chopped capers

1 teaspoon very finely *minced* shallots or green onion bulbs
2 tablespoons *minced* parsley, tarragon, and chervil

> Use a peppermill for this. Freshly ground pepper is more vibrant than already-ground pepper. Both black and white peppercorns are available, the former being somewhat lustier.

Combine the vinegar with the salt and several twists of the peppermill in a bowl. Beat with a wire whisk until the salt has dissolved. Add the oil gradually, whisking constantly. Stir in the herbs and serve with cold artichokes. Also excellent for fish, hot or cold boiled beef, or other cold vegetables. Sufficient for 4.

> To peel, slice, mince, or dice onions, garlic, and shallots the easy way, see directions on page 306.
>
> To mince parsley—hold the blade of a heavy French chef's knife at both ends and chop with rapid up-and-down motions, pulling the ingredients back into a pile with the knife as you work.

FRESH STRAWBERRIES WITH
ICE CREAM SAUCE

EQUIPMENT:
Colander; paring knife.

INGREDIENTS:

Vanilla ice cream   Fresh ripe strawberries
Grand Marnier   Candied orange peel (commercial)

Thaw vanilla ice cream in the refrigerator. When melted, perfume with Grand Marnier to taste.

Wash the strawberries in a colander, under a stream of cool water. Allow to drain, then hull, using a paring knife. Dry thoroughly.

When dry, place in a handsome bowl. Pour the melted ice cream over the strawberries and garnish with the orange peel.

One-half pint ice cream as a sauce is about adequate for 2; and 1 box (1 pint) of strawberries will serve about 3.

Strawberries are always washed first under a stream of cool water, then hulled. If hulled, then washed, they soak up water. Serve at room temperature for best flavor.

PANCAKE TURNER

SLOTTED SPOON

LARGE LADLE

LARGE METAL SPOON

2-PRONGED FORK

BULB BASTER

THE KITCHEN SPOONS, ETC.

No cook can work efficiently without a large spoon for basting or a bulb baster, the slotted spoon to lift foods from liquids, pancake turner and ladle for obvious uses, 2-pronged fork for testing and turning meat, fowl, etc.

HAM

BAKED HAM WITH APRICOT GLAZE

English Mustard

Puréed Chestnuts   *Creamed Spinach*

Leeks, Vinaigrette

French Chocolate Cake with Chocolate Glaze

Coffee

YOUR COOKING SCHEDULE: The cake can be made the day before. If not, it must be baked and glazed the morning of the day it is to be served to give the glaze time to set and the cake time to become firm. Do not refrigerate. Since the ham calls for at least 3½ hours of baking, it should go into the oven no later than 3 o'clock. During that time, you can purée the chestnuts, cook the spinach and leeks and make both the English Mustard and the Sauce Vinaigrette (page 44). None of these is a very complicated chore. With all this behind you, dinner is as good as on the table.

BAKED HAM WITH APRICOT GLAZE

EQUIPMENT:

Paring knife; kitchen scissors; large roasting pan with a rack; bulb baster or large metal spoon; corkscrew; small saucepan; fine sieve.

You have a choice of cook-before-eating hams or fully cooked hams. Whatever type you choose, we recommend glazing it, if only for looks. This Apricot Glaze is an especially easy one, used by many fine chefs.

A whole ham offers many advantages in that every last scrap of the meat, right down to the bone, can be turned into a delicious meal. Since ham, unlike most other meats, keeps very well refrigerated, it doesn't have to be eaten up all in one gulp, as it were, boring everybody to death.

INGREDIENTS:

1 8- to 10-pound ham, bone in
Whole cloves

1 jar (12-ounce size) commercial
    apricot jam, not dietetic
Dry white wine (optional)

Preheat the oven to 325° (or slow) for 15 minutes before the ham goes in the oven.

Whatever the type ham, loosen the skin for about 2 inches at the shank end. Then, with scissors, make a sawtooth design around the edge. Scrape off any paper labels. Place the ham fat side up, on the rack in the roasting pan in the preheated oven and bake 3½ hours. *Baste* regularly with pan juices and/or wine, using a bulb baster or large metal spoon. A half hour before the ham is cooked take out of the oven and with a sharp knife *score* the fat in a diamond pattern. Insert whole cloves in each diamond.

To baste—spray, spoon, or brush a liquid or melted fat over food while it cooks.

To score—slash lightly with a knife the skin or outer fat of the ham.

While the ham is baking make the Apricot Glaze by placing the jar of jam without its cover in a small saucepan of hot water until the contents has melted. Then push the jam through a fine sieve.

Spoon the purée over the fat on the ham. Return the ham to the oven for the remainder of the prescribed cooking time, or until the glaze has set. Then place the ham on a hot serving platter and *allow to rest* 25 to 30 minutes before carving. Garnish with a bouquet of fresh watercress or parsley.

Allow meat to "rest" 15 to 20 minutes after it comes from the oven. This gives the juices time to settle and makes carving easier.

Cold Baked Ham accompanied by Scalloped Oysters and Mostarda di Frutta (commercial mustard fruits) followed by a green salad and Apple Pie (page 288) is a dinner to rival the ham served hot.

ENGLISH MUSTARD

EQUIPMENT:
Small spoon; small mixing bowl.

Mix dry mustard with enough tap water to make a thick, smooth, creamy paste. Do not use hot water because it will stop the enzyme action. Allow to stand about 10 minutes to mellow. Make only as much as you can use at one time and discard any that is not used up.

PURÉED CHESTNUTS

EQUIPMENT:

Can opener; saucepan; measuring cups and spoons; peppermill; rubber spatula; fine sieve or potato ricer; wooden spatula; double boiler.

INGREDIENTS:

Canned chestnuts (marrons entiers au naturel) are expensive, but it seems to us worth the price as against the arduous task of shelling fresh ones which are available only in the winter.

3 cans (11-ounce size) imported fresh *chestnuts*

4 tablespoons (½ stick) butter, melted

4 tablespoons heavy cream, heated

Salt

Freshly ground white pepper

Pinch of sugar

Use a peppermill for this. Both black and white peppercorns are available, the former being somewhat lustier.

Heat the chestnuts in their liquid to the boiling point only. Drain. With a rubber spatula, push the nuts through a fine sieve or put through a potato ricer. Beat in all remaining ingredients hard, using a wooden spatula. *Taste* for seasoning. Place in top of double boiler over *simmering* water to heat through and keep warm. Serves 5 to 6.

Learn to taste. One person's salt-and-pepper tolerance can be quite different from another's.

To simmer—cook liquid just below boiling (185°) so that it just shivers.

CREAMED SPINACH

EQUIPMENT:

Measuring cups and spoons; large heavy enameled saucepan; French chef's knife; wooden spatula; Saran.

INGREDIENTS:

3 packages (10-ounce size) frozen spinach

4 tablespoons butter

Salt

Freshly ground pepper

1½ tablespoons all-purpose flour

1 cup heavy cream (about)

Drop the frozen spinach into the large, heavy *enameled saucepan* of boiling salted water. Bring up to a boil again and cook, *uncovered,* for 2 to 3 minutes. Taste it to see if it is sufficiently tender. Drain at once, then run cold water into the saucepan to cool the spinach quickly. Squeeze the spinach to extract as much water as possible. Now chop very fine, using a big French chef's knife.

Dry the saucepan, then melt the butter. Add the chopped spinach and seasonings, and cook over a moderate heat just long enough to heat through and to evaporate any liquid. Sprinkle on the flour, stir in with a wooden spatula and cook for 2 minutes. Stir in about two-thirds of the cream and *simmer,* stirring often, for about 10 minutes. Add more cream if the spinach seems too dry. Spoon into a heated serving dish. Serves 6.

If not served at once, set aside and seal with Saran so the spinach won't dry out. Reheat very slowly.

Do not cook spinach in aluminum or cast iron or it will have a metallic taste.

Always cook green vegetables uncovered to retain their color.

To simmer—cook liquid just below boiling (185°) so that it just shivers.

LEEKS VINAIGRETTE

EQUIPMENT:
French chef's knife; large kettle; sharp paring knife; paper towels.

Allow about 4 leeks per person. Cut off the root ends and pull off any withered leaves. Slit the green tops lengthwise twice. Since leeks are inclined to be very gritty, wash thoroughly under cool running water, spreading the leaves apart. Cut off enough of the green tops to leave the leeks about 7 inches long.

Have ready a big kettle of boiling, salted water. Add the leeks and cook, uncovered, until the white bulbs are tender when pierced with the point of a sharp paring knife (about 15 to 20 minutes). Drain and run under cold water to stop the cooking. Drain again thoroughly and pat dry with paper towels.

When cold, cover with Sauce Vinaigrette (page 44), and allow to marinate for an hour or longer.

Leeks à la Grecque: Follow directions for cooking Onions à la Grecque (page 219).

FRENCH CHOCOLATE CAKE WITH CHOCOLATE GLAZE

EQUIPMENT:

Measuring cups and spoons; 8-inch round cake pan; waxed paper; electric blender; double boiler; electric beater or electric mixer; cake rack; small metal spatula.

INGREDIENTS:

½ cup (1 stick) butter, softened
1 cup almonds or filberts, skin on
¾ cup chocolate pieces or 4 squares (1-ounce size) semisweet chocolate

⅔ cup sugar
3 eggs
Grated rind 1 large orange
¼ cup very fine *bread crumbs*

To butter a pan—crumple up a little waxed paper, scoop up a bit of butter and coat the bottom and side of the cake pan generously.

To line—place the pan on a piece of waxed paper. Outline the shape with a pencil, then cut out with scissors and place in bottom of the pan.

Use firm day-old bread for bread crumbs (1 slice makes ¼ cup). Break into pieces and grind, crust and all, in the electric blender, or crumble by hand until very fine.

Melt chocolate over hot, not boiling, water because if steam rises, then condenses, the chocolate will tighten and become un-

Preheat the oven to 375° (or moderate) for 15 minutes before baking the cake.

Butter the bottom and sides of an 8-inch round cake pan thoroughly, then *line* the bottom with waxed paper and butter it, too. Set aside.

Grind the almonds as fine as possible in an electric blender and set aside. *Melt the chocolate* in the top of a double boiler over hot, not boiling, water.

Work or cream the remaining butter with your hands, an electric beater, or in an electric mixer, until very soft and light. Very gradually add the sugar, beating constantly. When all the sugar is in, add the eggs, one at a time,

manageable. Should this happen, add 2 tablespoons of vegetable shortening and work into the chocolate until it becomes soft again.

beating hard after each addition. The batter at this point will look curdled, but don't be alarmed. Stir in the melted chocolate, ground nuts, rind and bread crumbs thoroughly with a rubber spatula.

Pour into the prepared pan and place in the preheated oven for 25 minutes. Allow the cake to cool on a rack for about 30 minutes then run the metal spatula around the edge. Turn out onto a cake rack. If cake doesn't drop out easily, give the pan a bang with your hand. Very gently ease off the waxed paper. Cool completely before glazing.

The center of the cake will not seem thoroughly cooked, hence its soft texture and exceptionally delicious flavor.

GLAZE

INGREDIENTS:

2 squares (1-ounce size) unsweet-
    ened chocolate
2 squares (1-ounce size) semisweet
    chocolate, or ¼ cup chocolate
    pieces

¼ cup (½ stick) butter, softened
    and cut up
2 teaspoons honey
Toasted slivered almonds or whole
    filberts

Combine the two chocolates, butter, and honey in the top of a double boiler and melt over hot water. Take off the heat and beat until cold but still "pourable"—in other words, until it begins to thicken.

Place the cake on the rack over a piece of waxed paper and pour the glaze over all. Tip the cake so the glaze runs evenly over the top and down the side. Smooth side, if necessary, with a metal spatula. Garland the rim of the cake with toasted slivered almonds or filberts, placing them fairly close together.

This cake freezes very successfully if wrapped and sealed securely.

HAM SLICES BAKED IN MAPLE SYRUP

Buttered Baby New Potatoes (page 120)	*Buttered Broccoli* (page 74)
Lemon Butter Tartlets	*Coffee*

YOUR COOKING SCHEDULE: You can make the pastry whenever you feel like it, but the tarts should be baked early on the day they are to be served, and you might as well make the filling then, too. Since you have to stay in the kitchen for an hour—more or less—before dinner, to baste the ham, you'll have loads of time to cook the potatoes and broccoli, make the Hollandaise, and fill the tarts.

HAM SLICES BAKED IN MAPLE SYRUP

EQUIPMENT:

French chef's knife; measuring cups and spoons; shallow roasting pan just large enough to accommodate the meat; small mixing bowl; 2-pronged kitchen fork; bulb baster or large metal spoon.

INGREDIENTS:

2 ham slices, 1½ inches thick

Whole cloves

1½ teaspoons allspice

1 cup real maple syrup

Preheat the oven to 300° (or slow) for 15 minutes before baking the ham.

Slash the fat around the edge of the ham, then stud by pressing cloves into the meat at random. Place in roasting pan. Mix the allspice into the syrup, and pour the mixture over the meat.

Bake uncovered in a preheated oven for about 1 hour or until the meat is very tender when pierced with a fork. *Baste* every 15 minutes, using a bulb baster or large metal spoon.

To baste—spray or brush a liquid or melted fat over food while it cooks.

If the sauce becomes too thick—and it may—stir in a little boiling water.

Serves 4 to 6, depending on appetites.

LEMON BUTTER TARTLETS

EQUIPMENT:

Measuring cups and spoons; mixing bowl; pastry blender; pastry cloth or board; rolling pin, preferably with a sleeve; 1 5-to-6-inch cookie cutter; 6 or 8 tart pans of 3 to 3½ inches each; waxed paper; dried beans or rice; kitchen fork; flat grater; lemon squeezer; sharp knife; double boiler; wooden spatula.

INGREDIENTS:

If you haven't mastered the trick of separating egg yolks from egg whites, see directions on page 305.

Half the recipe for basic pastry
  (page 288)

3 whole eggs

1 egg *yolk*

1 cup sugar

Grated rind 2 lemons

Juice 2 lemons

½ cup butter

To grate rind of citrus fruit, which must be done before squeezing—work on a flat grater placed on top of a piece of waxed paper.

Combine all ingredients except pastry in the top of a double boiler and mix together well, using a wooden spatula. Place over *simmering* water and cook, stirring occasionally, until the mixture is as thick as mayonnaise. This will take from 25 to 30 minutes. Take off the heat and cool.

To simmer—cook liquid just below boiling (185°) so that it just shivers.

Preheat the oven to 450° (or hot) for 15 minutes before baking the tarts.

On a lightly floured pastry cloth—using a rolling pin with a lightly floured sleeve—roll out dough no more than ⅛ inch thick.

Do not stretch pastry or it will shrink when baked.

Cut the dough in squares one inch larger than the top of the tart pans. Fold in flour and *drop* (don't push it) the dough into the pans. Then push it into all the indentations until it touches all sides. Cut off with a sharp knife any dough that hangs over the edge. Prick the bottoms with the tines of a fork, then cut squares of wax paper and drop into each pastry shell. Fill with rice or dry beans to keep pastry from shrinking.

Place the pans on a baking sheet and bake in the preheated oven for 25 minutes. At this point lift the rice or beans from the shells (store and reuse rice or beans) and continue baking another five minutes or until centers are completely cooked. Take from the oven and while still hot, turn the patty shells out of the pans and cool on cake racks.

Fill each shell with Lemon Butter. This amount will fill 6 to 8 tart shells or one 8-inch pie shell.

SPLIT PEA SOUP

Rye Toast   *Sweet Butter*

Orange and Onion Salad
(page 19)
Rich Brownies

Vanilla Ice Cream with Ginger Sauce

Coffee

YOUR COOKING SCHEDULE: Once the soup is on the stove, it's as good as done, so it would seem to us to make sense to cook it early in the day and freeze any that's not needed for dinner. The Ginger Sauce can be made in jig time, anytime. If the ice cream is in the freezer, take it out about a half hour before dinner and place in the refrigerator to soften slightly before serving. Because onions are inclined to darken once sliced, the salad must be prepared shortly before it is served. It would be nice to make the toast in the dining room as it is needed, and thus serve it hot.

SPLIT PEA SOUP

EQUIPMENT:

Measuring cups and spoons; French chef's knife; large, heavy kettle with a cover; large fine sieve.

INGREDIENTS:

Ham bone

4 cups (two 1-pound boxes) quick-cooking split peas

2 onions *peeled*, each stuck with 2 cloves

2 cloves garlic, *peeled*

2 bay leaves

A few peppercorns

3 celery ribs, with tops, coarsely chopped

3 large carrots, washed, coarsely chopped

2 tablespoons tomato paste

Heavy cream

Minced parsley

To peel, slice, mince or dice onions, garlic, and shallots the easy way—see directions on page 306.

To mince parsley—hold the blade of a heavy French chef's knife at both ends and chop with rapid up-and-down motions, pulling the ingredients back into a pile with the knife as you work.

In the event you haven't a ham bone on hand when you feel like a big bowl of homemade pea soup, buy the butt end of a ham from the butcher. Cut off a thick slice and bake in maple syrup for one meal (page 172). Use the remainder (the real butt) to make the soup.

Place all ingredients except the tomato paste, cream, and parsley in a large kettle. Add enough cold water (5 to 6 quarts) to cover, and bring up to a boil. Reduce the heat, then *simmer*, covered, until the peas are very soft. Several hours. Lift the ham bone out of the kettle.

To simmer—cook liquid just below boiling (185°) so that it just shivers.

Push the soup and the vegetables through a fine sieve to make a thick purée. Then stir in the tomato paste. This should make about 4 generous quarts. Cut off any meat on the bone, and sliver it. Reserve for garnish. Discard the bone.

Use a peppermill for this. Freshly ground pepper is more vibrant than already-ground pepper. Both black and white peppercorns are available, the former being somewhat lustier.

To serve, dilute the purée with heavy cream (a cup or so to a quart). *Taste for seasoning.* At this point, you'll probably need both salt and *freshly ground pepper.* Bring up to a boil, but do not cook further.

Present the soup in a large heated tureen with a garnish of slivered ham and parsley.

This pea soup freezes perfectly. Best to freeze in relatively small quantities—certainly no more than 1-quart jars. Add heavy cream after thawing.

Learn to taste. This makes sense, since one person's salt-and-pepper tolerance can be quite different from another's.

RICH BROWNIES

EQUIPMENT:

Measuring cups and spoons; mixing bowl; flour sifter; 8-inch square baking pan; double boiler; rotary or electric beater; wooden spatula; cake rack; metal spatula.

INGREDIENTS:

½ cup (1 stick) butter

2 squares (1-ounce size) unsweetened chocolate

1 cup sugar

2 eggs

½ cup *sifted* all-purpose flour

½ teaspoon salt

1 cup coarsely chopped walnuts

½ teaspoon vanilla

To measure sifted flour properly, spoon it—after sifting—into a dry measuring cup well above the top, then level or cut off with the edge—not the flat surface—of a metal spatula or knife. Do not shake flour down.

Melt chocolate over hot—not boiling—water because if steam rises, then condenses, the chocolate will tighten and become unmanageable. Should this happen, add 2 tablespoons of vegetable shortening and work into the chocolate until it becomes soft again.

Preheat the oven to 350° (or moderate) for 15 minutes before baking the brownies.

Grease the pan and set aside.

Melt the chocolate in the double boiler top over hot water. In a bowl, cream or work the remaining butter until soft and fluffy, using your hands or an

To grease a pan—crumple up a little waxed paper, scoop up a bit of butter and coat the bottom and sides of the pan generously.

electric beater. Gradually work in the sugar. Add the eggs, one at a time, beating very hard with a rotary or electric beater after each addition. Combine the flour and salt in a sifter and sift straight into the mixture. Stir in with a wooden spatula. Finally, thoroughly mix in the nuts, melted chocolate, and vanilla.

Pour into the prepared pan and bake in the preheated oven for 25 to 30 minutes. Properly baked the brownies are soft to the touch when pressed lightly.

Cool in the pan set on a cake rack. Cut into 16 even squares in the pan. Lift out carefully with a metal spatula.

GINGER SAUCE FOR ICE CREAM

EQUIPMENT:
Measuring cups and spoons; lemon squeezer; small saucepan; candy thermometer.

Combine 1 cup water, ¾ cup sugar, and the juice of ½ lemon in a saucepan. Cook over a moderate heat until syrup reaches 230° on candy thermometer. Take off the heat and stir in 3 tablespoons finely chopped candied ginger. Bring up to a boil again. Makes 1 cup.

Serve hot or cold over vanilla ice cream.

This delicious sauce will keep beautifully, refrigerated, if made up in a quantity.

Chicken Consommé with Orange Zest

HAM MOUSSE

Country Salad   *Baked Toast*
(page 39)

Poached Fresh Peaches with Fresh Raspberry Sauce

Chocolate Cloud Cookies   *Coffee*
(page 257)

YOUR COOKING SCHEDULE: The Ham Mousse must be made early in the day (it needs at least 3 hours in the refrigerator), or if it suits you better, the day before. The poached peaches also need an interlude in the refrigerator—at least an hour—so they, too, can be prepared in the morning; also, the Raspberry Sauce, soup and Baked Toast. Actually, it makes sense to get all these little cooking chores out of the way about the same time. The salad is made right at the table by each person, so all you need to do is to see that the lettuce is washed and dried. Lacking garden lettuce, use Boston or Bibb. With all this finished, you have only to reheat the soup and dinner is as good as on the table.

CHICKEN CONSOMMÉ WITH ORANGE ZEST

EQUIPMENT:

Measuring spoons; can opener; grater; French chef's knife; 2 medium heavy saucepans; strainer; cheesecloth.

INGREDIENTS:

Use a peppermill for this. Freshly ground pepper is more vibrant than already-ground pepper. Both black and white peppercorns are available, the former being somewhat lustier.

Learn to taste. This makes sense, since one person's salt-and-pepper tolerance can be quite different from another's.

2 cans (10½-ounce size) condensed chicken broth
4 fresh, very ripe tomatoes
Salt

Freshly ground white pepper
Pinch sugar
Grated rind 1 large orange
2 to 3 tablespoons dry vermouth

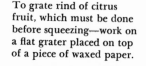

To grate rind of citrus fruit, which must be done before squeezing—work on a flat grater placed on top of a piece of waxed paper.

To simmer—cook liquid just below boiling (185°) so that it just shivers.

Chop the tomatoes coarsely. Combine with the soup, salt and pepper to *taste*, and sugar in a heavy saucepan.

Bring up to a boil, then reduce heat and *simmer* for about 30 minutes or until the tomatoes have completely disintegrated. Strain into a clean saucepan through a sieve lined with 2 or 3 layers of dampened cheesecloth. Add the orange rind and vermouth. Bring up to a boil, then serve immediately in heated soup cups. Serves 4 to 6.

HAM MOUSSE

EQUIPMENT:

Measuring cups and spoons; peppermill; can opener; French chef's knife; 2 heavy saucepans; wooden spatula; wire whisk; electric blender; rotary or electric beater; rubber spatula; paring knife or small spatula; 2-quart mold.

INGREDIENTS:

1 pound ham, diced, or 2 cups diced ham

3 tablespoons butter

3 tablespoons flour

2 cups chicken broth (your own or canned condensed)

Salt

Freshly ground white pepper

3 envelopes unflavored gelatin

3 egg *whites*

⅛ teaspoon cream of tartar

1 cup heavy cream, whipped

Use a peppermill for this. Freshly ground pepper is more vibrant than already-ground pepper. Both black and white peppercorns are available, the former being somewhat lustier.

Melt the butter in a saucepan over low heat. Make a roux by stirring in the flour until smooth, then cook slowly, stirring with a wooden spatula, until the butter and flour froth (about 3 minutes) without browning. Take off the heat, add the chicken broth and beat vigorously with a wire whisk until smooth. Put back over a moderately high heat and cook, whipping constantly, until the sauce comes to a boil. Boil for 1 minute, whipping steadily. Take off the heat and add salt and pepper to *taste*. *Sprinkle* the gelatin over the hot sauce. Place back over a moderate heat and cook, stirring constantly, with a spatula, until the gelatin has dissolved.

Place half the ham and half the sauce in the container of an electric blender. Blend at high speed for 35 to 40 seconds. Empty into a saucepan. Blend remaining ham and sauce. Combine the two and taste for seasoning. Add salt

If you haven't mastered the trick of separating egg yolks from egg whites, see directions on page 305.

Learn to taste. This makes sense, since one person's salt-and-pepper tolerance can be quite different from another's.

Note the word "sprinkle." Do not dump into the liquid, or the gelatin won't dissolve.

and pepper if necessary. Keep warm over low heat.

Beat egg whites only to the stiff, shiny stage. If beaten longer, they become granular.

Beat the egg whites and the cream of tartar with a rotary or electric beater until they stand in firm peaks when the beater is held straight up. With a rubber spatula *fold* at once into the hot ham mixture.

For exact folding technique —see directions on page 305.

Refrigerate, giving the mixture an occasional stir, until almost cool and beginning to set. Fold the whipped cream into the cooled mixture and spoon into a 2-quart mold. Refrigerate for at least 3 hours or until firm. Serves 6.

To unmold: First, rinse the serving plate in cold water. (This makes it easier to slide the mold into the center of the plate in case you miss it. Once the mold is in place, wipe the serving plate dry.)

Dip the mold briefly into warm, not hot, water just to the level of the mousse, then loosen around the edge with the tip of a small knife. Wipe the mold off and place serving dish on top of the mold. Invert. Give it a good shake, holding the mold tightly in place. If this doesn't work, repeat the operation.

Another way: Wring a cloth out in very hot water and wrap around the bottom of the inverted mold, taking care not to apply the heat too long or the shape may be ruined. Before serving wipe the plate around the mold in case there are drops of water.

Metal unmolds more easily than earthenware because metal conducts heat more quickly.

COUNTRY SALAD

Arrange in a large bowl as much lettuce as you think will be needed. Have at hand, salt, sugar, heavy cream and vinegar. Right at the table, just before serving, sprinkle the leaves with salt and sugar. Then pour on a little cream then a little vinegar. Toss gently. Serve at once. It is impossible to indicate how much of anything should be used as this salad is made entirely by feel.

POACHED FRESH PEACHES WITH FRESH RASPBERRY SAUCE

EQUIPMENT:
Measuring cups and spoons; large, heavy saucepan; bulb baster or large metal spoon; electric blender; very fine strainer.

The skin on very ripe peaches will often peel off easily. If not, cover with boiling water and allow to stand for about a minute.

Combine ¾ cup sugar, 2 cups water and a 2-inch piece of *vanilla bean*, split, in saucepan. Bring to a boil, then boil for 5 minutes. Add 6 or 8 whole *peeled* peaches or large peach halves to the boiling syrup. Reduce heat to *simmer* and poach until tender when pierced with the point of a sharp knife. *Baste* occasionally. Chill in syrup.

The vanilla bean can be washed, dried, stored, and reused.

To simmer—cook liquid just below boiling (185°) so that it just shivers.

To baste—spray, spoon, or brush a liquid or melted fat over food while it cooks.

Raspberry Sauce: Combine in the container of the electric blender all except a handful of 1 box fresh ripe raspberries with ¼ cup of the syrup in which the peaches poached. Blend to make a smooth purée. Strain, if you like, to eliminate the seeds. Perfume with a few drops of kirsch or some other liqueur.

To serve: Arrange the chilled strained peaches in a crystal serving dish. Just before serving, cover with the Raspberry Sauce. Garnish with a few fresh raspberries.

Another way: Arrange chilled canned peach halves, drained, in a serving dish. Thaw 1 package (10-ounce size) frozen raspberries. Purée in the electric blender and pour over the peach halves.

VEGETABLE PEELER   FRENCH TOMATO KNIFE   BREAD KNIFE   3½"- 8"- AND 12"-BLADE RIVETED KNIVES   CARVING SET   CARBORUNDUM KNIFE SHARPENER

THE KNIVES

Cooks who care put function first in the kitchen, and you can't function without good and proper knives. With the exception of the peeler and the bread and tomato knives, all these are carbon steel. Stainless steel or other metals will not keep a good edge and they are a waste of money.

The razor-sharp serrated knives with blades about 4 inches long are primarily for slicing tomatoes, though they have many uses. They never need to be sharpened. The bread knife is a duplicate of the tomato knife, but it is 8 inches long. The "working" kitchen knives used by all chefs are made of carbon steel with riveted handles. They can be readily sharpened at home on a carborundum stone. In addition to the "working" knives, every kitchen should have a knife and fork for carving at the table. The swivel-bladed vegetable peeler is one of the handiest tools in your batterie de cuisine. We recommend the stainless-steel version. The carborundum knife sharpener is ideal for giving an edge to all knives.

PORK

ROAST LOIN OF PORK

Roast Apples   *Roast Potatoes*   *Roast Onions*

Belgian Endive, Vinaigrette
(page 34)

Chocolate Soufflé   *Coffee*

YOUR COOKING SCHEDULE: The soufflé can be mixed, except for the egg whites, any time you feel like it. Probably best to get it out of the way early in the afternoon. As for the pork, it should go into the oven 3½ hours before you plan to sit down at the dinner table. Forty-five minutes before the meat comes out of the oven you should have the potatoes and onions parboiled and ready to go in; the apples, pealed and cored, waiting their turn. Exclusive of the soufflé, there are just three little chores to do while the meat is resting: the gravy, the Sauce Vinaigrette, the endive. While the meat is being carved, whip up the egg whites and finish the soufflé. It can be baking while you enjoy your dinner. Best to take a timer to the dining room with you unless you have built-in radar.

ROAST LOIN OF PORK

EQUIPMENT:

Peppermill; vegetable peeler (preferably) or paring knife; measuring cups and spoons; meat thermometer (zero to 220° range); large roasting pan; 2 medium saucepans; apple corer; kitchen scissors; small kitchen bowl; wooden spatula.

The loin, the leg (fresh ham), and the shoulder are the most desirable cuts from a "porker."

INGREDIENTS:

1 5- to 6-pound loin of pork, with fat on	6 medium yellow onions, all of a size
Salt	6 tart green apples, all of a size
Freshly ground pepper	1 tablespoon cornstarch
6 medium potatoes, all of a size	1 cup sweet cider
	½ cup applejack or calvados

Use a peppermill for this. Freshly ground pepper is more vibrant than already-ground pepper. Both black and white peppercorns are available, the former being somewhat lustier.

Preheat the oven to 325° (or slow) for 15 minutes before putting the roast in.

When you buy the loin of pork insist (and you will have to insist) on the butcher leaving a layer of fat about ½ inch deep on the meat. At the same time ask him to crack the chine bone to make carving easier, and then to tie the loin.

To score—slash the skin or outer fat lightly with a small sharp knife.

Score the fat as you would for ham, dust with salt and pepper. Place in roasting pan in the preheated oven and roast approximately 3 hours or 35 minutes per pound (165° to 170° F. on meat thermometer). Do not overcook or you will have strings instead of succulent, tender meat.

To peel, slice, mince or dice onions, garlic, and shallots the easy way, see directions on page 306.

Peel the potatoes (using a vegetable peeler). Peel onions. *Parboil* separately in boiling salted water for about 10 minutes. Core the apples, using an apple corer. Forty-five minutes before roasting time is up, place potatoes and onions in the pan with the pork, rolling them around in the pan drippings. Fifteen minutes later, add the apples. Roll them around in the fat, too.

To parboil—simply partially cook.

When pork is cooked, take it out of the pan, cut off any strings, place on a warm serving platter and keep warm. Meat should *rest* 20 to 25 minutes before carving. Test the potatoes and onions with the point of a sharp knife to make sure they are cooked just right. Arrange vegetables in separate warm serving dishes and keep warm. Arrange apples around the pork.

Allow meat to "rest" 15 to 20 minutes after it comes from the oven. This gives the juices time to settle and makes carving easier.

Pour off all the fat from the pan. Mix the cornstarch in a small bowl with a little water to make a smooth paste. Add to the roasting pan with the cider and applejack or calvados. Cook over high heat, using a wooden spatula to scrape down all the rich brown particles that cling to the pan, until sauce begins to get syrupy. If sauce seems too thick, add a bit more cider and, perhaps, a dash more of the spirits. Season with salt and pepper to *taste*. Serves 6 or more.

Cold Loin of Pork is simpatico with Potato Salad along with Glazed Apple Rings (page 198).

Learn to taste. This makes sense, since one person's salt-and-pepper tolerance can be quite different from another's.

CHOCOLATE SOUFFLÉ

EQUIPMENT:
Measuring cups and spoons; 1½-quart soufflé dish; double boiler; wooden spatula; Saran; electric beater or mixer; wire whisk; rubber spatula; flour sifter or sieve.

INGREDIENTS:

Butter

Granulated sugar

3 squares (1-ounce size) semisweet chocolate or ½ package (6-ounce size) chocolate pieces

2 tablespoons *powdered instant* coffee

1 recipe for Crème Pâtissière

7 egg *whites*

Salt

Sifted confectioners' sugar

If you haven't mastered the trick of separating egg yolks from egg whites, see directions on page 305.

Do not use freeze-dried coffee; it does not dissolve readily in this mixture.

Preheat the oven to 375° (or moderate) for 15 minutes before baking the soufflé.

Butter the soufflé dish. Add several tablespoons of granulated sugar to the buttered mold. Then, holding it over the sink, tip the mold back and forth so the sugar coats the bottom and sides. Turn upside down and give it a good thump to knock out any excess. Refrigerate.

Melt the chocolate in a double boiler over hot, not boiling, water. Beat the melted chocolate and the instant coffee into the hot Crème Pâtissière thoroughly with a wooden spatula. (The soufflé can be prepared in advance to this point and set aside, sealed with Saran.)

Add a good pinch of salt to the egg whites and *beat* with an electric beater, or preferably in an electric mixer, until the whites hold stiff shiny peaks when the beater is held straight up. Then beat in 1 tablespoon of granulated sugar. Whip about a third of the whites into the soufflé base very hard with a wire whisk. *Fold* in the remainder with a rubber spatula.

Bake in the preheated oven for 35 minutes. Sift a light coating of confectioners' sugar over the top and continue baking for another 10 minutes. Serve at once with Crème Chantilly which is nothing more than heavy cream, preferably two days old, whipped, sweetened with sifted confectioners' sugar to taste and perfumed with vanilla or rum.

Melt chocolate over hot, not boiling, water because if steam rises, then condenses, the chocolate will tighten and become unmanageable. Should this happen, add 2 tablespoons of vegetable shortening and work into the chocolate until it becomes soft again.

Beat egg whites only to the stiff, shiny stage. If beaten longer, they become granular.

For exact folding technique —see directions on page 305.

BAKED PORK CHOPS, NORMANDY STYLE

Turmeric Rice   *Brussels Sprouts à la Crème*

Iced Grenadine Soufflé   *Coffee*

YOUR COOKING SCHEDULE: As is true of many desserts, the soufflé can be made way ahead, even a day, if sealed with Saran and refrigerated. Rice, of course, can always be cooked in advance and heated up over simmering water. It can even be frozen, then reheated in boiling water (not cooked further, however). Since the sprouts take hardly any time at all, it would be simplest to cook them shortly before you take the chops from the oven. They, of course, should be in the oven an hour, or slightly better, before dinner is to be served.

BAKED PORK CHOPS, NORMANDY STYLE

EQUIPMENT:
Measuring cups and spoons; French chef's knife; large ovenproof baking dish with cover, large enough to accommodate the chops flat, and attractive enough

to go to the table; peppermill; apple corer; vegetable peeler; waxed paper; aluminum foil.

INGREDIENTS:

Butter

6 loin pork chops (1 to 1½ inches thick)

Salt

Freshly ground pepper

3 large tart cooking apples

1 teaspoon sugar

1 teaspoon cinnamon

1 bay leaf

3 whole cloves

2 or 3 shallots, *minced,* or the equivalent in green-onion bulbs

½ cup hard cider

½ cup beef broth

Minced parsley

Use a peppermill for this. Freshly ground pepper is more vibrant than already-ground pepper. Both black and white peppercorns are available, the former being somewhat lustier.

To butter a dish—crumple up a little waxed paper, scoop up a bit of butter and coat the bottom and sides of the dish generously.

To peel, slice, mince, or dice onions, garlic, and shallots the easy way—see directions on page 00.

To mince parsley—hold the blade of a heavy French chef's knife at both ends and chop with rapid up-and-down motions, pulling the ingredients back into a pile with the knife as you work.

Slash fat on steaks, chops, etcetera, to keep the meat from curling while cooking.

Preheat the oven to 350° (or moderate) for 15 minutes before putting the chops in to bake.

Butter baking dish generously. *Slash* the fat on the edges of the chops. Arrange in the dish and sprinkle with salt and pepper.

Using an apple corer, core, then peel the apples with a vegetable peeler. Slice thin and arrange on top of the chops. Mix the sugar and cinnamon together and sprinkle over the apple slices. Dot with butter (about 1 tablespoon). Tuck in the bay leaf, add the cloves and scatter the shallots on top. Mix the hard cider with the broth and pour over all.

Cover tightly (or lacking a cover, use heavy-duty foil) and place in preheated oven for 45 minutes. Uncover and continue baking 15 to 20 minutes to allow apples to brown lightly. Garnish with minced parsley. Serves 4 to 6.

BRUSSELS SPROUTS À LA CRÈME

EQUIPMENT:

Measuring cups and spoons; peppermill; large kettle; paring knife; heavy saucepan large enough to accommodate the sprouts.

INGREDIENTS:

1½ pounds Brussels sprouts	Salt
½ cup heavy cream	*Freshly ground* white pepper
Butter	

Do not cut the stems too short or the outer leaves will fall off during cooking.

Always cook green vegetables uncovered to retain their color.

Allow plenty of time for the sprouts to drain, otherwise any water they retain will dilute the sauce.

To simmer—cook liquid just below boiling (185°) so that it just shivers.

Try to find very small, young sprouts. Trim and *cut* the stalks and remove two or three of the outer leaves. Wash well, then drop into a big kettle of boiling, salted water and boil, *uncovered*, for 10 to 12 minutes, or until the point of a small sharp knife will pierce the stem ends easily. Take care not to overcook them. *Drain* thoroughly immediately.

Pour the cream into the saucepan. Bring to a boil, then *reduce* to about half. Add the sprouts, about 1 tablespoon of butter, salt and pepper to *taste*. Shake the pan well to mix the contents thoroughly. Place over a very low heat and *simmer* just long enough for the sprouts to heat through and to mix their flavor with that of the cream. Serves 4 to 6.

Use a peppermill for this. Freshly ground pepper is more vibrant than already-ground pepper. Both black and white peppercorns are available, the former being somewhat lustier.

To reduce—simply boil liquid over a high heat until the amount left is what the recipe specifies.

Learn to taste. This makes sense, since one person's salt-and-pepper tolerance can be quite different from another's.

TURMERIC RICE

Cook the rice in the Chinese manner (page 29) stirring ½ teaspoon of turmeric into the water before adding it to the rice.

ICED GRENADINE SOUFFLÉ

EQUIPMENT:

Measuring cups and spoons; electric blender; double boiler; large mixing bowl; wooden and rubber spatulas; rotary or electric beater; 1-quart soufflé dish.

INGREDIENTS:

1 envelope unflavored gelatin	¼ teaspoon salt
1 cup (6-ounce bag) almonds, *blanched*	½ cup grenadine syrup
	½ teaspoon almond extract
4 eggs	1 cup heavy cream
½ cup sugar	

To blanch—drop almonds into boiling water and boil 1 minute. Drain. Then slip off skins between thumb and forefinger.

Note the word "sprinkle." Do not dump into the liquid, or the gelatin won't dissolve.

Sprinkle gelatin over ½ cup water to soften. Grind the almonds in the electric blender until very fine. Set aside.

Separate the eggs, dropping the yolks into the top of double boiler, the whites into a large mixing bowl.

If you haven't mastered the trick of separating egg yolks from egg whites, see directions on page 305.

Add the sugar and salt to the yolks and cook over simmering water, stirring constantly with a wooden spatula until the mixture thickens. Take off the heat, stir in the softened gelatin and all remaining ingredients except the cream. Cool.

Beat egg whites only to the stiff, shiny stage. If beaten longer, they become granular.

For exact folding technique —see directions on page 305.

Beat the egg whites with a rotary or electric beater until they stand in firm, shiny peaks when the beater is held straight up.

Fold the whites into the grenadine mixture, using a rubber spatula. Whip the cream until it, too, holds a shape. Then fold it in, too.

Pour into soufflé dish and refrigerate until firm (several hours).

CHINESE SPARERIBS

Boiled Rice, the Chinese Way
(page 29)
Sliced Tomatoes and Onions

French Bread   Butter

Cheese   Fresh Pears

YOUR COOKING SCHEDULE: Since the dessert is, in a sense, already prepared, the spareribs are the only time-consuming job and not much, at that. If you can, it's best to start marinating them the day before and, as you can see from reading the recipe, they take only about an hour all told in the oven. In that time you can prepare the salad and make the sauce for the spareribs. As for cheeses, many taste good with pears. We suggest Brie—if you are feeling expansive and can track down some that is perfectly ripe; or one of the blues, domestic or imported; or a good Camembert, domestic or imported. Present the washed pears on individual plates with dessert or fruit knives so they can be peeled.

SPARERIBS CHINESE STYLE

EQUIPMENT:

Measuring cups and spoons; can opener; sharp, paring knife; large polyethylene bag; pan; paper towels; large roasting pan with a rack; bulb baster or large metal spoon; small mixing bowl; small saucepan.

INGREDIENTS:

6 pounds spareribs, all in one piece

4 cloves garlic

½ cup honey

¼ cup soy sauce

1 can (10½-ounce size) condensed chicken or beef broth

1 cup (1 8-ounce can) tomato sauce

½ teaspoon dry mustard

1 tablespoon cornstarch

Preheat the oven to 325° (or slow) for 15 minutes before placing the ribs in.

Peel and *mince* the garlic. Mix thoroughly with ¼ cup of the honey, the soy sauce, broth, and tomato sauce. *Taste* at this point to see if it needs salt.

Place the ribs in a very large polyethylene bag, add the *marinade* and turn the bag several times so the ribs are well coated. Place in a pan in case of leakage and refrigerate several hours or, preferably, overnight. Turn as often as possible so all surfaces soak up the flavors.

Dry the spareribs with paper towels. Arrange on a rack in a large roasting pan and bake in the preheated oven for 45 minutes. With a bulb baster, suck up (or spoon out) and discard any fat that accumulates. *Baste* the ribs occasionally with a little of the marinade. At the end of 45 minutes, using a spoon, coat the ribs with the remaining honey mixed with the dry mustard. Increase

To peel, slice, mince, or dice onions, garlic and shallots the easy way—see directions on page 306.

Learn to taste. This makes sense, since one person's salt-and-pepper tolerance can be quite different from another's.

To marinate—soak or steep meats or other foods in a marinade (seasoned liquid) to impart flavor and, in some instances, to tenderize.

To baste—spray, spoon or brush a liquid or melted fat over food while it cooks.

the heat to 450° (or very hot) and bake just long enough to give the ribs a handsome glaze.

While the spareribs are cooking, bring the marinade to a boil in small saucepan. Reduce heat and *simmer* until you have about 1½ cups left. Mix the *cornstarch* with enough cold water to make a smooth paste. Stir into the marinade and cook for several minutes or until sauce is clear and slightly thick. Serves 4 to 6.

As a thickening agent, one tablespoon of cornstarch is the equivalent of 2 tablespoons of flour. The resulting sauce is more translucent than when flour is used.

To simmer—cook liquid just below boiling (185°) so that it just shivers.

SLICED TOMATOES AND ONIONS

EQUIPMENT:
Sharp paring knife; serrated knife (preferable) or French chef's knife; deep bowl or saucepan.

Allow about 3 ripe tomatoes and 3 Bermuda onions for 4 to 6 people. Cut out stem ends of the tomatoes, *peel*, and slice very thin. *Peel* the onions, and slice them very thin, too. Arrange on individual plates and serve with cruets of oil and vinegar, a bowl of kosher salt, and a peppermill on the side. Or if you like, dress with Sauce Vinaigrette (page 44) before serving.

To peel tomatoes, cover with boiling water and allow to stand for about 20 seconds. (Unripe tomatoes may take a few seconds longer.) Plunge into cold water. Start peeling at the stem end.

To peel, slice, mince, or dice onions, garlic and shallots the easy way—see directions on page 306.

PORK SAUSAGES IN ONION SAUCE

Mashed Potatoes   *Glazed Apple Rings*
(page 11)

Green Bean Salad, Vinaigrette

Hot Gingerbread with Whipped Cream

Coffee

YOUR COOKING SCHEDULE: The goodness of the individual dishes in this menu —except for the beans, which must be cooked in advance—depends, to a large extent, on their being cooked and eaten promptly. Since the onion sauce that accompanies the sausages takes about an hour to cook, you can boil and finish the potatoes, keeping them warm over simmering water. With the potatoes out of the way, you can make and bake the gingerbread. That leaves only the apple slices, and the time they will take depends on your speed and how many apples you are cooking. Give yourself at least 30 minutes.

PORK SAUSAGES IN ONION SAUCE

EQUIPMENT:
Measuring cups and spoons; peppermill; large, heavy skillet with a cover; slotted spoon; paper towels; French chef's knife.

INGREDIENTS:

1 pound little pork sausages

3 or 4 yellow onions

1 cup white wine

Salt

Freshly ground white pepper

½ teaspoon caraway seeds

⅛ teaspoon sugar

Use a peppermill for this. Freshly ground pepper is more vibrant than already-ground pepper. Both black and white peppercorns are available, the former being somewhat lustier.

Place the sausages in the cold skillet. Add 2 or 3 tablespoons of water, cover tightly, and cook slowly 7 or 8 minutes. Take off the cover, drain off all the fat, and continue cooking slowly until brown and well done. Toss the pan occasionally to turn the sausages over. Lift the sausages from the pan with a slotted spoon onto a paper towel. Set aside.

While the sausages are cooking, *peel* and slice the onions very thin. Pour off all but about 3 tablespoons of the fat from the skillet. Add the onions, wine, salt and pepper to *taste*, caraway and sugar. Bring up to a boil again, reduce heat to *simmer*, cover, and cook for about 50 to 60 minutes or until onions are very tender and almost all the liquid has boiled away. Add the sausages and simmer until the sauce has cooked down a bit more and thickened slightly. Serve immediately. Serves 4 to 5.

To peel, slice, mince, or dice onions, garlic and shallots the easy way, see directions on page 306.

Learn to taste. This makes sense, since one person's salt-and-pepper tolerance can be quite different from another's.

To simmer—cook liquid just below boiling (185°) so that it just shivers.

GLAZED APPLE RINGS

EQUIPMENT:

Apple corer; lemon squeezer; French chef's knife; kitchen bowl or polyethylene bag; heavy skillet; metal spatula; bulb baster or large metal spoon; kitchen fork.

INGREDIENTS:

1 apple per person	Salt
Juice 1 lemon (about)	Sugar
Butter	

Wash and core big, ripe, but firm cooking apples, using an apple corer. Then slice into ½-inch slices. Drop into a bowl or a polyethylene bag with the *lemon juice.* Turn over so the slices are coated.

Use lemon juice to keep the apples from discoloring, also to add flavor.

Heat butter (about 2 tablespoons or ¼ stick, for each apple) in the skillet. When hot, add the apple slices, sprinkle lightly with salt. As they *sauté,* sprinkle with sugar. Turn the rings occasionally, using a metal spatula, and *baste* with the pan juices, using a bulb baster or heavy metal spoon. As apple rings cook, place in a heated serving dish, and keep warm. Add more butter and sugar to the pan as needed. Cooked perfectly, the apples are tender when pierced with a fork and have a slightly shiny glaze. Serve with pan juices spooned over them.

To sauté—cook or brown food in a very small amount of very hot fat.

To baste—spray, spoon or brush a liquid or melted fat over food while it cooks.

Also good as a dessert, served with heavy or sour cream.

GREEN BEAN SALAD, VINAIGRETTE

To cook the beans, see page 49. Once the beans are cooled, as directed, dress with Sauce Vinaigrette (page 44), allowing approximately 1 tablespoon per person or just enough to coat the beans. Don't drown them in the sauce.

HOT GINGERBREAD

EQUIPMENT:

Measuring cups and spoons; flour sifter; 9-inch square baking pan; small saucepan; large mixing bowl; rubber or wooden spatula; toothpick; rotary or electric beater.

INGREDIENTS:

½ cup (1 stick) butter	¾ teaspoon baking soda
1 cup molasses	1 teaspoon ground ginger
1 cup commercial sour cream	1 teaspoon ground cinnamon
2⅓ cups *sifted* all-purpose flour	¼ teaspoon ground cloves
⅛ teaspoon salt	Heavy cream, whipped

To measure sifted flour properly spoon it—after sifting—into a dry measuring cup (or spoon), well above the top, then level or cut off with the edge—not the flat surface—of a metal spatula or knife. Do not shake flour down.

Preheat the oven to 350° (or moderate) for 15 minutes before baking the gingerbread.

Butter bottom and sides of baking pan generously. Set aside.

Combine the butter and molasses in a saucepan and heat to the boiling point. Take off the heat, pour into a large mixing bowl, and cool slightly. Then stir in the sour cream with a spatula. Sift the flour with the salt, baking soda, and spices. Mix into molasses combination thoroughly.

To butter—crumple up a little waxed paper, scoop up a bit of butter and coat the bottom and sides of the pan generously.

Pour into the prepared pan and bake in the preheated oven for 35 to 40 minutes or until a toothpick inserted in the center comes out dry. Turn out of the pan onto a cake rack. Cut into squares and serve warm with whipped cream.

———◆———

GOULASH, CZECHOSLOVAKIAN STYLE

Dumplings   *Onion and Beet Salad*

Eggnog Mousse   *Coffee*

YOUR COOKING SCHEDULE: The nice thing about this Goulash is that you can make it a day, even two, ahead and reheat it just before serving time. As for the dumplings, they can be made early in the day but, unlike this good goulash, they do not improve by resting in the refrigerator. There's no reason under the sun why the Mousse could not be made a day ahead, too, sealed with Saran and refrigerated. As is always true, the salad greens should be washed, wrapped in a fresh dishcloth and refrigerated so they will be dry when needed. With all these chores out of the way, the only before-dinner-is-served jobs left are the salad, heating the goulash and dumplings, garnishing the mousse with whipped cream.

GOULASH, CZECHOSLOVAKIAN STYLE

EQUIPMENT:
French chef's knife; measuring cups and spoons; kitchen scissors; frying pan;

slotted spoon; corkscrew; paper towels; heavy, deep casserole; 2-pronged fork.

INGREDIENTS:

1 loin of pork, boned
1 pound bacon
2 medium onions, *peeled* and *minced*
2 cloves garlic, *peeled* and *minced*
3 tablespoons sweet paprika
2 tablespoons hot paprika
8 juniper *berries*

1½ teaspoons caraway seeds
Salt
2 cups dry white wine
2 cups (1-pound-size can or bag) sauerkraut
3 cups commercial sour cream at room temperature

To peel, slice, mince, or dice onions, garlic, and shallots the easy way, see directions on page 306.

Use about ¼ cup of gin if berries are not available.

Have the butcher bone the pork for you and cut the meat into 1-inch cubes. Holding the bacon in a bundle, cut it with scissors into 1-inch pieces and place it in a cold frying pan. Fry over low heat, turning frequently until brown and crisp. Lift out of the fat with a slotted spoon and drain on paper towels. Drain off all except a film of the bacon fat, add the cubes of pork—don't crowd the pan—and brown on all sides. As you finish each batch, lift out of the pan with a slotted spoon and set aside.

If goulash is prepared a day or even two ahead, refrigerate. To serve, reheat to the boiling point only. Then add the cream and bacon. Bring to a boil again, but do not cook further.

Add the onions and garlic, with 1 cup of water, bring up to a boil, reduce heat to moderate, and cook until all the water has boiled away and the onions are transparent. Now combine, in the casserole, all ingredients except the sour cream and bacon. Add the browned meat, bring to boil, reduce heat to *simmer*, cover, and cook for about 30 minutes or until the meat is very tender when pierced with a fork.

To simmer—cook liquid just below boiling (185°) so that it just shivers.

Just before serving, stir in the sour cream and bacon. Serves 8.

DUMPLINGS

Measuring cups and spoons; wire whisk; large mixing bowl; large kettle; sharp kitchen knife; colander; dish towel.

INGREDIENTS:

4 level cups all-purpose flour	1 teaspoon salt
1¾ cups milk	1 cup croutons
2 egg *yolks*	

If you haven't mastered the trick of separating egg yolks from egg whites, see directions on page 305.

Whip the yolks slightly with a wire whisk. Combine with the flour, milk, and salt in a large bowl and work together thoroughly with your hands. Then mix in the croutons.

Divide the dough into four parts and roll each one into a tube about 2½ inches in diameter. Drop into a large kettle of boiling salted water and cook for 30 minutes. Start timing after the water comes to a boil a second time. When properly cooked, the dumplings will have a slight glaze. In the beginning give the kettle an occasional shake so the dumplings won't stick to the bottom. Once they start to cook, they will float to the top.

Removing the dumplings from the kettle is quite tricky, since they are extremely fragile. The easiest way is to drain off most of the water, then lift them out, using two small plates like a scoop. Better put on a pair of "mitten" pot holders to protect hands. To serve, slice about half an inch thick. Serves 8.

If dumplings are made ahead, reheat just before serving time by *steaming.*

Croutons: Take half a loaf of sliced firm bread and cut it into small cubes. Brown in hot butter. Any croutons that are left over can be stored and used some other time.

To steam—place the sliced dumplings in a colander that will sit on the rim of a saucepan but above the simmering water. Cover lightly with a fresh dish towel.

ONION AND BEET SALAD

EQUIPMENT:
Can opener; paring knife; French chef's knife.

INGREDIENTS:
2 cans (12-ounce size) beets
2 sweet Spanish white or Italian
   red onions

Sauce Vinaigrette (page 44)
Lettuce

Drain the beets, then slice very thin. Peel and slice the onions, also very thin. Arrange the slices, more or less alternately on top of crisp lettuce. Spoon Sauce Vinaigrette all over. Serves 8.

EGGNOG MOUSSE

EQUIPMENT:
Measuring cups and spoons; small saucepan; rotary or electric beater or electric mixer; rubber spatula; wire whisk; 2-quart mold.

INGREDIENTS:
2 envelopes unflavored gelatin
8 eggs, *separated*
3/4 cups good bourbon
2 teaspoons vanilla

1/4 teaspoon salt
1 cup sugar
Heavy cream

If you haven't mastered the trick of separating egg yolks from egg whites—see directions on page 305.

Sprinkle the gelatin over 1 cup of cold water in saucepan, then place over a moderate heat and stir until gelatin has dissolved. Five minutes or so.

Note the word "sprinkle." Do not dump into the liquid, or the gelatin won't dissolve.

Beat the yolks with a rotary or electric beater until very thick and creamy. With a rubber spatula, stir in the bourbon and vanilla, mixing well. Lastly mix in the gelatin thoroughly. Chill until the mixture begins to set (that is, has body enough to barely hold other foods in suspension). Give it an occasional whipping with a wire whisk.

Sprinkle the salt over the whites and beat with an electric or rotary beater or in an electric mixer until frothy. Gradually beat in the sugar until you have a smooth, shiny meringue. Whip about a third of the meringue into the gelatin mixture vigorously with a wire whisk, then *fold* in the remainder with a rubber spatula. Finally, whip the cream and fold it into the mixture. Pour into a 2-quart mold and refrigerate until firm (a matter of several hours).

For exact folding technique—see directions on page 305.

The wire whip or whisk (fouet in French) is available from the 8-inch size up to the 13½-inch balloon. We suggest that two or three medium-sized whips (10- to 14-inch) made of piano wire are adequate for most households.

WIRE WHIPS

ELECTRIC BEATER

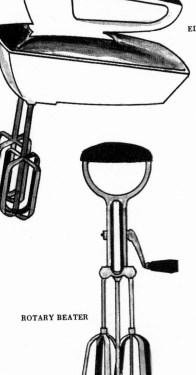

ROTARY BEATER

ELECTRIC MIXER

THE BEATERS

Operated by hand, the rotary beater can beat up whole eggs, yolks, whites, frostings, etc., but can't cope successfully with heavy batters. The portable electric beater, usually with three speeds, is a real "work horse" in the kitchen. Broadly speaking, it can do everything from mixing pie crust to whipping cream. The stationary electric mixer may well be one of the greatest inventions since the wheel. Ideal for long mixing jobs, such as kneading bread (use the bread hook); for making pastry (use the flat beater); for making cakes (use the whip); for "working" all heavy batters. Expensive but to the dedicated cook worth every dollar.

LAMB

ROAST LEG OF LAMB

Baked Stuffed Tomatoes
(page 156)

Green Beans
(page 49)

Fresh Mushroom Salad

Rice Pudding　　　**Coffee**

.

YOUR COOKING SCHEDULE: Both the tomatoes and the beans can be prepared ahead, the beans actually cooked ready to reheat. The Rice Pudding must be done far enough in advance to allow it to chill. Figure on a minimum of 2 hours in the refrigerator. When the lamb comes out of the oven and is resting, the tomatoes can be baked and the beans heated up in butter. While that is going on, slice the mushrooms and make the salad.

ROAST LEG OF LAMB

EQUIPMENT:

French chef's knife; can opener; large roasting pan with a rack; meat thermometer; bulb baster or large metal spoon; peppermill; wooden spatula; strainer.

The question of garlic always comes up when the subject of roast lamb comes up. If you are a garlic aficionado, insert 3 or 4 slivers in the meat at the shank end, or make several incisions in the meat itself and insert garlic slivers, or instead add 3 or 4 unpeeled cloves to the roasting pan a half hour before the lamb has finished cooking.

If you like your lamb cooked with garlic, then do NOT serve Baked Stuffed Tomatoes, since they, too, are cooked with garlic. Rather serve potatoes roasted with the meat. To do this, place mature peeled potatoes (cut in two, if large) around the meat when you add the other vegetables. Roll around in the fat to coat them. Turn once during roasting.

INGREDIENTS:

1 6-pound leg of young lamb
Butter, softened
1 large carrot, coarsely chopped
1 large onion, *peeled* and coarsely
    chopped

1 can (10½-ounce size) beef broth
Watercress

To peel, slice, mince, or dice onions, garlic, and shallots the easy way, see directions on page 306.

Preheat the oven to 450° (or hot) for 15 minutes before roasting the lamb.

With your hands, rub 3 or 4 tablespoons softened butter all over the leg of lamb.

To baste—spray, spoon, or brush a liquid or melted fat over food while it cooks.

To roast to the well-done stage, allow approximately 30 to 35 minutes per pound, 160° to 165° on the meat thermometer. We recommend a thermometer that registers from zero to 220°

Allow meat to rest 15 to 20 minutes after it comes from the oven. This allows juices to settle and makes carving easier.

Place the leg on a rack in a roasting pan in the hot oven for about 20 minutes, *basting* with a bulb baster or large metal spoon every 5 minutes or so, or until it is browned on all sides. Reduce the heat to 350° (moderate), add the vegetables to the pan and *roast* the meat to the pink stage—approximately 1¼ hours. To test properly, insert the meat thermometer into the thickest part of the meat without touching a bone. It should read 130° to 135° for pink. Place the meat on a warm serving platter, sprinkle with salt and *freshly ground* pepper and allow it to *rest* for 20 to 30 minutes before carving.

Dump a pan of ice cubes into the roasting pan so the fat congeals around them. Lift out and discard.

Add the beef broth to the pan, return to the fire and boil over a high heat, scraping up any coagulated juices and mashing the vegetables into the broth with a wooden spatula. *Reduce* to about 1 cup. Strain into a warm sauceboat to serve. Garnish the lamb with fresh watercress (or parsley or celery tops) just before serving. A 6- to 7-pound roast of lamb will serve 6 to 8 people.

Cold Roast Lamb, a delicious byproduct of the hot roast, makes a marvelous dinner accompanied by Potatoes Dauphinois (page 7), a mixed green salad tossed in Sauce Vinaigrette (page 44), and for dessert, coffee ice cream and Sugar Cookies (page 245).

Use a peppermill for this. Freshly ground pepper is more vibrant than already-ground pepper. Both black and white peppercorns are available, the former being somewhat lustier.

To reduce—simply boil a liquid over a high heat until the amount left is what the recipe specifies.

FRESH MUSHROOM SALAD

EQUIPMENT:
Paring knife; small mixing bowl; French chef's knife.

Take 1 pound of raw medium-size mushrooms. Wipe with a clean damp cloth or run under a light stream of cool water. *Dry* thoroughly.

Nip off the tips of the stems with a sharp knife, then slice, stems and all,

Never soak mushrooms in water; never peel, unless shriveled and old.

very thin. Toss in ½ cup Sauce Vinaigrette (page 44) with ¼ cup *finely* *minced* parsley. Serve with or without lettuce. Serves 6 to 8.

Variations: Use chopped fresh mint leaves or minced chives in place of parsley; or, like James A. Beard, add a handful of fresh violets before serving.

To mince parsley—hold the blade of a heavy French chef's knife at both ends and chop with rapid up-and-down motions, pulling the ingredients back into a pile with the knife as you work.

RICH RICE PUDDING

EQUIPMENT:

Measuring cups and spoons; small mixing bowl; double boiler; rotary or electric beater; rubber or wooden spatula; kitchen spoon.

INGREDIENTS:

½ cup uncooked long-grain rice	¼ teaspoon salt
½ cup raisins	4 eggs
2 cups light cream	2 cups heavy cream
2 cups milk	2 teaspoons vanilla
¾ cup sugar	*Freshly grated* nutmeg

Pour ½ cup water over raisins and allow them to soak.

Combine rice, light cream, milk, sugar and salt in the top of a double boiler. Place over simmering water, cover, and cook for 1 hour, giving mixture an occasional stir.

Beat the eggs together with a rotary or electric beater. Mix two or three tablespoons of the hot rice mixture into the eggs, using a rubber or wooden spatula. Then combine the two in the top of the double boiler, stirring constantly. Place back over simmering water and cook until the mixture is thick enough to make a film that coats a spoon. *Take off the heat* and cool completely.

Beat heavy cream until it holds a definite shape, then *fold* into the cold rice

For this, you need a small nutmeg grater and, of course, whole nutmegs. Like cheese and pepper, freshly grated nutmeg makes all the difference in the finished dish because the flavor is so delicious.

Do not cook beyond this point or the custard will certainly curdle.

For exact folding technique —see directions on page 305.

mixture. Mix in the well-drained raisins and the vanilla. Spoon into a handsome serving dish, sprinkle with freshly grated nutmeg and chill until firm.

———◆·◆———

Vichyssoise

BROILED LAMB CHOPS

Carrots with Marsala
(page 161)

Coleslaw
(page 116)

Spiced Figs   *Coffee*

YOUR COOKING SCHEDULE: The Vichyssoise, Coleslaw, and Spiced Figs—all three—can be made the day before. Failing that, they must be made early in the day so the soup and figs can chill, the slaw mellow. The Vichyssoise makes a fairly large quantity, so there is sufficient for two meals. The potatoes should be in the oven at least an hour before you plan to sit down at the dinner table; the chops in their marinade at the same time. Once the potatoes are baked, broil the chops.

VICHYSSOISE

EQUIPMENT:

French chef's knife; vegetable peeler or paring knife; can opener; measuring cups and spoons; heavy deep kettle with a cover; electric blender; fine sieve.

INGREDIENTS:

4 leeks, the bulb part only

2 or 3 tablespoons sweet butter

1 medium onion, *peeled*, and
    chopped fine

5 medium potatoes, peeled and
    sliced thin

4 cups chicken broth or 3 cans
    (10½-ounce size)

1 tablespoon salt (about)

3 cups milk

2 cups heavy cream

Minced chives

To peel, slice, mince, or dice onions, garlic, and shallots the easy way, see directions on page 306.

Chop the green leaves off the leeks and discard them. Wash the bulbs well, then slice thin.

Melt the butter in the kettle, add the leeks, onion, potatoes, broth, and salt. Bring to a boil, reduce heat to moderate, cover and cook for about 35 minutes or until the potatoes are extremely tender.

Purée the vegetables a few at a time, in the blender, along with a little of the broth, until very smooth. Pour back into the kettle, add the milk and 1 cup of the cream. Bring up to a boil again. Take off the heat and cool. When cold, push through a very fine sieve. Chill. Add the remaining cream and chill again. Serve in chilled soup cups with a garnish of chives. (Vichyssoise can also be served hot.)

To mince chives—hold the blade of a heavy French chef's knife at both ends and chop with rapid up-and-down motions, pulling the herb back into a pile with the knife as you work.

BROILED LAMB CHOPS

EQUIPMENT:
Peppermill; polyethylene bag; broiling pan with rack.

INGREDIENTS:

Double (2-inch) lamb *chops* (1 per person)	Salt
Olive oil	Pepper
Garlic	Butter
	Minced parsley

If possible, buy loin lamb chops. They are the best, but they are also the most expensive. Rib or French chops are very small and therefore, less practical.

To marinate—soak or steep meat or other foods in a marinade (seasoned liquid) to impart flavor and, in some instances, to tenderize.

To peel, slice, mince, or dice onions, garlic, and shallots the easy way—see directions on page 306.

Marinate the chops for 1 hour in olive oil, seasoned with garlic, salt, and freshly ground pepper. For 6 chops combine 6 tablespoons of oil, 1 clove garlic, *peeled* and split, ½ teaspoon salt, and several twists of the peppermill. Tie securely in a polyethylene bag. Add the chops and place in a pan in case of leakage. Turn occasionally so chops are well saturated.

Preheat the broiler for 15 minutes to highest heat before broiling the chops. Place the chops on a cold rack about 2 or 3 inches from the source of the heat in the preheated broiler. Brown on both sides, *broiling* a total of 10 minutes for rare; 15 minutes for medium rare. Place the cooked chops on a warm platter, sprinkle with salt and pepper, and add a small pat of butter to each chop. Garnish with minced parsley.

To mince parsley—hold the blade of a heavy French chef's knife at both ends and chop with rapid up-and-down motions, pulling the ingredients back into a pile with the knife as you work.

For "well done," broil a total of 16 to 20 minutes. However, rare or medium rare is recommended for best flavor.

SPICED FIGS

EQUIPMENT:
Measuring spoons; medium saucepan; bulb baster or large metal spoon.

INGREDIENTS:

1 can (1-pound size) figs

2 sticks cinnamon

3 tablespoons brown sugar

¼ teaspoon ground ginger

Combine all the ingredients in the saucepan. Bring up to a boil, then reduce heat and cook very slowly, uncovered, for about 15 minutes or until the syrup is about as thick as molasses. *Baste* the fruit occasionally during the cooking. Pour into a dish, cover and refrigerate. Serve cold with or without cream.

To baste—spray, spoon, or brush a liquid or melted fat over food while it cooks.

IRISH STEW FOR EIGHT

Green Salad, Vinaigrette
(page 44)

Orange Custard   Coffee

YOUR COOKING SCHEDULE: Allowing about 30 minutes to make the custard and an hour to bake it, it should be finished early in the afternoon to have sufficient time in the refrigerator to chill properly. The salad greens should be washed thoroughly, wrapped in a clean dishcloth, tucked into a polyethylene bag, tied, and refrigerated early in the day. Twenty or, at the most, thirty minutes is all that's needed to prepare the stew. It takes approximately an hour and a half to cook. That means you should be in the kitchen no later than 5 o'clock if dinner is to be at 7. The last little job: whip up the Sauce Vinaigrette (page 44).

IRISH STEW FOR EIGHT

EQUIPMENT:

French chef's knife; measuring spoons; vegetable peeler; can opener; large, heavy fireproof casserole with a cover; peppermill; medium saucepan.

INGREDIENTS:

4 pounds boned shoulder of lamb, cut into 1¼-inch cubes
4 leeks, well washed and sliced
1 rib celery, chopped
2 tablespoons salt
6 peppercorns, *crushed*
2 cloves garlic, peeled and *crushed*
Dash Worcestershire sauce
3 cans (10½-ounce size) condensed beef broth
Bouquet garni: 2 stalks parsley; 1 bay leaf; ½ teaspoon dried thyme

12 small potatoes, peeled, or 6 medium, peeled and quartered
16 small white onions, *peeled*
8 small whole carrots, peeled, or 3 large carrots, peeled and quartered
2 white turnips, peeled and cut into 1-inch cubes
1 pound fresh green peas, shelled, or 2 packages (10-ounce size) frozen peas
Minced parsley

To crush garlic and peppercorns, give them a good whack with the side of a cleaver, heavy knife or any heavy implement.

To make a bouquet garni combine spices in a little cheesecloth or bag, to make it easy to remove. (Even if other seasonings are used it is still called a bouquet garni.

To peel, slice, mince, or dice onions, garlic, and shallots the easy way—see directions on page 306.

To mince parsley—hold the blade of a heavy French chef's knife at both ends and chop with rapid up-and-down motions, pulling

Place the meat, and all ingredients except potatoes, white onions, carrots, turnips and peas in the casserole. Add enough water to almost cover. Bring up to

the ingredients back into a pile with the knife as you work.

a boil slowly. Reduce heat, add the lid, and *simmer* for 1 hour. Meanwhile, prepare the vegetables. At the end of an hour, add all vegetables except the peas. Fifteen minutes later, add the fresh peas. (If frozen peas are used, add just 5 minutes before cooking time is up.) Continue cooking another 15 to 20 minutes. By that time the meat, as well as the potatoes and onions, should be tender when pierced with a fork. Total cooking time about 1½ hours. Remove the bouquet garni. Garnish with the minced parsley and serve straight from the casserole.

To simmer—cook liquid just below boiling (185°) so that it just shivers.

ORANGE CUSTARD

EQUIPMENT:
Measuring cups; grater; orange squeezer; 2-quart soufflé dish or ovenproof baking dish; wooden spatula; large mixing bowl; skillet; electric beater or electric mixer; roasting pan; metal knife; aluminum foil.

INGREDIENTS:

1½ cups sugar

5 eggs

3 egg *yolks*

Grated rind from 2 oranges

1 cup heavy cream

1½ cups fresh orange juice, strained (about 6 juicy oranges), or pasteurized orange juice

If you haven't mastered the trick of separating egg yolks from egg whites, see directions on page 305.

To grate rind of citrus fruit —which must be done before squeezing—work on a flat grater placed on top of a piece of waxed paper.

Place the soufflé dish or baking dish in a saucepan of hot water.

Place ¾ cup of the sugar in a heavy skillet over high heat and cook, stirring constantly, with a wooden spatula, until the sugar has caramelized. Pour at once into the warm soufflé dish. Tip the dish back and forth until the bottom is completely coated. When sugar is no longer running, turn the dish upside down. Refrigerate.

At this point, preheat the oven to 400° (or hot) for 15 minutes before baking the custard.

Combine the whole eggs, yolks and remaining sugar in a bowl and beat hard with an electric beater, or in an electric mixer, until very thick and creamy. Thoroughly stir in the orange rind, juice, and heavy cream, using a wooden spatula. Pour into the cold prepared dish.

Place in a roasting pan and add enough hot water to reach to about two thirds the depth of the soufflé dish. Bake in the preheated oven for 1 hour or until a knife comes out clean when inserted into the custard about 1 inch from the outer edge. If custard seems to be browning too much as it cooks lay a piece of aluminum foil lightly on top. Cool, then refrigerate.

MOUSSAKA FOR TEN

French Bread   *Onions à la Grecque*

Glazed Carrot Cake   *Coffee*

YOUR COOKING SCHEDULE: This entire menu can be prepared a day ahead most satisfactorily, making it an ideal supper for a party of ten or so. You should know that the cake must be done in advance, but glazed the day it will be served. So it would seem to make sense to do all three major cooking jobs the day before and have the day of the party off—more or less. A total of two hours in the kitchen should wrap up all the cooking.

MOUSSAKA

EQUIPMENT:

Measuring cups and spoons; French chef's knife; peppermill; nutmeg grater; cheese grater; vegetable peeler; electric blender; wire whisk; kitchen bowl; paper towels; large, heavy skillet; medium saucepan; wooden spatula; 11 × 16-inch ovenproof baking dish.

Of Greek origin, Moussaka (pronounced moos-ah-kah) makes a marvelous addition to the buffet, but it can also stand alone. Of its many advantages, it must be prepared ahead (a day, if you like), and it should be served either lukewarm or at room temperature. To reheat, place in a 140° (low) oven just long enough to barely warm.

INGREDIENTS:

4 medium-size eggplants
Salt
Flour
½ cup vegetable oil
10 tablespoons (1 stick plus 2 tablespoons) butter
3 large onions, *minced*
2 pounds ground lamb
3 tablespoons tomato paste
20 to 30 parsley sprigs, *minced*

½ cup dry red wine
A few twists of the peppermill
¼ teaspoon cinnamon
2 whole eggs, beaten until frothy
¾ cup *freshly grated* Parmesan cheese
½ cup fine *bread crumbs*
3 cups milk, heated
Freshly ground nutmeg
4 egg *yolks*, slightly beaten

To peel, slice, mince, or dice onions, garlic, and shallots the easy way, see directions on page 306.

To mince parsley—hold the blade of a heavy French chef's knife at both ends and chop with rapid up-and-down motions, pulling the ingredients back into a pile with the knife as you work.

Cut Parmesan cheese into relatively small chunks and grate in the blender.

Use firm day-old bread for bread crumbs (1 slice makes about ¼ cup). Break into pieces and grind in the electric blender, or crumble by hand until very fine.

For this, you need a small nutmeg grater and, of course, whole nutmeg.

If you haven't mastered the trick of separating egg yolks from egg whites—see directions on page 305.

Peel the eggplant, using a vegetable peeler, then slice lengthwise into pieces about ½ inch thick. Sprinkle with salt on both sides, place in a bowl and allow to stand for 30 minutes. Cover with cold water and allow to stand 10 minutes longer. Squeeze out the water and blot the slices dry with paper towels. Coat lightly with flour. Heat the vegetable oil in a large skillet. When hot, fry the eggplant slices until golden. Don't crowd the pan. Drain on paper towels. Set aside.

Add 4 tablespoons of the butter to the skillet. Add the onions and meat. *Sauté* until the meat has browned, giving it an occasional stir. Stir in the tomato paste, wine, parsley, salt and pepper to *taste*, and ½ cup water. *Simmer* stirring frequently, until all the liquid has been absorbed. Take off the heat and cool. Then stir in the cinnamon, the two beaten whole eggs, ½ cup of the cheese and ¼ cup of the bread crumbs. Set aside.

Preheat the oven to 350° (or moderate) 15 minutes before baking the moussaka.

To make the sauce: Melt the remaining butter in a saucepan over a low heat. With a wooden spatula, stir in 6 tablespoons of flour until smooth. Cook, stirring constantly, for about 3 minutes. Do not brown. Then add the hot milk, beating constantly with a wire whisk. Put back over a moderate heat and cook, whipping constantly, until the sauce is thick and smooth. Stir in salt, pepper, and nutmeg to taste. Beat a little of the hot sauce into the egg yolks, then combine the two, whipping steadily. Cook over very low heat for 2 minutes, still whipping. Do not cook further or the sauce will curdle.

Butter the baking dish. Sprinkle the remaining crumbs over the bottom. Cover with a layer of the eggplant slices, then a layer of the meat mixture. Continue until all ingredients are used, finishing with a layer of eggplant. Cover with the sauce, sprinkle with remaining cheese and bake in a preheated 350° (or moderate) oven for 1 hour or until the top is golden. Cool for about 25 minutes before serving. Serves 8 to 10.

To sauté—cook or brown food in a very small amount of very hot fat.

To simmer—cook liquid just below boiling (185°) so that it just shivers.

To butter a baking dish—crumple up a little waxed paper, scoop up a bit of butter and coat the bottom and sides of the dish generously.

Learn to taste. This makes sense, since one person's salt-and-pepper tolerance can be quite different from another's.

ONIONS À LA GRECQUE

EQUIPMENT:

Measuring cups and spoons; French chef's knife; lemon squeezer; paring knife; large, heavy saucepan with a cover; slotted spoon.

INGREDIENTS:

1 cup olive oil

Juice 1 lemon

1 rib celery, coarsely chopped

1 clove garlic, peeled and split

½ teaspoon rosemary

2 or 3 shallots, *minced*

⅛ teaspoon fennel seeds or 1 sprig fresh

½ teaspoon thyme or 2 sprigs fresh

½ bay leaf

6 to 8 coriander seeds

12 peppercorns

¾ teaspoon salt

6 parsley sprigs

36 very small onions, all of a size, peeled

To peel, slice, mince, or dice onions, garlic, and shallots the easy way, see directions on page 306.

Combine all the ingredients except the onions with 2 cups of water in a large, heavy saucepan. Bring to a boil, reduce heat, cover, and *simmer* for 10 minutes. Add the onions, bring up to a boil again, reduce heat, cover, and simmer until the onions are tender when pierced with the point of a paring knife. With a slotted spoon lift the onions from the bouillon to a bowl. Return the bouillon to the fire and *reduce* to half to concentrate the flavors. Then pour over the onions and refrigerate overnight. Serve cold. Serves 10.

To simmer—cook liquid just below boiling (185°) so that it just shivers.

To reduce—simply boil liquid over a high heat until the amount left is what the recipe specifies.

Many vegetables can be prepared à la Grecque; such as: artichoke hearts, celery hearts, cauliflowerets, leeks, mushroom caps, green onions, et cetera.

GLAZED SWISS CARROT CAKE

EQUIPMENT:

Measuring cups and spoons; electric blender; vegetable peeler; lemon squeezer; 8-inch spring-form pan; waxed paper; flat grater; rotary or electric beater; wire whisk; rubber spatula; large mixing bowl; medium mixing bowl; toothpicks; metal spatula.

Don't let the name throw you off, for this is a most delicious and interesting cake which can be made ahead of time. In fact, it benefits by mellowing a few days.

INGREDIENTS:

Vegetable shortening	½ teaspoon cinnamon
1 cup fine dry *bread crumbs*	¼ teaspoon ground cloves
3 to 4 medium carrots, about	6 eggs, *separated*
1⅔ cups almonds or filberts, with	1¼ cups sugar
skins on	*Grated* rind and juice of 1 lemon

Dry unseasoned bread crumbs are available packaged, or firm bread can be dried in a low (200° oven), then ground in the electric blender or rolled into crumbs with a rolling pin.

To grease a pan—crumple up a little waxed paper, scoop up a bit of butter and coat the bottom and sides of the pan generously.

If you haven't mastered the trick of separating egg yolks from egg whites, see directions on page 305.

To grate rind of citrus fruit—which must be done before squeezing—work on a flat grater placed on top of a piece of waxed paper.

To line a pan—place the pan on a piece of waxed paper. Outline the shape with a pencil, then cut out with scissors and place in bottom of the pan.

Preheat the oven to 350° (or moderate) 15 minutes before baking cake.

Grease the bottom of the spring form. Cut a circle of *waxed paper* to fit the bottom of the pan, then grease the paper and, at the same time, grease the sides of the pan. Add about 3 spoonfuls of bread crumbs. Working over the sink, tip the pan back and forth so the crumbs coat the bottom and sides of the pan. Then give the pan a good whack to knock out any surplus.

Peel the carrots with a vegetable peeler, then grate fine (you need ⅔ cup packed down tight). Grind the nuts in the electric blender until fine. Mix carrots, nuts, remaining bread crumbs and spices in a large mixing bowl.

Combine egg yolks, sugar, and lemon juice in a medium bowl and beat vigorously with a rotary or electric beater until thick. Then stir into the carrot mixture along with the lemon rind. *Beat* the whites until they stand in firm, shiny peaks when the beater is held straight up. Using a whisk, whip about a third of the whites into the batter. *Fold* in remainder carefully with rubber spatula.

For exact folding technique —see directions on page 305.

Beat egg whites only to the stiff, shiny stage. If beaten longer, they become granular.

Spoon into the prepared pan and bake in the preheated oven for 45 to 60 minutes or until a toothpick inserted in the center comes out dry. Cool on a rack. When cold, release the sides of the pan, turn upside down to remove the bottom and pull off the waxed paper. Wrap in foil or Saran and allow to mellow in the refrigerator 2 or 3 days.

Finish with this glaze: Combine 2 cups sifted confectioners' sugar with 4½ tablespoons water and ¼ teaspoon lemon extract or fresh lemon juice. Mix until perfectly smooth. Then pour over the top of the cake, smoothing with a metal spatula.

This cake does not call for flour, because it is replaced by the crumbs.

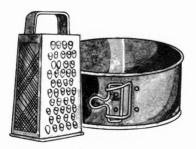

SHELLFISH
AND FISH

SHELLFISH

CURRIED SHRIMP

Boiled Rice, the Chinese Way   **French Fried Onion Rings**
(page 29)
Sliced Ripe Bananas   **Chutney**

Chilled Beer

Almond Pudding   **Coffee**
with Chocolate Glaze

YOUR COOKING SCHEDULE: The Almond Pudding should be steamed early in the day to allow for cooling and glazing. Both the curry sauce and the rice can be cooked a day ahead. The latter can even be cooked and frozen. Onion rings are best if served immediately after they've been fried, but they can be kept warm in a low, 140° oven, if necessary. It seems almost superfluous to add that the beer should be properly chilled.

CURRIED SHRIMP

EQUIPMENT:
Paring knife; can opener.

INGREDIENTS:

2 pounds medium shrimp, thawed,   Recipe for Curry Sauce (page 28)
   shelled, deveined

To shell—push the shell with your thumb and forefinger; it will come off easily; to devein—make a thin cut with the point of a sharp paring knife along the curve of the body and lift out the little black "string." Not always there, by the way.

Make up the recipe for the sauce as directed, substituting 4 cans (10½-ounce size) chicken broth for homemade. Add the raw shrimp at the same time recipe indicates adding the chicken. The time it will take to heat the sauce after the addition of the cream and lemon juice will be just enough to cook the shrimp. Serves 8.

You may, if you wish, serve the same condiments as suggested for the curried chicken (page 29) rather than the onion rings and ripe *bananas*.

Sprinkle the bananas with lemon juice to keep them from turning dark.

CURRIED CRABMEAT

Substitute crabmeat for the shrimp in the same amount.

FRENCH FRIED ONION RINGS

EQUIPMENT:
Two medium kitchen bowls; peppermill; sharp paring knife; French chef's knife; deep-fat fryer; slotted spoon; paper towels; candy thermometer.

INGREDIENTS:

8 large, sweet white onions

Vegetable oil

Milk

Flour

Salt

Freshly ground pepper

To peel, slice, mince, or dice onions, garlic, and shallots the easy way—see directions on page 306.

For exact technique of deep-fat frying—see directions on page 306.

Cut the ends off the onions, *peel* off the outer skin and slice about ½ inch thick. Carefully push out the middle slices to separate them into rings.

Heat the oil in a *deep-fat* fryer to 380° on the thermometer, or until a cube of bread browns in 1 minute. Dip each onion ring in milk, then in flour, shaking off any excess, and drop, a few at a time, into the hot fat. Cook about 5 minutes or until golden brown and crisp. Lift from the fat with slotted spoon. Check the temperature between each batch to make sure it maintains 380°. Drain the cooked onions on paper towels and season with a good sprinkling of salt and pepper. Keep warm in a low (140°) oven. Serves 8.

Use a peppermill for this. Freshly ground pepper is more vibrant than already-ground pepper. Both black and white peppercorns are available, the former being somewhat lustier.

ALMOND PUDDING WITH CHOCOLATE GLAZE

EQUIPMENT:

Measuring cups and spoons; corkscrew; 6-inch spring form or 4-cup metal mold; electric blender or hand-operated nut grater; small saucepan; mixing bowl; wooden spatula; rubber spatula or kitchen spoon; rotary or electric beater; roasting pan; kitchen scissors; toothpick; cake rack; double boiler; wire whisk.

INGREDIENTS:

1 cup (15-ounce can) whole blanched almonds

½ cup sugar

2 tablespoons Cognac or rum

4 egg *whites*

Pinch salt

If you haven't mastered the trick of separating egg yolks from egg whites, see directions on page 305.

GLAZE:

2 squares (1-ounce size) unsweetened chocolate

2 squares (1-ounce size) semisweet
chocolate

2 teaspoons liquid honey

4 tablespoons (½ stick) butter,
softened

Preheat the oven to 300° (or slow) for 15 minutes before baking the pudding.

Butter well the spring-form pan or the metal mold and set aside. Grind the almonds in the electric blender or put through a hand-operated nut grater. Set them aside, too.

Combine the sugar with 3 tablespoons of water in a small saucepan. Place over a moderate heat and stir with a wooden spatula until the sugar has dissolved. Stir in the ground nuts and cook over a very low heat, stirring constantly with wooden spatula until the mixture forms a ball in the center of the pan. Watch out to see that it doesn't scorch. Take off the heat and cool. When cold, it will be hard. Break it up somewhat, then grind in the electric blender until very fine. Pour into a bowl and with a rubber spatula or spoon work in the Cognac or rum. *Beat* the egg whites and salt with a rotary or electric beater until they stand in firm, shiny peaks when the beater is held straight up. *Fold* into ground-nut mixture. Pour into the prepared pan. Place in a roasting pan with enough boiling water to reach to about two-thirds the depth of the pudding mold. The pan will probably float, making it necessary to put a weight on top. Here you will have to use your ingenuity. A pair of kitchen scissors or shears or a heavy tool long enough to go across and to rest on the rim of the pan are possibilities.

Place the pan in the center of the preheated oven and bake for 1 hour and 10 minutes or until a toothpick plunged in the center comes out dry. Cool on a cake rack.

To butter—crumple up a little waxed paper, scoop up a bit of butter and coat the bottom and sides of the pan generously.

Beat egg whites only to the stiff, shiny stage. If beaten longer, they become granular.

For exact folding technique —see directions on page 305.

To make the glaze: Combine both chocolates and the honey in the top of a double boiler. Melt over hot—not boiling—water. Take off the heat. Add the butter in chunks, beating constantly with a wire whisk. Continue beating until the glaze is cold and begins to thicken. Pour over the pudding and allow to set. Do not refrigerate. When glaze is firm, lift pudding with metal spatula to serving plate.

This odd but interesting, rich pudding is served in small wedges.

Senegalese Soup

SHRIMP SALAD IN SPICY SAUCE

Italian Bread   *Sweet Butter*

Baked Pears with Ginger   *Iced Tea*

YOUR COOKING SCHEDULE: Since the pears must be baked in time to cool, they should certainly be finished early in the afternoon. This marvelous soup can be made whenever you feel like cooking and have the time—then frozen. But if made the day it is to be served, you must allow time for it to chill, once it's made. It can be whipped together in a matter of minutes, but needs to simmer for 1 hour and you should certainly give it a good 2 hours in the refrigerator.

As for the Shrimp Salad, blender mayonnaise is essentially instant and the shrimp take no more than 3 or 4 minutes to cook. Both could be done while the soup is bubbling along. Do not, however, arrange the salad until just before you sit down at the table.

SENEGALESE SOUP

EQUIPMENT:

Measuring cups and spoons; French chef's knife; can opener; peppermill; large, heavy saucepan; wooden spatula; large, metal spoon; wire whisk; fine strainer; shallow baking pan.

INGREDIENTS:

5 tablespoons (½ stick plus 1 tablespoon) butter

1 small onion, *peeled* and coarsely chopped

1 carrot, washed and coarsely chopped

1 rib celery, coarsely chopped

1 heaping teaspoon curry powder

3 small cinnamon sticks

2 bay leaves

1 teaspoon whole cloves

3 or 4 cans (10½-ounce size) condensed chicken broth

1 tablespoon tomato purée

2 heaping tablespoons commercial almond paste

1 tablespoon red currant jelly

3 tablespoons flour

Salt

Freshly ground white pepper

2 cups heavy cream

Toasted flaked coconut

To peel, slice, mince, or dice onions, garlic, and shallots the easy way, see directions on page 306.

Use a peppermill for this. Freshly ground pepper is more vibrant than already-ground pepper. Both black and white peppercorns are available, the former being somewhat lustier.

Heat 2 tablespoons of the butter in the saucepan. Add the vegetables and cook over a moderate heat until the vegetables have taken on a little color. Stir occasionally. Stir in the curry powder with a wooden spatula until well mixed.

Add cinnamon stick, bay leaves, cloves, broth, tomato purée, almond paste, and currant jelly. Mix well. Bring up to a boil, reduce heat, and *simmer* for 1 hour. Skim off with a large metal spoon any foam that rises to the surface. Knead the remaining butter together with the flour to make a beurre manié. Add, bit by bit, to the soup, whipping constantly with a wire whisk until smooth. Cook for about 5 or 6 minutes over a moderate heat until the soup has thickened slightly. Strain, *taste* for seasonings, and refrigerate.

To serve, combine with the heavy cream and serve in chilled soup cups with a garnish of toasted coconut.

The basic soup can be made ahead of time, and refrigerated for several days, or frozen. Makes about 2 quarts.

To toast coconut: Sprinkle thinly in a shallow baking pan. Bake in a pre-heated 350° (or moderate) oven for 8 to 12 minutes or until lightly browned. Shake pan often to help it toast evenly.

To simmer—cook liquid just below boiling (185°) so that it just shivers.

Learn to taste. This makes sense, since one person's salt-and-pepper tolerance can be quite different from another's.

SHRIMP SALAD IN SPICY SAUCE

EQUIPMENT:
Measuring cups and spoons; French chef's knife; big mixing bowl; rubber spatula.

INGREDIENTS:

1½ pounds medium shrimp, cooked, *shelled, deveined*

1½ cups Mayonnaise (page 38)

1 tablespoon chopped capers, well drained

4 to 5 shallots, *minced*, or green onion bulbs

1 tablespoon chopped gherkins or small French sour pickles

4 to 5 sprigs parsley, *minced*

Crisp, curly endive

Cherry tomatoes

Ripe olives

To mince parsley—hold the blade of a heavy French chef's knife at both ends and chop with rapid up-and-down motions, pulling the ingredients back into a pile with the knife as you work.

To peel, slice, mince, or dice onions, garlic, and shallots the easy way, see directions on page 306.

To shell—push the shell with your thumb and forefinger; it will come off easily; to devein—make a thin cut with the point of a sharp paring knife along the curve of the body and lift out the little black "string." Not always there, by the way.

Cook the shrimp (page 235) first so they'll have time to cool.

In the mixing bowl, combine the Mayonnaise with the capers, shallots, gherkins, and parsley. When well mixed, *fold* in the whole cold shrimp, using a rubber spatula. Refrigerate.

To serve, arrange endive on a suitable platter. Mound the Shrimp Salad in the center; garnish with tomatoes and ripe olives. Serves 4 to 6.

For exact folding technique —see directions on page 305.

BAKED PEARS WITH GINGER

EQUIPMENT:

Large saucepan; ovenproof baking dish; bulb baster or large metal spoon; sharp, paring knife.

INGREDIENTS:

6 fresh firm pears
1 cup light brown sugar
Whole cloves

Few slivers candied ginger
Heavy cream

Preheat the oven to 350° (or moderate) for 15 minutes before baking the pears.

To simmer—cook liquid just below boiling (185°) so that it just shivers.

Combine the sugar with ¾ cup of water in a generous saucepan. Bring to a boil, then *simmer* for 5 minutes. Arrange the pears in the baking dish, stick each one with a clove, and add the bits of ginger. Pour the syrup over the pears and bake in the preheated oven, using a bulb baster or large metal spoon to *baste* frequently with the syrup. Bake for 20 to 30 minutes or until the fruit is tender, but still shapely, when pierced with the point of the paring knife.

To baste—spray, spoon, or brush a liquid or melted fat over food while it cooks.

Serve at room temperature with heavy cream.

ICED TEA

To brew tea properly, you need a perfectly clean earthenware teapot and freshly boiled water. Heat the pot with boiling water. Pour off the water and add 1 teaspoon loose tea or 1 tea bag for every ¾ cup of water with an extra teaspoon or bag "for the pot." Add the boiling water and allow to brew (which simply means to stand) about 3 minutes at the very least, 5 minutes at the very most. Overbrewing makes tea bitter. Final caution: Never boil tea.

To make Iced Tea: Increase the amount of tea by 50 percent to allow for dilution by the ice. Cool the brew to room temperature, but do not *refrigerate*. To serve pour the cold tea over ice cubes. Serve with lemon slices and sugar.

Tea that has been refrigerated and turned cloudy can be restored to its clear amber color by the addition of a small amount of boiling water.

SHRIMP MORNAY

Boiled Rice, the Chinese Way
(page 29)

Fresh Mushroom Salad
(page 208)

French Dinner Rolls   *Sweet Butter*

Fresh Pineapple with Kirsch

Shortbread   *Coffee*

YOUR COOKING SCHEDULE: With the exception of the shortbread, which must be baked ahead in time to cool, most of this dinner is last minute, and very fast. You can, of course, cook the rice in advance and heat it up over boiling water but, at most, it takes only 20 minutes to cook. The Sauce Vinaigrette for the salad can be whipped up any old time. Shortly before you make the Shrimp Mornay, prepare the pineapple, but not too far in advance or it may turn dark. The mushroom salad, too, is best done just before serving for the same reason. But these are little jobs that take hardly any time at all.

SHRIMP MORNAY

EQUIPMENT:

Measuring cups and spoons; grater; peppermill; heavy skillet with a cover; heavy, medium saucepan; 6 ramekins or scallop shells; wooden spatula; wire whisk; rotary beater; rubber spatula; baking sheet.

INGREDIENTS:

2 pounds medium shrimp, cooked, *shelled, deveined*

5 tablespoons butter

4 tablespoons all-purpose flour

2 cups milk

3 egg *yolks*

½ cup freshly *grated* Swiss or Gruyère cheese

¼ cup heavy cream

Salt

A few twists of the peppermill (white pepper)

Grate on fine, flat grater over waxed paper.

To shell shrimp, push the shell with your thumb and forefinger; it will come off easily; to devein, make a thin cut with the point of a sharp paring knife along the curve of the body and lift out the little black "string." Not always there, by the way.

If you haven't mastered the trick of separating egg yolks from egg whites, see directions on page 305.

A very simple way to cook shrimp: Wash thawed shrimp in cold water. Without draining, place in a heavy skillet with all the water that clings to them. Cover tightly and cook over a moderate heat for 3 to 4 minutes or until the shrimp turn pink. Shell and devein.

Butter the ramekins or scallop shells. Set aside.

Melt the remaining butter in a heavy saucepan, then to make a smooth roux, stir in the flour. Cook, stirring constantly with a wooden spatula for 2 to 3 minutes to cook the flour. Gradually stir in the milk. Bring to a boil, whipping constantly with a wire whisk. Take off the heat.

Beat the egg yolks slightly with a wire whisk or rotary beater. Beat in 2 or 3 tablespoons of the hot sauce. Then combine the two, beating hard and fast with

To butter—crumple up a little waxed paper, scoop up a bit of butter and coat the inside of each ramekin generously.

For exact folding technique
—see directions on page 305.

Learn to taste. This makes
sense, since one person's
salt-and-pepper tolerance
can be quite different from
another's.

a whisk. *Fold* in all but 2 tablespoons of the Swiss cheese with a rubber spatula
(not a wire whisk or the cheese will "string"). Then stir in the cream and salt
and pepper to *taste*. Finally, the shrimp. Spoon into the prepared ramekins and
sprinkle with the remaining cheese. Place on a baking sheet and slide under a
preheated broiler, 4 to 5 inches from source of heat, until bubbling and
golden on top. Serves 6.

CRABMEAT MORNAY

Crabmeat Mornay is made exactly the same way, substituting 1-pound can
lump crabmeat, or 1 pound frozen crab, thawed, for the shrimp.

FRESH PINEAPPLE WITH KIRSCH

EQUIPMENT:
French chef's knife; sharp paring knife; medium mixing bowl; measuring
spoons.

Bright, fresh appearance;
some orange-yellow at base;
and fresh, green plume are
signs of ripeness. Thump
with index finger and if
the sound is like a thump
on your wrist, the fruit is
solid.

Choose a large, fresh *ripe pineapple* and cut into six wedges by slicing
through from top to bottom with the chef's knife. Leave the plume attached—
just cut right through it. Take the meat off each wedge by running a sharp
knife between rind and meat. To avoid too many "eyes," try not to come too
close to the rind. Lift out with paring knife any eyes that remain. Cut into
chunks, cutting out the woody core as you work. Even if the pineapple is dead
ripe, it may need a sprinkling of superfine sugar. Then mix in 2 to 3 tablespoons of Kirsch.

SHORTBREAD

EQUIPMENT:

Measuring cups and spoons; flour sifter; mixing bowl; electric beater; square 9-inch baking pan; fork; toothpicks.

INGREDIENTS:

To measure sifted flour properly, spoon it—after sifting—into a dry measuring cup (or spoon), well above the top, then level or cut off with the edge —not the flat surface—of a metal spatula or knife. Do not shake flour down.

2 cups *sifted* all-purpose flour
1 cup (2 sticks) butter

½ cup sifted confectioners' sugar

Preheat oven to 350° (or moderate) for 15 minutes before baking the shortbread.

Sift the flour 3 times. Then work the butter with your hands or an electric beater until very soft and creamy. Add the sugar gradually, creaming constantly. Sift in the flour, a small amount at a time, mixing it in quickly and lightly with a fork. Refrigerate the dough for 30 minutes.

Press the dough into the ungreased baking pan. Prick the surface all over with the prongs of a fork. Place in the oven and bake for 5 minutes. Reduce oven heat to 300° (or slow) and bake another 20 to 25 minutes or until a toothpick inserted in the center comes out dry, that is, without any dough clinging to it. Correctly, shortbread should be a pale biscuit color. Cool. Then cut into squares.

LOBSTER POACHED IN COURT BOUILLON

Lemon Butter Sauce   *Shoestring Potatoes*

Cucumber Salad, French Style

Chilled Melon Bowl   *Coffee*

YOUR COOKING SCHEDULE: The Melon Bowl must be prepared a good bit ahead, several hours really, and the time it will take to complete it depends on the speed of the cook. Figure about an hour all told. As for the lobsters, the court bouillon needs a full hour. While it is simmering away, the Lemon Butter Sauce, the Sauce Vinaigrette, and the salad can all be prepared, the last mixed just before serving. The lobsters themselves will cook in a matter of minutes, but they still must be "readied" for the table. Time here is difficult to determine, since it depends on the number of lobsters. While this is going on, the canned shoestring potatoes can be dumped into a pan and heated up in a low (140°) oven.

LOBSTER POACHED
IN COURT BOUILLON

EQUIPMENT:
Measuring cups and spoons; French chef's knife; large, heavy kettle; strainer; nutcracker; tongs.

Although cooked lobster meat is available in almost every conceivable form, no lobster tastes as fresh, delicious, and succulent as that you cook yourself—preferably in court bouillon. Not alone because you do it yourself but because lobster cooked "to sell" is rarely cooked à point (to the right moment). In this country lobster is usually boiled in salted water or sea water, but we string along with the French notion that anything as good as lobster deserves a good court bouillon. We suggest that the word boiled be dropped and the word poached replace it.

The following is a good basic court bouillon in which to poach any shellfish:

INGREDIENTS:

2 quarts water

1 cup dry white wine

1 tablespoon salt

3 or 4 stalks parsley

1 bay leaf

½ teaspoon thyme

1 rib celery, chopped coarsely

1 small carrot, coarsely chopped

Few peppercorns

Combine all the ingredients in a large heavy kettle (not aluminum because foods cooked with wine tend to discolor in aluminum). Bring to a boil, then

To simmer—cook liquid just below boiling (185°) so that it just shivers.

Allow one 1½-pounds lobster per person.

Be absolutely certain the lobster is alive—and this is essential. You may be sure it is if it curls its tail under its body when picked up.

reduce heat to *simmer* and cook for 40 to 50 minutes. Strain.

To cook lobsters: Bring the cooked, strained court bouillon to a rolling boil. Grab the *lobsters* from behind the head and plunge head first into the boiling broth. Start timing when liquid comes to a boil again. Reduce heat to simmer, cover, and cook 5 minutes for the first pound and 3 minutes for each additional pound. Using tongs, lift the lobsters from the broth immediately.

Lay the lobster on its back, and split it in half, with a large heavy knife, from end to end, starting at the head. Remove the stomach, which is just back of the head, and the intestinal vein, which runs from the stomach to the tip of the tail. Crack the claws with a nutcracker. Take care not to miss those great delicacies the green liver and the coral roe (in hen lobsters only).

Frozen Rock Lobster Tails call for a minimum of cooking. Drop the thawed tails into boiling salted water (1 teaspoon salt to 1 quart water)—enough to cover—or a court bouillon (above). When the liquid comes to a boil a second time, reduce heat to simmer, and cook as many minutes as the tail weighs in ounces (your market should give you the weight of the individual tails when you buy them). A 4-ounce tail, for instance should be cooked 4 minutes after the water comes to a boil the second time.

The suggested menus for Poached Lobsters (pages 238 and 243) can be used with equal success for Frozen Rock Lobster Tails.

LEMON BUTTER SAUCE

Use a peppermill for this. Freshly ground pepper is more vibrant than already-ground pepper. Both black and white peppercorns are available, the former being somewhat lustier.

EQUIPMENT:

Lemon squeezer; peppermill; medium saucepan; paring knife; wire whisk.

Combine juice 1 lemon with ⅛ teaspoon of salt and a pinch of *freshly ground* white pepper in a saucepan. *Reduce* over a high heat to 1 tablespoon.

To reduce—simply boil a liquid over a high heat until the amount left is what the recipe specifies.

Take off the heat. Cut ½ cup (1 stick) cold butter into 4 pieces. Place pan over a very low heat, add 1 piece of the butter, and beat with a wire whisk until creamy. Keep adding the butter, one piece at a time, beating constantly. Set aside.

To warm the sauce before serving, beat in about 2 tablespoons of hot water. Serve in a just-warm sauceboat. This sauce is not served hot. Makes ½ cup but recipe can be doubled or tripled successfully.

This is a good sauce to serve with broiled or poached fish, shellfish, and such vegetables as asparagus, cauliflower, broccoli.

CUCUMBER SALAD, FRENCH STYLE

EQUIPMENT:
Vegetable peeler; small kitchen spoon; sharp, paring knife; mixing bowl.

Peel 3 large, firm cucumbers, using a vegetable peeler. Then cut in half, lengthwise. Scoop the seeds out of the halves with the spoon. Slice very, very thin. Sprinkle with salt and allow to stand for half an hour. Drain, then dress with Sauce Vinaigrette (page 44) made without mustard but with either minced fresh chervil, if available, or *minced* parsley sprigs. Serves 6.

To mince parsley—hold the blade of a heavy French chef's knife at both ends and chop with rapid up-and-down motions, pulling the ingredients back into a pile with the knife as you work.

CHILLED MELON BOWL

EQUIPMENT:
French chef's knife; melon-ball cutter; large kitchen spoon; large mixing bowl; electric blender.

Cut the top off the stem end of a large *melon* and set aside to use as a "lid." Remove all the seeds, scoop out about two-thirds of the flesh with a melon-ball cutter and set aside. Remove the remainder with a large spoon and discard. Turn the shell upside down to drain. Combine the melon balls with an attractive mélange of fruits and berries that are in season, such as seedless grapes; sweet cherries, pitted; sliced fresh peaches and apricots; diced fresh pineapple (see page 256). Combine all the fruits in the large bowl. Thaw, then purée 1 package (10-ounce size) frozen raspberries in the electric blender. Perfume with kirsch (optional) to taste and mix with the fruit. Fill the melon bowl, cover with the "lid" and chill well before serving. Number of servings depends on size of melon.

Use any of the big melons in season such as a Crenshaw, Casaba, Persian, or the Christmas (also called Santa Claus).

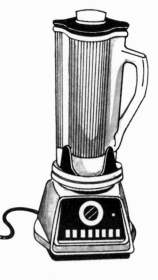

COLD POACHED LOBSTER
(page 238)

Mayonnaise with Capers
or Sauce Rémoulade

Hard-cooked Eggs
(page 306)

Baked Protein Toast
(page 39)

Green Gage Plum Ice

Sugar Cookies

Coffee

YOUR COOKING SCHEDULE: Every course in this menu can be prepared ahead. The lobsters early in the day, also the eggs. All else, the Mayonnaise or Rémoulade, the toast, the Plum Ice, and the cookies even a day ahead.

COLD POACHED LOBSTER

Poach lobsters according to directions on page 238. Cool quickly in cold running water just long enough to stop the cooking. Do not refrigerate the lobster unless absolutely essential. Serve in the shell or remove the lobster meat and arrange on a bed of fresh, crisp salad greens, garnished with hard-cooked eggs.

SAUCE RÉMOULADE

EQUIPMENT:
Measuring cups and spoons; medium mixing bowl; French chef's knife.

Into 1½ cups Mayonnaise (page 38) stir 1 generous teaspoon Dijon mustard, 2 tablespoons each of chopped gherkins and capers (both well drained), *minced* parsley, fresh tarragon or chervil (or about 2 teaspoons dried, crumbled fine), and a "whisper" of anchovy paste. Allow the sauce to stand for a couple of hours to mellow. Makes 1¾ cups.

To mince parsley—hold the blade of a heavy French chef's knife at both ends and chop with rapid up-and-down motions, pulling the ingredients into a pile with the knife as you work.

GREEN GAGE PLUM ICE

EQUIPMENT:
Can opener; electric blender; refrigerator tray; rotary or electric beater.

Open 2 cans (1-pound, 14-ounce size) green gage plums. Remove all pits (there aren't too many), then purée plums and syrup in the electric blender, half at a time. Pour into a refrigerator tray and freeze until firm. Before serving, transfer from freezer to refrigerator about ½ hour ahead of time so the ice can be served easily.

Serve with lightly sweetened whipped cream or sour cream. Cool and delicious.

SUGAR COOKIES

EQUIPMENT:
Measuring cups and spoons; flour sifter; nutmeg grater; 2 cookie sheets; medium mixing bowl; waxed paper; electric beater or electric mixer (desirable); wooden or rubber spatula; teaspoon; metal spatula; cake rack.

INGREDIENTS:

Vegetable shortening	¼ teaspoon *freshly grated* nutmeg
2 cups *sifted* all-purpose flour	1 cup (2 sticks) butter
½ teaspoon baking soda	¾ cup sugar
1 teaspoon cream of tartar	2 eggs
⅛ teaspoon salt	1 teaspoon vanilla

To measure sifted flour properly, spoon it—after sifting—into a dry measuring cup (or spoon), well above the top, then level or cut off with the edge —not the flat surface—of a metal spatula or knife. Do not shake flour down.

To grease a cookie sheet —crumple up a little waxed paper, scoop up a bit of shortening, and grease the surface of the pan well.

For this, you need a small nutmeg grater and, of course, whole nutmegs. Like cheese and pepper, freshly grated nutmeg makes all the difference in the finished dish because the flavor is so delicious.

Preheat the oven to 400° (or hot) for 15 minutes before baking the cookies.

Grease 2 cookie sheets with vegetable shortening; sift flour, baking soda, cream of tartar, salt and nutmeg together. Set aside.

Cream or work the butter with your hands, an electric beater or in an electric mixer until soft. Gradually work in the sugar, beating constantly. Add the eggs, one at a time, beating hard after each addition. Then stir in the vanilla and the flour mixture thoroughly, using a wooden or rubber spatula.

Spoon the batter by heaping teaspoons onto the prepared cookie sheets, leaving plenty of room for spreading.

Bake in the preheated oven for 8 to 10 minutes. The minute the cookies come from the oven, sprinkle the tops with granulated sugar. Then, with a broad metal spatula, lift onto a wire cake rack to cool.

Makes 3 to 4 dozen, but because they're so rich, they store well in a closely covered tin container.

—◆◆—

Chilled Madrilène with Lemon

LOBSTER NEWBURG

Boston Lettuce with Parsley and Chives

Fresh Grapefruit in Syrup   *Coffee*

YOUR COOKING SCHEDULE: It would be a good idea to put the madrilene in the refrigerator a day ahead, so it will not only be chilled but jellied. As for the lobsters, if you plan to poach them yourself, it would certainly make sense to do it the day before, but if you are buying the lobster meat from the market, that's a horse of a different color.

The Newburg is best made just in time to serve it, although in a dire emergency you could make it ahead and heat it up over hot water—if you watch it like a hawk. As always, the salad greens should be washed, dried, and refrigerated early.

The grapefruit can be prepared almost any time during the day it is to be served. Not earlier, because it doesn't "stand" well.

CHILLED MADRILÈNE WITH LEMON

EQUIPMENT:
Can opener; French chef's knife.

Chill canned madrilène in the refrigerator. Then spoon into chilled soup cups, cutting it slightly so it's more attractive and elegant. Then top each serving with a slice of fresh lemon, sprinkled with a little *minced* parsley.

To mince parsley—hold the blade of a heavy French chef's knife at both ends and chop with rapid up-and-down motions, pulling the ingredients back into a pile with the knife as you work.

LOBSTER NEWBURG

EQUIPMENT:
Measuring cups and spoons; baking sheet; French chef's knife; large, heavy skillet; small saucepan; wire whisk; double boiler; wooden spatula.

INGREDIENTS:

6 frozen patty shells
6 tablespoons (¾ stick) butter
Cooked meat from 2 1½-pounds
    lobsters (Recipe for poaching,
    p. 238)

⅓ cup Cognac
2 cups heavy cream
6 egg *yolks*, slightly beaten
Salt
Cayenne

If you haven't mastered the trick of separating egg yolks from egg whites, see directions on page 305.

Bake the patty shells according to directions.

Slice the tail meat of the lobsters, but leave the claw meat intact. Melt the butter in a large heavy skillet. When hot, add the lobster meat and *sauté* over a high heat for 5 minutes. Take off the heat.

To sauté—cook or brown food in a very small amount of very hot fat.

Beat the egg yolks with a whisk until well mixed. Heat the Cognac in a small saucepan, ignite, and pour over the lobster. Shake the pan and when the flames die out, stir in the cream. Place back over the heat, and bring up to a boil. Take off the heat.

Spoon a couple of tablespoons of the hot sauce into the yolks, whipping briskly with a wire whisk. Combine with the lobster mixture in the top of a double boiler and cook, stirring constantly with a wooden spatula, over *simmering* water until the sauce has thickened slightly. Season to *taste* with salt and cayenne. Correctly, the sauce should be rather light. Whatever happens, don't allow the sauce to boil or it will curdle. Spoon into the heated patty shells. Serves 6.

To simmer—cook liquid just below boiling (185°) so that it just shivers.

Learn to taste. This makes sense, since one person's salt-and-pepper tolerance can be quite different from another's.

BOSTON LETTUCE WITH PARSLEY AND CHIVES

EQUIPMENT:
Fresh dish towel; French chef's knife.

Wash the lettuce leaves under a gentle stream of cool water, shake off any excess, then wrap in a fresh dish towel to dry. Refrigerate. *Mince* a generous quantity of parsley sprigs and chives. Make the Sauce Vinaigrette (page 44) in the salad bowl. Add the dry lettuce, then the herb mixture and toss just before serving.

To mince parsley or chives —hold the blade of a heavy French chef's knife at both ends and chop with rapid up-and-down motions, pulling the ingredients back into a pile with the knife as you work.

FRESH GRAPEFRUIT IN SYRUP

Prepare exactly the same as oranges in syrup (page 30), grapefruit replacing the oranges.

RICH OYSTER STEW

Pilot Crackers   or   *Crusty French Bread*

Hearts of Lettuce, Roquefort Dressing

Poached Seckel Pears   *Coffee*

YOUR COOKING SCHEDULE: A very easy meal. Cook the pears ahead, allowing sufficient time for them to chill. The Roquefort Dressing can be made in advance. As for the stew, it's a twenty-five minute job from start to finish.

RICH OYSTER STEW

EQUIPMENT:
Measuring cups and spoons; French chef's knife; peppermill; 2 large, heavy saucepans, one with a lid; strainer.

INGREDIENTS:

3 dozen oysters in their liquor

¼ cup (½ stick) butter

2 medium onions, *peeled* and coarsely chopped

2 cloves garlic, *peeled* and coarsely chopped

2 carrots, chopped

2 ribs celery, chopped

Few stalks parsley

½ teaspoon dried thyme

2 cups milk

2 cups heavy cream

2 teaspoons *salt*

Freshly ground pepper

Good dash Worcestershire sauce

Good dash Tabasco

To peel, slice, mince, or dice onions, garlic, and shallots the easy way, see directions on page 306.

Melt the butter in the saucepan. Add the onions, garlic, carrot, celery, parsley, thyme, and 1 cup of water. Cover and cook over a good heat for 10 minutes, or until all the water has evaporated.

Add the milk, cream, and the liquor from the oysters. Heat to the boiling point, but do not boil. Strain into another saucepan. Add the oysters and heat only until the oysters curl at the edges. Season to *taste* with salt, pepper, Worcestershire, and Tabasco. Ladle into *heated* soup bowls. Serves 6 or better.

Take care with the salt because sometimes oysters are salty enough.

Use a peppermill for this. Freshly ground pepper is more vibrant than already-ground pepper. Both black and white peppercorns are available, the former being somewhat lustier.

Heat soup bowls by filling them with boiling water and allowing them to stand briefly. Then dump out the water and wipe the bowls dry.

Learn to taste. This makes sense, since one person's salt-and-pepper tolerance can be quite different from another's.

ROQUEFORT DRESSING

EQUIPMENT:

Kitchen fork; mixing bowl.

Using a fork, mash 2 or 3 tablespoons Roquefort or other blue cheese and stir into the basic Sauce Vinaigrette (page 44).

POACHED SECKEL PEARS

EQUIPMENT:
Measuring cups; heavy saucepan; paring knife.

Combine ½ cup sugar and 1 cup water in a heavy saucepan. Bring to a boil. Wash about 1½ pounds of pears, leaving the stems on, and place in the pan with the syrup. Cook over a low heat until the pears are tender but still firm when pierced with the point of a paring knife. Cool in the syrup. Serve with or without cream.

————————◆————————

OYSTERS À LA JACQUES PÉPIN

Tartare Sauce
(page 273)

Avocado Halves, Vinaigrette

Snow Sherbet   Coffee

YOUR COOKING SCHEDULE: A look at the dessert will tell you it must be done in advance. A day ahead, if you like. The Tartare Sauce, too, can be made ahead.

The avocados should be prepared and filled at the last minute, otherwise they will darken. To cook the oysters, allow yourself a total of 20 to 25 minutes from start to finish.

OYSTERS À LA JACQUES PÉPIN

EQUIPMENT:

Measuring cups and spoons; French chef's knife; electric blender; heavy saucepan; polyethylene bag; pan or bowl; paper towels; rotary or electric beater; deep-fat fryer; candy thermometer.

INGREDIENTS:

3 dozen oysters with their liquor	2 eggs
1 cup dry white wine	2½ cups fresh *bread crumbs*
4 shallots or scallions, *minced*	Oil for deep-fat frying

To peel, slice, mince, or dice onions, garlic, and shallots the easy way, see directions on page 306.

Place the oysters with their liquor, the wine, and the shallots in a polyethylene bag, then in a pan against the possibility of leakage. Allow to *marinate* for 2 hours or more. Turn the bag occasionally so that the oysters are well bathed. At the end of this period, pour into the saucepan, bring to a boil, and *simmer* just long enough for the edges of the oysters to curl (about 2 to 3 minutes). Drain and dry with paper towels.

Beat the eggs well with 2 tablespoons of water, using a rotary or electric beater. Dip the oysters in the egg mixture, then roll in the bread crumbs.

Pour oil into a deep-fat fryer to a depth of about 4 inches and heat slowly to

Use firm day-old bread for bread crumbs (1 slice makes ¼ cup). Break into pieces and grind, crust and all, in the electric blender, or crumble by hand until very fine.

To marinate—soak or steep meats or other foods in a marinade (seasoned liquid) to impart flavor, and in some instances, to tenderize.

To simmer—cook liquid just below boiling (185°) so that it just shivers.

Without a thermometer: Heat the fat slowly. Drop into it a 1-inch cube of 1-day-old bread. If the bread browns in 40 seconds, the fat is ready for frying cooked food. If the bread browns in 1 minute, the fat is ready for frying uncooked foods. For more information on deep-fat frying, see page 306.

moderate or 350° on the candy *thermometer*. Drop the oysters, a *few* at a time, into the hot fat and fry until golden (1 to 2 minutes). Drain on paper towels and keep each batch warm in a low (140°) oven. Serve at once to about 6.

Do not fry too many at one time. It will lower the temperature too much and the final results will not be good.

AVOCADO HALVES, VINAIGRETTE

EQUIPMENT:
Heavy French chef's knife; mixing bowl; lemon squeezer.

Allow ½ avocado per person. Cut in half the long way, twisting gently to separate the halves. Whack with a sharp, heavy knife directly into the seeds and twist to lift out. Place each half on a large lettuce leaf and fill the centers with Sauce Vinaigrette (page 44) or, if you like, fresh lemon juice.

SNOW SHERBERT

EQUIPMENT:
Measuring cups and spoons; grater; lemon squeezer; large mixing bowl; ice-cube tray; rotary or electric beater.

INGREDIENTS:
2 cups buttermilk
Grated rind and juice 1 lemon
¼ cup sugar
¾ cup light corn syrup

To grate rind of citrus fruit, which must be done before squeezing—work on a flat grater placed on top of a piece of waxed paper.

Combine all ingredients in the bowl and mix very thoroughly. Pour into an ice-cube tray and place in the freezer or ice-cube compartment. If the latter, set at the coldest point. Freeze until the mixture is mushy.

Pour into a chilled bowl and beat with a rotary or electric beater until smooth and the ice crystals have broken up.

Pour back into the tray and again freeze to the mushy stage. Beat again until smooth. Repeat a third time before freezing until firm. This means a lot of beating, but it's what makes a smooth sherbet.

———— ◆ ◆ ————

CLAM CHOWDER

Pilot Crackers   or   *French Bread*

Macédoine of Fresh Fruits

Chocolate Cloud Cookies   *Coffee*

YOUR COOKING SCHEDULE: Both the Cookies and the Macedoine of Fruits must be done ahead. The cookies the day—or even days—before, if you like. Fresh fruit, on the whole, does not improve on standing, so it should be prepared early in the afternoon—only long enough in advance to allow for a brief marinating period in the refrigerator.

If you bought the clams from a fishman, the clam chowder should not take you, all told, more than an hour. If, on the other hand, you dug the clams, it will take time to clean them properly, then open them. The time this takes depends on how adept you are at the job.

CLAM CHOWDER

EQUIPMENT:
Measuring cups and spoons; French chef's knife; vegetable peeler; pepper-mill; 2 medium heavy saucepans; small, sharp, paring knife; wooden spatula.

INGREDIENTS:

1 quart (shucked) clams with their
    liquor
¼ pound salt pork, chopped fine
2 medium onions, *minced*
4 medium potatoes, peeled and
    cubed
3 tablespoons butter

Minced parsley
4 cups half and half (cream and
    milk) or 2 cups light cream and
    2 cups whole milk
Salt
Freshly ground pepper
Thyme
Paprika

To peel, slice, mince, or dice garlic, onions, and shallots the easy way, see directions on page 306.

Peel the potatoes, wash, dry, then cube as you would onions (page 306).

To mince parsley—hold the blade of a heavy French chef's knife at both ends, chop with rapid up-and-down motions, pulling the ingredients back into a pile with the blade as you work.

Use a peppermill for this. Freshly ground pepper is more vibrant than already-ground pepper. Both black and white peppercorns are available, the former being somewhat lustier.

Combine clams, their liquor and 1 cup of cold water in one of the saucepans. Bring up to a boil over moderate heat. Drain, reserving the broth. Cut off and discard the necks and coarse membranes from the clams. Mince the rest and set aside.

Fry the pork in the other saucepan until lightly brown. Stir in the onions and cook until limp but not brown. Add the reserved broth and the potatoes.

To simmer—cook liquid just below boiling (185°) so that it just shivers.

Bring to a boil, then *simmer* until the potatoes are just tender when pierced with the point of a small sharp knife. Do not cook until they are soft and mushy. Stir in the butter. Then add the half-and-half slowly, stirring constantly with a wooden spatula. Season with salt and pepper to *taste*.

Add the clams and a good pinch of thyme, crumbled very fine. Bring to a boil, but do not cook further. Serve immediately in large, heated soup bowls with a sprinkling of paprika and a garnish of parsley. Serves 8 or better.

Learn to taste. This makes sense, since one person's salt-and-pepper tolerance can be quite different from another's.

MACÉDOINE OF FRESH FRUITS

EQUIPMENT:
Small paring knife; French chef's knife; large mixing bowl; Saran.

This can be any combination of fresh fruits and it makes sense to choose compatible fruits that are in season and, therefore, at their best. Arrange in layers in a large bowl whichever of these fruits are available; pears, quartered, cored, peeled and diced; peeled, sliced bananas; *pineapple*, peeled, cored, and cut into chunks; whole, hulled strawberries; grapes; melon balls; raspberries if not too ripe and soft.

Sprinkle each layer with superfine sugar and a few teaspoons of a liqueur such as kirsch or maraschino. Mix with your hands. Seal with Saran and refrigerate for about two hours.

Since pears and bananas are inclined to turn dark, sprinkle them with fresh lemon juice or roll them around in lemon juice before adding to the bowl.

To dice a fresh pineapple —slice off the crown and stem, using a heavy French chef's knife. Then cut off the rind by slicing down the sides from the top to bottom all around. Slice off any "eyes" that remain and cut out recalcitrant ones with a paring knife. Slice the pineapple in quarters, cut out the core, then cube in approximately three-quarter-inch pieces.

CHOCOLATE CLOUD COOKIES

EQUIPMENT:

Measuring cups and spoons; nut grater; flour sifter, double boiler; electric beater or electric mixer; wooden spatula; mixing bowl; baking or cookie sheet.

INGREDIENTS:

½ cup semisweet chocolate pieces

2 cups (4 sticks) butter

1 egg *yolk*

¼ cup sugar

2 tablespoons Cognac or bourbon

1 teaspoon vanilla

1 cup (4-ounce can) walnuts, *grated*

6 cups *sifted* cake flour

If you haven't mastered the trick of separating egg yolks from egg whites, see directions on page 305.

Melt chocolate over hot, not boiling, water, because if steam rices, then condenses, the chocolate will tighten and become unmanageable. Should this happen, add 2 tablespoons of vegetable shortening and work into the chocolate until it becomes soft again.

Grate nuts with a hand-operated grater (1 cup or about 5 ounces, by weight, yields 2 cups grated); or in the electric blender where the same amount yields 1½ cups grated. Either method can be used in this recipe.

To measure sifted flour properly, spoon it—after sifting—into a dry measuring cup (or spoon), well above the top, then level or cut off with the edge—not the flat surface —of a metal spatula or knife. Do not shake flour down.

Preheat the oven to 325° (or slow) for 15 minutes before baking.

Melt the chocolate in a double boiler over hot, not boiling water. Cream or work the butter with an electric beater or, preferably, electric mixer until very soft, fluffy and creamy. Beat in the egg yolk, then dump in the sugar, Cognac or bourbon, and vanilla. Continue beating until very well mixed. Finally, using a wooden spatula, thoroughly stir in the melted chocolate, nuts, and flour. Correctly, the dough at this point should be heavy, slightly moist, but not sticky.

Shape the dough into little balls about the size of a walnut, place on an ungreased baking or cookie sheet, an inch or so apart to allow for spreading, and bake for 15 or 20 minutes or until the cookies can be lifted easily from the cookie sheet with a metal spatula. Cool right on the sheet, however. Makes around 7 to 8 dozen that keep well in a tin with a tight cover.

STEAMED CLAMS

Poached Lobster　　　　　*Corn on the Cob*
(page 238)

Sliced Ripe Tomatoes with Basil
(page 39)

Bread Sticks

Blueberries with Brown Sugar　　　　*Coffee*
and Sour Cream

YOUR COOKING SCHEDULE: Once the clams are cleaned (and this takes quite a bit of doing), steaming is quite literally a matter of minutes. The lobsters, on the other hand, take a bit more time, especially if they are to be served hot. It would be our impulse to cook and prepare the lobsters first, then steam the clams. Obviously, the corn should be cooked at the same time as the clams. The tomatoes need to be sliced and dressed and the blueberries washed. Both these little jobs should be finished by the time the clams are cooked. And that's it.

STEAMED CLAMS

EQUIPMENT:
Two large kettles with covers (one for the clams, one for the lobsters); small saucepan; cheesecloth; strainer.

Allow about 15 clams, in the shell, per person. Wash and scrub the clams well and rinse several times to get rid of the *sand*. Place in a large kettle with about ½ inch of water in the bottom. Cover the kettle tightly and cook until the clams steam *open*—no more—about 6 to 10 minutes.

Serve immediately with small bowls of melted butter and cups of the broth, *strained*. Better *taste* the broth for seasoning.

Live clams, like oysters, open, once cooked. If they don't, they were dead before cooking and must be discarded.

Strain through a cheesecloth-lined fine strainer, leaving a residue of the broth in the bottom of the kettle in case some of the sand eluded you.

Learn to taste. This makes sense, since one person's salt-and-pepper tolerance can be quite different from another's.

To desand clams you have dug yourself, cover with fresh cold water, add some salt and a handful of cornmeal for the clams to feed on. Allow to stand overnight in a cool place.

CORN ON THE COB

EQUIPMENT:
Large kettle with a cover; tongs.

To cook the corn: drop the *husked* ears into rapidly boiling water to which a tablespoon or so of sugar has been added. Do not add salt. It tends to make the corn tough. When the water comes to a boil the second time, boil the corn 3 to 5 minutes. Very tender, young corn will take only 3 minutes. Lift from the water at once with tongs. Wrap in a big linen napkin and place in serving dish.

Do not husk until just before using. If fresh corn must be kept, wrap it (unhusked) in plastic bags and refrigerate, or it will lose half its flavor in one hot summer day.

———◆◆———

Ripe Olives, Pimientos, Chicken Liver Pâté

Crusty Italian Bread   *Sweet Butter*

LINGUINE WITH WHITE CLAM SAUCE

Chianti

Pêches en Crème Brulée   *Coffee*

YOUR COOKING SCHEDULE: Both the Chicken Liver Pâté and the White Clam Sauce can be made any time during the day, and the peaches can be peeled and covered with cream. Do not add brown sugar until broiling time.

Before starting the pasta, arrange the olives and pimientos in a suitable dish and cut the bread. The pasta is at most a 10-minute job once the water is boiling. While it's cooking, the sauce can be heated up. Just before you go to the table, finish the Pêches en Crème Brulée and heat the broiler. Don't, however, put the dessert in the broiler until a few minutes before you serve it.

CHICKEN LIVER PÂTÉ

EQUIPMENT:

Measuring cups and spoons; peppermill; French chef's knife; heavy skillet; meat grinder or electric blender; mixing bowl; Saran; can opener; saucepan.

INGREDIENTS:

½ pound *chicken livers*

2 tablespoons butter

2 *hard-cooked* eggs, *shelled*

1 package (8-ounce size) cream
    cheese, softened

Few sprigs parsley, *minced*

¾ teaspoon salt

2 or 3 twists of the peppermill

2 tablespoons Cognac

Frozen chicken livers are readily available, but if you've been freezing those that came with chickens you've bought, thaw and use them.

To hard-cook eggs—see page 306. To shell an egg the easy way, tap all over with the back of a knife until it is "mapped." Then, holding the egg in the palm of your hand, peel off the shell and inner skin. If small shell particles cling to the egg, dip the egg in cold water.

To mince parsley—hold the blade of a heavy French chef's knife at both ends and chop with rapid up-and-down motions, pulling the ingredients back into a pile with the knife as you work.

To sauté—cook or brown food in a very small amount of very hot fat.

Heat the butter in a heavy skillet. When hot, add the chicken livers and *sauté* until they are lightly brown outside but still somewhat pink inside. To determine this, cut one open. Chop fairly fine. Work the livers and the hard-cooked eggs through a meat grinder, using the finest blade, or blend, a small amount at a time, in the electric blender. Grind or blend a second time to make a very smooth mixture.

Work the cheese until very soft and malleable. Best done with your hands. Then work in the liver mixture, parsley, salt, and Cognac thoroughly. Makes about 1½ cups.

Spoon into a suitable serving dish and seal with Saran or dress it up with a coating of aspic. A seal is important because the pâté darkens when exposed to air. Serve with dry or buttered toast points or unseasoned crackers.

To make the aspic: Sprinkle 1 envelope unflavored gelatin over ½ cup cold water to soften. Combine with 1 can of consommé (10½-ounce size) in a saucepan and stir over a low heat until dissolved. Pour a ¼-inch layer of the aspic on top of the pâté and refrigerate until firm. A couple of hours possibly. This is attractive if the pâté is to be served for a "cocktail."

This pâté cannot be frozen because of the eggs.

Since most of the aspic will be left over, refrigerate and use up some other way. For instance, melt over a low heat, refrigerate until mixture has the consistency of unbeaten egg whites, then combine with cooked vegetables cut in small dice. Pour into a mold and refrigerate until firm. Good with Mayonnaise (page 38) and sliced cold meat.

TUNA PÂTÉ

For the chicken livers and butter substitute 1 can (7-ounce size) tuna packed in oil. Break the tuna apart and blend a small amount at a time in the blender. From here on in follow the same instructions as for Chicken Liver Pâté, eliminating the salt.

LINGUINE WITH CLAM SAUCE

EQUIPMENT:

Measuring cups and spoons; French chef's knife; peppermill; grater; large, heavy kettle with cover; fine sieve; cheesecloth; large saucepan; wooden fork; colander.

INGREDIENTS:

To peel, slice, mince, or dice onions, garlic, and shallots the easy way, see directions on page 306.

4 dozen clams in the shell
1 medium onion, *peeled* and coarsely chopped
1 rib celery, coarsely chopped

1 carrot, washed and coarsely chopped
1 cup dry white wine or vermouth
½ cup olive oil

3 cloves garlic, minced
Handful parsley sprigs, *minced*
1 heaping tablespoon dried basil,
    crumbled
Salt

Freshly ground pepper
1 pound linguine, spaghetti, or spa-
    ghettini
Freshly grated Parmesan cheese

To mince parsley—hold the blade of a heavy French chef's knife at both ends and chop with rapid up-and-down motions, pulling the ingredients back into a pile with the blade as you work.

Use a peppermill for this. Freshly ground pepper is more vibrant than already-ground pepper.

Cut Parmesan cheese into relatively small chunks and grate in the blender.

To desand clams you have dug yourself, cover with fresh cold water, some salt, and a good handful of cornmeal for them to feed on. Allow to stand overnight in a cool place.

Wash and scrub the clams well and rinse several times to get rid of the *sand*. Combine the onion, celery, carrot, wine, and clams in the kettle. Cover tightly and steam until the clams open (about 6 to 8 minutes). Discard any clams that don't open. When cooked and cool enough to handle, remove the clams from their shells, mince and set aside.

Strain the broth through a fine sieve lined with dampened cheesecloth, leaving a small residue at the bottom in case some of the sand escaped you.

Rinse out the kettle and return the strained broth. Bring to a rolling boil and *reduce* to about half.

To reduce—boil the liquid over a high heat until the amount left is what the recipe specifies.

Heat the olive oil in a large saucepan. Add the garlic, parsley, basil, salt and pepper to *taste*, and the broth. Bring up to a boil. Add the clams. Heat just before serving, but do not cook further.

Learn to taste. This makes sense, since one person's salt-and-pepper tolerance can be quite different from another's.

To cook the linguine (spaghetti or spaghettini): Bring 7 quarts of water to a rolling boil, with 2 tablespoons of salt per quart. Add the pasta gradually so as not to stop the water boiling. Long pastas such as linguine should never be broken. Lower a handful at a time into the boiling water. The pasta will curl in the kettle as the water softens it.

Boil briskly, uncovered, stirring occasionally with a wooden fork. After 4 minutes (it's wise to time yourself), taste a piece—it should be al dente (firm to the tooth). Continue cooking and testing until the pasta is very slightly resistant. *Drain* immediately and thoroughly in a colander.

Do not run under cold water to keep the strands from sticking together. All this does is cool the pasta.

Pour the linguine into a heated dish, cover with the hot clam sauce and serve with lots of grated cheese on the side. Serves 4 to 6.

PÊCHES EN CRÈME BRULÉE

EQUIPMENT:

Sifter; sharp paring knife; 1-quart soufflé dish; metal spatula.

INGREDIENTS:

8 ripe, fresh peaches, *peeled*

Superfine sugar

Kirsch (optional)

Commercial sour cream

Light brown sugar, sifted

To peel peaches, cover with boiling water for 1 minute, then plunge into cold water. Cut in half, peel, pit, and slice. If peeled very far in advance, roll in fresh lemon juice to prevent darkening.

Slice the peaches fairly thin and arrange in the soufflé dish. You should have enough fruit to almost fill the dish. If the peaches are not really sweet, sprinkle lightly with superfine sugar, then perfume with 3 or 4 tablespoons of kirsch. Spoon a thick layer of commercial sour cream over the top and smooth with a metal spatula. Cover with a ½-inch layer of sifted light brown sugar. Slide under a preheated broiler, 4 to 5 inches from the source of heat, just long enough to caramelize the sugar. Watch sharply. Don't even close the oven door. Serve at once. A delicious mixture of cool peaches, rich cream, and crunchy sugar.

Nectarines, blueberries, strawberries, or raspberries can be used in place of the peaches.

Chicken Consommé à la Portugaise

COQUILLES SAINT-JACQUES

Marinated Carrots with Black Olives

French Bread   *Sweet Butter*

French Upside-down Apple Tart   *Coffee*

YOUR COOKING SCHEDULE: Everything in this menu can be made somewhat ahead. The soup, the coquilles and the carrots the day before, then refrigerated. Only the apple tart must be made the day it is served, because pastry is at its best if eaten the day it is baked; it should never be refrigerated. Make the pastry any time, but bake the tart in the late afternoon. Allow yourself a total of fifteen minutes to "gratiné" the coquilles and heat the soup.

CHICKEN CONSOMMÉ À LA PORTUGAISE

EQUIPMENT:

Can opener; French chef's knife; measuring spoons; peppermill; flat grater; 2 large heavy saucepans; sieve; cheesecloth.

INGREDIENTS:

4 cans (10½-ounce size) condensed chicken broth

4 to 5 very ripe tomatoes, coarsely chopped

1 teaspoon sugar

Salt

Freshly ground white pepper

Grated rind 1 orange

Dry vermouth (optional)

Use a peppermill for this. Freshly ground pepper is more vibrant than already-ground pepper. Both black and white peppercorns are available, the former being somewhat lustier.

To simmer—cook liquid just below boiling (185°) so that it just shivers.

Combine the broth, full strength, tomatoes, and sugar in the saucepan. Bring up to a boil, reduce heat to *simmer* and cook until the tomatoes are very soft. Season with salt and pepper to *taste*. Take off the heat and push through a sieve, lined with a dampened cheesecloth, into another saucepan. Add the orange rind and bring to a boil. Stir in 2 or 3 tablespoons of vermouth (or to taste). Do not cook further. Serve hot or chilled to about 6.

To grate rind of citrus fruit, which must be done before squeezing—work on a flat grater placed on top of a piece of waxed paper.

Learn to taste. This makes sense, since one person's salt-and-pepper tolerance can be quite different from another's.

COQUILLES SAINT-JACQUES

EQUIPMENT:

Measuring cups and spoons; French chef's knife; peppermill; flat grater; sharp, paring knife; large enameled saucepan; slotted spoon; strainer; wire whisk; large mixing bowl; 8 scallop shells, individual ramekins or soufflé dishes; cookie or baking sheet.

INGREDIENTS:

There are two types of scallops: the tiny, sweet, tender bay scallops and the large, less sweet sea scallops. If you are using sea scallops, cut them in half.

The button mushrooms, the least expensive, are best in cooked dishes. Mushrooms need not be peeled.

To dice or chop scallions (green onions)—peel off any withered skin and cut off the long roots. Take as much of the scallions, including the green top as you think you'll need. Slice lengthwise, four times. Then slice across into small dice.

1½ pounds *scallops*, fresh or frozen (thawed)
½ pound *button mushrooms*
1½ cups dry white wine
3 or 4 stalks parsley
3 or 4 green onions, *chopped* or 1 small onion, peeled, coarsely chopped
1 bay leaf
½ teaspoon thyme

1 teaspoon salt
Several twists of the peppermill (white pepper)
½ cup (1 stick) butter (about)
4 tablespoons flour
3 egg *yolks*
½ cup milk
1 cup heavy cream, about
Grated Swiss cheese

If you haven't mastered the trick of separating egg yolks from egg whites, see directions on page 305.

Rinse the scallops well and pick out any bits of shell lurking around. Wipe the mushrooms with a damp cloth, slice off the tips of the stems, then slice thin. Combine the wine, parsley, green onions, bay leaf, thyme, salt and pepper in the saucepan. Bring up to a boil, then *simmer* for about 5 minutes.

Add the scallops and mushrooms and enough cold water to just cover. Bring to a boil again, reduce heat and simmer 3 to 4 minutes, depending on the size of the scallops.

To simmer—cook liquid just below boiling (185°) so that it just shivers.

Lift the scallops and mushrooms from the broth with a slotted spoon and set aside.

Return the pan with the broth to the fire, bring to a boil, and *reduce* to about 1½ cups. Strain. Meanwhile, work 3 tablespoons of the butter and the flour together to make a beurre manié. Drop, by small bits, into the broth, whipping constantly and hard with a wire whisk until the sauce is smooth and thickened.

To reduce—simply boil liquid over a high heat until the amount left is what the recipe specifies.

Combine the egg yolks, milk and cream in a big bowl and whip together. Dribble in the hot sauce, whipping constantly. Season to *taste* with salt, pepper, and lemon juice. If the sauce seems too thick, add a bit more cream to bring it to the right consistency. Take off the heat. Combine the scallions with the scallops and mushrooms, and add to the sauce.

Learn to taste. This makes sense, since one person's salt-and-pepper tolerance can be quite different from another's.

Butter scallop shells or ramekins. Spoon some of the coquilles into each. Sprinkle the top with the grated cheese and dot with butter. Can be prepared in advance to this point and refrigerated.

To butter—crumple up a little waxed paper, scoop up a bit of butter and coat the ramekins generously.

Place the shells on a baking sheet and broil in a preheated broiler 8 to 9 inches from the source of the heat so the coquilles can heat through gradually, the cheese melt and the top brown. Serve immediately.

MARINATED CARROTS WITH BLACK OLIVES

EQUIPMENT:
Measuring cups and spoons; vegetable peeler; lemon squeezer; French chef's knife; cheesecloth; large saucepan.

INGREDIENTS:

1½ pounds small young carrots
Bouquet garni: few parsley stalks;
   1 bay leaf; good pinch thyme;
   good pinch tarragon
1 tablespoon salt
1½ cups dry white wine
1 large clove garlic, *crushed*

3 teaspoons sugar
Juice ½ lemon
6 to 8 peppercorns
8 tablespoons olive oil
Big handful parsley sprigs, *minced*
Ripe olives

To crush garlic, give it a good whack with the side of a cleaver, heavy knife or any heavy, flat implement. No need to peel.

To mince parsley—hold the blade of a heavy French chef's knife at both ends, and chop with rapid up-and-down motions, pulling the ingredients back into a pile with the knife as you work.

Peel the carrots, using a vegetable peeler, then cut in quarters, lengthwise. Set aside for the moment.

Tie the bouquet garni in a little cheesecloth bag and combine in a large saucepan with all remaining ingredients—except carrots, olives and minced parsley—plus 1 cup of water. Bring to a boil, then reduce heat and *simmer* for 10 minutes to make the marinade.

To simmer—cook liquid just below boiling (185°) so that it just shivers.

Add the carrots, bring to a boil again and cook, over moderate heat, until they are tender but still a little bit crisp to the tongue. Refrigerate, covered, in the *marinade*.

To marinate, soak or steep meats or other foods in a marinade (seasoned liquid) to impart flavor and, in some instances, to tenderize.

To serve, arrange the carrots in a suitable serving dish. Spoon some of the marinade over them, sprinkle with the minced parsley and garnish with the olives. Serves 6.

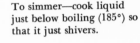

FRENCH UPSIDE-DOWN APPLE TART

EQUIPMENT:

Measuring cups; vegetable peeler; French chef's knife; large round glass baking dish, 2 inches deep; small saucepan; metal spatula; sharp paring knife.

INGREDIENTS:

Basic pastry for a 1-crust pie
   (page 288)
½ cup (1 stick) butter, softened
1 cup sugar

5 tart cooking apples
Heavy cream or commercial sour
   cream, chilled

Make the pastry and refrigerate. Preheat the oven to 400° (or hot) for 15 minutes before baking the tart.

Choose a large round glass baking dish about 2 inches deep. Spread some of the butter in a thick layer over the bottom with a metal spatula or scoop up the butter with some waxed paper and spread with that. Sprinkle heavily with sugar. Place remaining sugar and butter in a small saucepan over low heat to melt the butter.

Using a vegetable peeler, peel the apples. Cut into quarters and cut out the core. Arrange on top of the butter in the baking dish. Pour the melted butter-sugar combination over all. Cover with a circle of pastry rolled very thin, just large enough to fit on top of dish. Bake for 30 minutes in the preheated oven. At this point, check to see if the apples are cooked by lifting up a corner of the pastry with a metal spatula. They should be golden and slightly caramelized. If not, cook a bit longer.

To serve, loosen the crust all around with the point of a sharp paring knife. Unmold by placing a serving platter upside down over the pie dish and invert quickly. Serve hot or warm with chilled cream.

Prosciutto and Melon

SOFT-SHELL CRABS MEUNIÈRE

Tartare Sauce

Brown Bread   *Sweet Butter*

Mousse Aux Marrons   *Coffee*

YOUR COOKING SCHEDULE: Both the dessert and the Tartare Sauce can be made a day ahead if you are so inclined, although it is not essential. The dessert needs only a short time in the refrigerator to chill slightly. With these out of the way there is really very little to do except prepare the melon and arrange on individual plates with the sliced prosciutto. Remember to have a peppermill on the table.

The crabs, of course, must be sautéed just before you sit down at the table, a matter of about fifteen minutes.

PROSCIUTTO AND MELON

Prosciutto, one of the loveliest of all the cured hams, is of Italian origin. However, we have a very good prosciutto type in this country. Prosciutto should always be cut in the thinnest possible slices. Serve with wedges of ripe melon or, as is often done in Italy, fresh figs and freshly ground pepper.

SOFT-SHELL CRABS MEUNIÈRE

EQUIPMENT:

French chef's knife; sharp, paring knife; large, heavy skillet; peppermill.

INGREDIENTS:

To clean, unless already done by the market—wash the crabs in several waters. Place the live crab, face down on a board. Make an incision just back of the eyes with a small, sharp pointed knife. Lift the tapering points on each side of the back shell to remove sandbags and spongy gills. Turn crab on its back and remove the small apron on the front.

Soft-shelled crabs, *cleaned* (allow 2 or 3 per person)
Flour
Butter (approximately 1 cup or 2 sticks)

Salt
Freshly ground pepper
Handful parsley sprigs, *minced*
Lemon wedges

Use a peppermill for this. Freshly ground pepper is more vibrant than already-ground pepper.

To mince parsley—hold the blade of a heavy French chef's knife at both ends and chop with rapid up-and-down motions, pulling the ingredients back into a pile with the knife as you work.

To sauté—cook or brown food in a very small amount of very hot fat.

Dip the cleaned crabs in flour. Set aside. Heat the butter in the skillet, 2 or 3 tablespoons at a time, and *sauté* the crabs a few at a time (do not crowd the pan) until lightly brown and crisp on one side. Turn and cook the second side. About 8 to 10 minutes all told. Add more butter as needed. Arrange the crabs, as they are cooked, on a heated platter and keep warm.

To serve, pour the pan juices over the crabs and sprinkle with salt, pepper, and parsley. Garnish with lemon wedges.

TARTARE SAUCE

EQUIPMENT:

Measuring cups and spoons; mixing bowl; French chef's knife; lemon squeezer; Saran.

INGREDIENTS:

2 cups Mayonnaise (page 38)

½ small yellow onion, *minced*

2 teaspoons lemon juice

8 to 10 parsley sprigs, *minced*

1 large dill pickle, minced, or 2 tablespoons minced fresh dill

Combine all ingredients well in the mixing bowl, seal with Saran and allow to mellow for 2 hours or better.

To peel, slice, mince, or dice onions, garlic, and shallots the easy way—see directions on page 306.

To mince parsley—hold the blade of a heavy French chef's knife at both ends and chop with rapid up-and-down motions, pulling the ingredients back into a pile with the knife as you work.

MOUSSE AUX MARRONS

EQUIPMENT:

French chef's knife; measuring cups; rubber spatula; fine sieve; mixing bowl; rotary or electric beater.

INGREDIENTS:

1 jar (9½-ounce size) marrons glacé (chestnuts in syrup)

1 package (8-ounce size) cream cheese, softened

¼ cup coarsely chopped pecans, walnuts or blanched almonds

2 tablespoons finely *chopped* candied ginger or mixed candied fruits

1 cup heavy cream, whipped

When chopping sticky foods such as candied ginger or candied fruits, keep a damp cloth handy to wipe off the knife blade occasionally.

Set aside 3 of the marrons glacé. Using a rubber spatula, push the remainder with the syrup through the sieve to make a smooth purée. The electric blender won't work here.

Combine the purée with the cheese and work together thoroughly with a rubber spatula or, better, your hands. Then stir in the nuts and ginger. Last of all, *fold* in the whipped cream. Pour into a pretty serving dish and garnish with the reserved chestnuts sliced in two. Chill.

For exact folding technique —see directions on page 305.

FRENCH FOOD MILL

FRENCH PASSOIRE

THE PURÉES

With the handy mouli *you can make fine, medium or coarse purées. The* passoire *(also called a* chinois) *can function both as a strainer or sieve and as a means of puréeing foods. We find it invaluable.*

THE SIEVES AND SIFTERS

One each (small, medium, large) rustless aluminum sieves are adequate for the average kitchen, augmented by a colander for draining vegetables, pasta, etc.; flour sifters in two sizes (1-cup and 5-cup) expedite things in the kitchen.

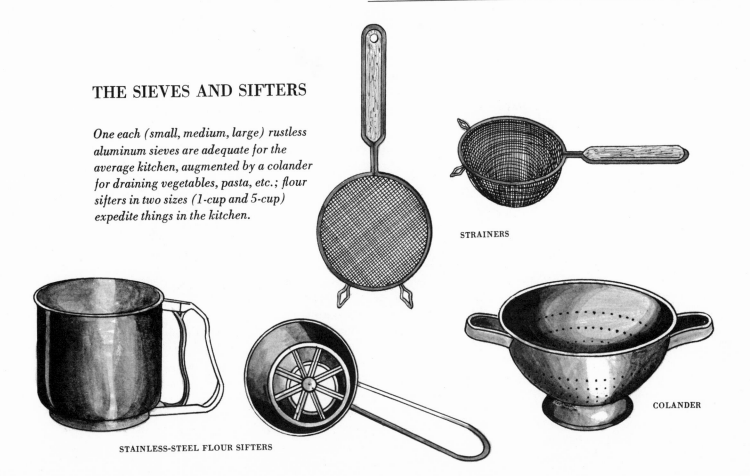

STRAINERS

STAINLESS-STEEL FLOUR SIFTERS

COLANDER

FISH

POACHED SALMON WITH EGG SAUCE

Buttered Baby New Potatoes
(page 120)

New Peas Steamed, French Style

Peach Shortcake   Coffee

YOUR COOKING SCHEDULE: The cake for the peach shortcake can be made early in the day, but the fruit and cream should be added just before it is served, otherwise the cake will be soggy. The peaches themselves, however, can be made ready. When sliced sprinkle peaches with lemon juice to keep them from turning dark.

The potatoes, depending on size, will need 20 to 25 minutes, so they must go on the stove before the salmon. If the fish is to be poached in court bouillon, you have to plan on cooking the bouillon for an hour before adding the fish. Otherwise it's just a matter of bringing enough salted water to a boil. The peas, once shelled, will steam in just about the time it takes to poach the salmon.

POACHED SALMON WITH EGG SAUCE

EQUIPMENT:
Cheesecloth. For a whole fish, a fish cooker with cover is ideal, but any flame-proof container, with a cover, large enough to hold the fish can be used. In the old days, cooks often used a big washboiler.

Whether you are poaching a whole fish or a piece, the principle is the same. It is poached in enough Court Bouillon (page 239) or salted water to cover. Tie up the fish (which must be at room temperature) in a piece of cheesecloth with long ends so that it can be lifted easily from the hot liquid. The fish is always added to the cooking kettle when the liquid has reached a rolling boil.

To simmer—cook liquid just below boiling (185°) so that it just shivers.

Once the liquid comes to a fast boil a second time, the heat is reduced to *simmer* and the fish is cooked, covered, 10 minutes per inch. If, for example, the fish or piece, measures 2 inches in depth at the thickest point (don't guess, measure with a ruler exactly), simmer it a total of 20 minutes. This is far more accurate than minutes per pound. Once the fish is cooked, lift it from the liquid immediately. Properly cooked fish flakes when *tested* with a fork.

A whole salmon, weighing 6 to 8 pounds, makes a spectacular show. Whether or not you cook it with the head on is a matter of choice. In Europe and England they do; here we are inclined not to, in which case the fishman cleans and scales the fish, and removes the head.

To test for doneness, probe the thickest part of the flesh gently with a fork. If the flesh separates and falls easily into its natural divisions, the fish is cooked perfectly. Properly cooked, fish becomes opaque, but is still moist.

Serve on a warm platter with a bouquet of watercress at the head. Traditionally, the skin is left on the fish when served hot, the person serving it skinning as he goes along. Serves 8 very comfortably.

EGG SAUCE

EQUIPMENT:

Measuring cups and spoons; peppermill; nutmeg grater; medium saucepan; wooden spatula; strainer; wire whisk.

INGREDIENTS:

4 tablespoons butter	Salt
3 tablespoons flour	*Freshly ground* white pepper
1 cup of the fish broth, strained	*Freshly ground* nutmeg
1 cup milk	2 hard-cooked eggs (page 306)

Make a roux by melting the butter in a saucepan and stirring in the flour with a wooden spatula until smooth. Cook over a moderate heat for about 2 or 3 minutes, stirring constantly so the roux cooks and takes on a little color— just off the white

Stir in the hot fish broth and cook, whipping constantly with a wire whisk, until smooth. Add the milk gradually and continue to cook, whipping, for about 5 minutes or until the sauce has thickened.

Add salt, pepper, and nutmeg to *taste*. Makes about 2 cups.

Shell the eggs, chop coarsely and stir into the Velouté, taking care not to break the eggs more than necessary. Pour into a warm sauceboat.

To shell an egg the easy way, tap all over with the back of a knife until it is "mapped." Then, holding the egg in the palm of your hand, peel off the shell and inner skin. If small shell particles cling to the egg, dip the egg in cold water.

Use a peppermill for this. Freshly ground pepper is more vibrant than already-ground pepper. Both black and white peppercorns are available, the former being somewhat lustier.

For this you need a small nutmeg grater and, of course, whole nutmegs. Like cheese and pepper, freshly grated nutmeg makes all the difference in the finished dish because the flavor is so delicious.

Learn to taste. This makes sense, since one person's salt-and-pepper tolerance can be quite different from another's.

NEW PEAS STEAMED, FRENCH STYLE

EQUIPMENT:

Measuring spoons; peppermill; large heavy saucepan with a tight-fitting lid; colander.

INGREDIENTS:

3 pounds fresh young peas in the shell

Several large outside lettuce leaves

6 tablespoons (¾ stick) butter

Salt

Freshly ground pepper

Shell the peas just before they are to be cooked. Place 2 tablespoons of the butter in the saucepan. Wash the lettuce leaves and place enough leaves (still wet) on top of the butter, to cover the bottom of the pan.

Heap the peas on top and dot with the remaining butter. Cover completely with more wet lettuce leaves. Add the lid and cook over a high heat until the butter is bubbling hot.

Reduce the heat to low and allow the peas to steam very gently until tender. This should take about 15 minutes, depending on the age of the peas, longer than if cooked the usual way, but worth the effort.

To serve, discard the lettuce, season the peas with salt and pepper to *taste*, and pour into a warm vegetable dish. Serves 6 to 8.

Use a peppermill for this. Freshly ground pepper is more vibrant than already-ground pepper. Both black and white peppercorns are available, the former being somewhat lustier.

Learn to taste. This makes sense, since one person's salt-and-pepper tolerance can be quite different from another's.

PEACH SHORTCAKE

EQUIPMENT:

Round 8-inch cake pan; metal spatula; cake rack; paring knife; serrated bread knife; rotary or electric beater; mixing bowl.

INGREDIENTS:

1 recipe for shortcake (page 35)

Milk

6 medium very ripe peaches

Superfine sugar

1 cup heavy cream

When the batter for the cake is made, pat into a round 8-inch cake pan. Smooth the surface with a metal spatula dipped in milk. Bake as directed.

When baked, turn out on a cake rack and cool.

Cut the *peeled* peaches in half, remove the pit and slice the fruit rather thin. Sprinkle lightly with sugar.

Split the baked, cooled cake with the knife. Place on a serving plate. Arrange half the peaches on the bottom layer, top with the second layer and cover with remaining peaches.

Whip the cream and spoon over the top of the cake. If you like, garland the perimeter of the cake with thin peach slices. Serve immediately.

To peel peaches drop into boiling water for 1 minute, then into cold water. The skin peels off like a breeze.

To whip heavy cream, the cream, bowl, and beater should be cold, preferably chilled. Whip until the beater leaves light traces on the surface of the cream and a bit of cream lifted and dropped will just retain its shape.

POACHED SALMON SERVED COLD

Mayonnaise Verte

Stuffed Hard-cooked Eggs   **Cucumber Salad, Swedish Style**
(page 25)

Cherry Tomatoes   **Hot Biscuits**

Cold Lemon Soufflé   **Coffee**

YOUR COOKING SCHEDULE: Broadly speaking, the salmon will taste best if served at room temperature the day it is cooked. If left over from a previous meal, inevitably it will be chilled from the refrigerator. In which case, we recommend taking it from the refrigerator a couple of hours before it is to be served to bring it to room temperature. If, however, the salmon must be cooked, then cooled, you should allow all told about 4 hours from start to finish.

Both the Lemon Soufflé and the Mayonnaise Verte can be made ahead, even a day early, and refrigerated. Otherwise, the soufflé needs two to three hours in the refrigerator to become firm.

The cucumbers can be prepared almost any time, and sealed with Saran. The biscuits, too, can be made ahead, ready to slide in the oven. Refrigerate until baking time. Bake about 10 minutes before you wish to serve them.

The eggs can be hard-cooked any old time, but it is best to shell them shortly before serving, since they are inclined to darken if they stand too long.

To skin a cooked salmon that is to be served cold: Lift from the broth onto several layers of newspaper or paper towels to absorb liquid. Untie the cheesecloth, but leave the fish lying on it. Now, taking great care not to break the flesh, peel off the skin. It slips off, really, when the fish is hot. Under the outside skin, there is a thin layer of gray flesh which must also be removed. Using a small dull knife, scrape it off very gently. Carefully pull out any protruding bones. Now, with the aid of the cheesecloth, roll the fish over, starting from the split side, and skin the second side. Once skinned, seal all the exposed flesh of the fish with Saran to keep it moist and from turning dark.

To present your salmon: Place the fish on a platter large enough to hold it comfortably and garnish with bouquets of fresh watercress, stuffed eggs, cherry tomatoes, and lemon slices. Serve Mayonnaise Verte on the side.

MAYONNAISE VERTE

EQUIPMENT:

French chef's knife; measuring cups and spoons; lemon squeezer; electric blender.

INGREDIENTS:

20 spinach leaves, coarsely chopped
2 whole eggs
¾ teaspoons dry mustard
¾ teaspoon salt
Juice 1 lemon
4 tablespoons *minced* chives
½ cup watercress leaves, coarsely chopped

½ cup parsley sprigs, coarsely chopped
2 teaspoons dried tarragon or 1 heaping tablespoon fresh, chopped
2 cups vegetable oil

To mince chives—hold the blade of a heavy French chef's knife at both ends and chop with rapid up-and-down motions, pulling the herb back into a pile with the knife as you work.

Rip the ribs from the spinach leaves and chop the leaves coarsely, using a French chef's knife. Place in the container of the electric blender with all other ingredients except the oil. Then add exactly ¼ cup of the oil. Cover. Turn the motor to high. Immediately remove the cover and quickly add the remaining oil in a steady stream. Turn the motor off once all the oil is added. Makes about 2½ cups.

STUFFED HARD-COOKED EGGS

EQUIPMENT:

Large saucepan; kitchen knife; kitchen spoon; kitchen fork; French chef's knife; Saran.

Hard-cook 6 eggs (page 306). Peel off the *shell*, then cut in half, lengthwise. Scoop out the yolks carefully, taking care not to break the whites.

Mash the yolks with a fork and combine with about 2 tablespoons of regular Mayonnaise (page 38), 1 teaspoon of minced chives, and about 6 sprigs of parsley, minced. Heap into the whites, place on a platter, seal with Saran, and refrigerate.

To shell an egg the easy way, tap all over with the back of a knife until it is "mapped." Then, holding the egg in the palm of your hand peel off the shell and inner skin. If small shell particles cling to the egg, dip the egg in cold water.

HOT BISCUITS

EQUIPMENT:
Measuring cups and spoons; flour sifter; pastry blender; mixing bowl; kitchen fork; waxed paper; pastry cloth and sleeve for rolling pin, or board and rolling pin; cookie cutter; cookie or baking sheet.

INGREDIENTS:

2 cups *sifted* all-purpose flour
2 teaspoons baking powder
Pinch or ½ teaspoon salt

½ cup (1 stick) butter, cold
Cold milk

To measure sifted flour properly, spoon it—after sifting—into a dry measuring cup (or spoon), well above the top, then level or cut off with the edge—not the flat surface —of a metal spatula or knife. Do not shake flour down.

Preheat the oven to 450° (or hot) for 15 minutes before baking the biscuits.

Sift the flour, baking powder, and salt together. Cut the butter into chunks and add half to the flour. Then, with a pastry blender, work the butter into the flour until the mixture is mealy. Add the remaining butter and work together only until the fat "clumps" into pieces about the size of peas. If the butter is "cut in" too much and the dough is overworked, the biscuits will be tough. Too much milk also makes them tough.

Sprinkle 3 tablespoons of milk over the mixture. Toss with a fork. Then, with your hands, work the mixture into a ball. If it doesn't hold, add a tiny bit more milk. If there's time, wrap the dough in waxed paper and chill. (This helps to make the dough more tender.)

Lightly flour a pastry cloth and the sleeve on the rolling pin (or a board and rolling pin). Roll out the dough about ½-inch thick. Cut with a medium-size cookie cutter.

Place on a baking sheet in the preheated oven for about 10 minutes, or until the biscuits are golden.

Serve at once, split and buttered, in a napkin-lined bowl. Makes about 12.

The biscuits can be made in advance, ready to bake, and refrigerated. Slide into the preheated oven about 10 minutes before going to the table.

COLD LEMON SOUFFLÉ

EQUIPMENT:

Measuring cups and spoons; grater; lemon squeezer; double boiler; wooden spatula; large mixing bowl; rotary or electric beater; wire whisk; rubber spatula; 2-quart soufflé dish; Saran.

INGREDIENTS:

1 envelope unflavored gelatin	1 cup sugar
4 eggs, *separated*	½ teaspoon salt
Grated rind 1 lemon	1 cup heavy cream
Juice 2 lemons	

If you haven't mastered the trick of separating egg yolks from egg whites, see directions on page 305.

To grate rind of citrus fruit, which must be done before squeezing—work on a flat grater placed on top of a piece of waxed paper.

Sprinkle gelatin—do not dump it all at once—over ½ cup cold water to soften. Combine egg yolks, lemon juice, ½ cup of the sugar, and the salt in the top of a double boiler. Cook over simmering water, stirring constantly with a wooden spatula until the mixture has thickened and is custardy.

Take off the heat, stir in the gelatin until dissolved, then add the lemon rind. Cool.

Beat egg whites with a rotary or electric beater until they hold a shape. Gradually beat in the remaining sugar and continue beating until the meringue (mixture is now a meringue) holds stiff, shiny peaks when the beater is held straight up. Beat the cream until it, too, holds a soft shape.

Vigorously whip about a third of the meringue into the yolk custard, using a wire whisk. Then *fold* in the remainder with a rubber spatula. Finally fold in the whipped cream. Pour into soufflé dish, seal with Saran, and refrigerate for 2 to 3 hours or until firm.

Beat egg whites only to the stiff, shiny stage. If beaten longer, they become granular.

For exact folding technique —see directions on page 305.

BROILED SWORDFISH STEAK

Sautéed Potatoes   Lemon Wedges

Radish and Cucumber Salad

Apple Pie   Coffee

YOUR COOKING SCHEDULE: Well, the first job is the apple pie. It can be baked fairly early in the day, but it is well to remember that baked pastry is best served the day it is made and, preferably, not refrigerated.

The vegetables for the salad can be prepared ahead and refrigerated (dressed just before serving), but both the potatoes and the fish must be cooked immediately before dinner—the potatoes first, then the swordfish.

BROILED SWORDFISH STEAK

EQUIPMENT:

Measuring cups and spoons; French chef's knife; lemon squeezer; peppermill; small saucepan; broiling pan; bulb baster or large metal spoon.

INGREDIENTS:

4 pounds *swordfish steak*, 1 inch thick (if frozen, thaw)

½ cup (1 stick) butter, melted

6 to 10 parsley sprigs, *minced*

1 small clove garlic, *minced*

Juice 1 lemon

Vegetable oil

Salt

Freshly ground white pepper

Lemon wedges

Allow from ½ to ¾ pound swordfish steak, per person. Thaw frozen fish before broiling.

To mince parsley—hold the blade of a heavy French chef's knife at both ends, and chop with rapid up-and-down motions, pulling the ingredients back into a pile with the knife as you work.

To peel, slice, mince, or dice onions, garlic and shallots the easy way—see directions on page 306.

To baste—spray, spoon, or brush a liquid or melted fat over food while it cooks.

Preheat the broiler at highest heat for 15 minutes.

Combine the butter, parsley, garlic, and lemon juice.

Place the steak on the *cold* broiling pan which has been well oiled. Pour the butter mixture all over it. Broil 3 to 4 inches from the source of heat for 3 minutes (time yourself exactly) on the first side. Turn and broil 5 minutes, *basting* each side twice during the broiling period.

Place on a heated platter, season with a sprinkling of salt and pepper and garnish with the lemon wedges. Serves about 6.

Halibut, striped bass, salmon, and cod, 1 inch thick, can all be used in place of the swordfish. For halibut, allow a minute longer on the first side;

Use a peppermill for this. Freshly ground pepper is more vibrant than already-ground pepper. Both black and white peppercorns are available, the former being somewhat lustier.

Remove broiling pan before preheating broiler or the fish will stick.

for striped bass, broil 4 minutes on each side; for salmon, broil the same length of time, both sides, as for swordfish; for cod, broil 5 minutes on each side.

SAUTÉED POTATOES

EQUIPMENT:
Vegetable peeler; measuring cups; peppermill; French chef's knife; heavy skillet; wooden spatula.

INGREDIENTS:
6 medium-size mature new potatoes
¼ cup (½ stick) butter
Salt
Freshly ground white pepper

Peel the potatoes, using the vegetable peeler; wash and dry thoroughly. Slice about ⅛ inch thick. Heat the butter in the skillet. When hot, add the potatoes, sprinkle with salt and pepper and cook, over medium heat, stirring often with a wooden spatula. When beautifully brown, crisp and tender, the potatoes are cooked. Taste to find out. Serves about 6.

Use a peppermill for this. Freshly ground pepper is more vibrant than already-ground pepper. Both black and white peppercorns are available, the former being somewhat lustier.

RADISH AND CUCUMBER SALAD

EQUIPMENT:
Measuring cups and spoons; peppermill; French chef's knife; large mixing bowl; wire whisk.

INGREDIENTS:

2 cucumbers, skin on
Big bunch red radishes
1 bunch, about 8, green onions
   (scallions)
1 cup commercial sour cream

Salt
Freshly ground pepper
2 teaspoons prepared horseradish
   sauce
Watercress

Use a peppermill for this. Freshly ground pepper is more vibrant than already-ground pepper. Both black and white peppercorns are available, the former being somewhat lustier.

Slice off both ends of the cucumbers, then slice very thin (leaving the skin on). Cut off both tops and roots of the radishes, and slice thin—enough to make 1 generous cup. Slice off the roots of the green onions. Discard any wilted leaves. Then cut into approximately 1-inch pieces.

Learn to taste. This makes sense, since one person's salt-and-pepper tolerance can be quite different from another's.

Combine all in a salad bowl and refrigerate. With a wire whisk mix together the sour cream, salt and pepper to *taste*, and the horseradish. Just before serving, pour over the vegetables and mix together. Garnish with a garland of fresh watercress. Serves 6.

APPLE PIE

EQUIPMENT:

Flour sifter; measuring cups and spoons; mixing bowl; 9-inch pie plate; pastry blender; kitchen fork; waxed paper; pastry cloth and rolling pin with sleeve (preferably) or board and rolling pin; apple corer; flat grater; paring knife.

To measure sifted flour properly, spoon it—after sifting—into a dry measuring cup (or spoon), well above the top, then level or cut off with the edge—not the flat surface —of a metal spatula or knife. Do not shake flour down.

BASIC PASTRY FOR A 2-CRUST, 9-INCH PIE

INGREDIENTS:

2 cups *sifted* all-purpose flour
1 teaspoon salt

$\frac{2}{3}$ cup (10 tablespoons) vegetable
   shortening
5 to 6 tablespoons ice water

Sift the flour together with salt into a bowl. Work half the shortening into the flour with a pastry blender, using a cutting motion, until mixture looks mealy. Work in the remainder the same way, but only until the fat particles "clump" together in pieces about the size of small peas. Sprinkle the ice *water*, 1 tablespoon at a time, over the flour and toss lightly with a fork. Then work together quickly with your hands until the ball of dough holds together. Wrap in waxed paper and chill for a half hour or so at least.

Be careful not to use too much liquid. It makes pastry tough. Overmixing and overhandling also make pastry tough.

To roll out pastry, divide in half. Refrigerate one half. Place the other half on a lightly floured board or pastry cloth. Lightly flour the rolling pin or sleeve. Then roll a few strokes to flatten the dough. Now roll lightly from the center to edge, lifting rolling pin on each stroke as it nears the edge. Roll very thin—less than ⅛ inch thick—into a circle large enough to extend 1½ inches all around the edge of the pie plate. Roll up loosely on rolling pin, lift over the pie plate, center, then unroll. *Fit* the pastry into the pan loosely. Trim edge with a sharp knife even with rim of pan. Refrigerate while you make Apple Filling.

Do not stretch pastry or it will shrink during baking.

APPLE FILLING

INGREDIENTS:

5 to 6 large tart cooking apples
1 cup sugar
¼ teaspoon salt
½ teaspoon cinnamon
½ teaspoon vanilla

Grated rind 1 lemon
Juice 1 lemon
2 tablespoons (¼ stick) butter
Heavy cream

To grate rind of citrus fruit, which must be done before squeezing—work on a flat grater placed on top of a piece of waxed paper.

At this point preheat the oven to 450° (or hot) for 15 minutes before baking the pie.

Peel, core, and slice apples very thin. Mix with all the ingredients except the butter and cream. Pile in the pie shell (high in the center because the apples cook down). Dot with bits of the butter.

Roll second half of the pastry exactly as you did the first. With a sharp knife make several 2-inch long slits near the center to permit steam to escape and forestall soggy pastry. Roll up loosely on rolling pin and center over the filling. Unroll. Trim top crust, allowing it to extend a good ½ inch over the rim. To seal, moisten the bottom edge and press top and bottom edges together. Then fold the edge of the top crust under the bottom crust and press together firmly. At this point carefully open the slits slightly with the point of a paring knife.

To flute, place right index finger on inside rim of pastry, left index finger and thumb on outside. Press pastry with right index finger into a V formed by pinching the dough with left thumb and index finger. Repeat all around the rim. Place in the preheated oven for 10 minutes. Reduce heat to 350° (or moderate) and continue baking 30 to 35 minutes longer. Five minutes before baking time is up, *brush* the pastry with cream and sprinkle generously with granulated sugar. Serve warm or at room temperature.

Use real hair or feather brush for this because they stay soft and flexible.

This amount of pastry will also make two 9-inch pie shells or about 15 (3½-inch) tart shells. Pastry can be frozen successfully. Freeze, then wrap securely.

To use up bits and pieces of pastry—make them into a ball, roll out thin, then cut into fingers about 1 × 2 inches (use a ruler as a guide). Sprinkle with finely grated Cheddar or Parmesan cheese. Place on a cookie or baking sheet and bake in a preheated 450° (hot) oven for 8 to 10 minutes. Good with salads or drinks.

SOLE LAUNAY

Steamed New Potatoes   *Salad of*
                             Fresh Cooked Vegetables

Strawberry Sherbet

Coffee

YOUR COOKING SCHEDULE: The strawberry sherbet and the vegetables for the salad can both be done a day ahead. Otherwise, early in the day to allow the vegetables to chill properly and the sherbet to freeze. Put the potatoes on to steam when you put the Sole Launay in the oven. While these are cooking, make the Sauce Vinaigrette for the salad.

SOLE LAUNAY

EQUIPMENT:
Measuring cups and spoons; French chef's knife; peppermill; electric blender; shallow baking pan (just large enough to hold all the filets flat); small mixing bowl; broad metal spatula; rubber spatula.

INGREDIENTS:

2½ pounds sole or flounder fillets, about

¼ cup (½ stick) butter, softened

1 generous cup parsley sprigs, *minced*

½ teaspoon dried tarragon or 1 teaspoon fresh, *minced*

Salt

Freshly ground pepper

2 cups sweet cider

1 tablespoon *cornstarch*

½ cup unseasoned *bread crumbs*

To mince parsley—hold the blade of a heavy French chef's knife at both ends, and chop with rapid up-and-down motions, pulling the ingredients back into a pile with the knife as you work.

To butter or coat—crumple up a little waxed paper, scoop up a bit of butter and coat the bottom and sides of the pan generously.

Use a peppermill for this. Freshly ground pepper is more vibrant than already-ground pepper.

Cornstarch gives a sauce a more translucent quality than flour—1 tablespoon is the equivalent of 2 of flour.

Use firm day-old bread for bread crumbs (4 or 5 slices make 2 cups). Break into pieces and grind crust and all in the electric blender, or crumble by hand until very fine.

Allow two fillets per person. Thawed, if frozen, before baking. Using about half the butter, *coat* a shallow baking pan just large enough to hold the fillets flat.

Preheat oven to 350° (or moderate), for 15 minutes before baking the fish.

Sprinkle half the parsley and half the tarragon over the butter. Lay the fillets on top and dot with the remaining butter, scatter with remaining parsley and tarragon. Sprinkle lightly with salt and pepper.

Mix the cornstarch with a little of the cider to make a smooth paste, then stir into the remaining cider. Pour over the fish and sprinkle with the bread crumbs.

Bake in the preheated oven for 15 minutes. Pour the cream over the fish and bake another 5 minutes.

With a broad metal spatula lift the baked fish from the pan onto a heated serving platter. The sauce at this point should have thickened to the consistency of a light cream sauce. If not, place the pan over a high heat and cook, stirring constantly with a rubber spatula, for a couple of minutes. Then pour over the fish. Serve at once.

STEAMED NEW POTATOES

EQUIPMENT:
Sharp paring knife or vegetable peeler; colander or sieve; large saucepan; double-duty foil.

Take 8 to 10 tiny new potatoes (or 2 to 3 per person) all of a size. Peel a little "belly" band, about an inch wide, from around the middle of each potato, using a sharp paring knife or vegetable peeler.

To steam, place the potatoes in a colander or sieve that can rest on the rim of a large pot of bubbling water but well above the water. Cover as securely as possible with double-duty foil. Steam for 15 to 20 minutes or until the potatoes are tender when pierced with the point of a paring knife. Place in a napkin-lined vegetable dish, wrapping the napkin around to keep them warm.

SALAD OF FRESH COOKED VEGETABLES

EQUIPMENT:
Sharp paring knife; 2 medium-size saucepans; colander; medium mixing bowl.

Cook vegetables separately because, in general, they do not cook for the same length of time.

Cook *separately*, equal quantities of fresh sliced green beans (page 49), peeled carrots and celery, both sliced on the bias; peas and lima beans. Drop into boiling broth or salted water and cook until barely tender (Italians say, al dente, firm to the tooth). Drain thoroughly. Cool each one immediately under cold water. Drain again and dry thoroughly. Combine in a serving bowl and toss in a good Sauce Vinaigrette (page 44). Garland with crisp lettuce before serving. Allow about ½ to ¾ cup of mixed vegetables per person.

STRAWBERRY SHERBET

EQUIPMENT:

Colander; measuring cups and spoons; paring knife; paper towels; large mixing bowl; electric blender; 2 freezer trays.

INGREDIENTS:

3 boxes strawberries
2 cups superfine sugar
Juice 3 oranges, strained

Juice 3 lemons, strained
⅓ cup Grand Marnier

Wash the berries thoroughly in a colander under a light stream of cool water. Lift out of the colander onto paper towels and dry well. Using a small paring knife, hull. Combine with the sugar and both juices in a large mixing bowl. Allow to stand 2 to 3 hours.

Blend, a small quantity at a time, in the electric blender. Stir in the Grand Marnier and pour into two freezer trays. Freeze until the sherbet has a solid edge about 1 inch thick. Transfer to a large bowl and beat with the rotary or electric beater until mushy. Return to trays and freeze until firm.

—•—

SAUTÉED FISH FILLETS MEUNIÈRE

Boiled Potatoes
(page 44)

Creamed Cucumbers

Tomato and Sweet Pepper Salad

French Bread

Meringues with Ice Cream

YOUR COOKING SCHEDULE: As is often the case, the dessert can be done way ahead. Actually, meringues keep so well they can be made whenever you have some extra egg whites on hand, then baked and stored in an airtight container.

The salad needs some marinating time, which means that the "work" can be done beforehand, except for dressing the tomatoes, which should be done at the last minute. Allow about 1½ hours for the cucumbers from the time you begin to prepare them until you take them out of the oven. During the last half hour they are baking, boil the potatoes. Last of all, and when everything else is ready, sauté the fish.

SAUTÉED FISH FILLETS MEUNIÈRE

EQUIPMENT:

Peppermill; lemon squeezer; French chef's knife; clean paper bag; heavy skillet; kitchen fork; broad metal spatula; wooden spatula.

Of all the ways there are to cook fish fillets or a whole fish, sautéeing, or pan frying as it is also called, is the easiest and quickest. It can also be the smelliest. A "fishy" odor can be avoided if the fat, whether butter or oil, is kept from reaching the smoking point, which is what causes the odor.

INGREDIENTS:

3 *pounds* fish fillets, fresh or frozen (thawed)	Salt
Flour	*Freshly ground* white pepper
Butter	Juice 1 lemon
	Minced parsley

Figure on ⅓ to ½ pound of fish per person when part of a dinner.

Drop the fillets into any clean bag with a few tablespoons of flour. Shake gently until the pieces are well coated. Lift from the bag and shake off any excess.

Heat the butter (allow 2 to 3 tablespoons for 3 fillets) in a heavy skillet. When hot, add as many fillets as the pan will hold comfortably without crowding, and *sauté* over a high heat until lightly browned on one side. Sprinkle with salt and pepper, then turn and sauté the second side—actually, a matter of seconds. Test for *doneness*. As the fillets are cooked, lift each one with a broad metal spatula onto a heated serving platter. Keep warm.

When all the fillets are cooked, take the pan off the heat to cool down a bit, then add a good lump of butter, the lemon juice and some minced parsley. Stir

To make the flake or doneness test, probe the thickest part of the flesh gently with a fork. If the flesh separates and falls easily into the natural divisions, the fish is cooked perfectly. Properly cooked, fish becomes opaque but is still moist.

Use a peppermill for this. Both black and white peppercorns are available, the former being somewhat lustier.

To mince parsley—hold the blade of a heavy French chef's knife at both ends, chop with rapid up-and-down motions, pulling the ingredients back into a pile with the knife as you work.

To sauté—cook or brown food in a very small amount of very hot fat.

with a wooden spatula over moderate heat until piping hot, then pour over the fish. Serve immediately to 6.

Another way to serve Sautéed Fish Fillets: *Peel, seed*, and chop 2 or 3 very ripe tomatoes. Combine in a saucepan with 4 tablespoons (½ stick) of butter. Cook over a moderate heat until the mixture is a thick paste. Season with 1 small clove garlic, minced very fine, salt, and curry powder to *taste*. Add ½ cup of dry white wine, bring to a boil, reduce heat to *simmer* and cook for 30 minutes. Pour over the sautéed fillets.

To simmer—cook liquid just below boiling (185°) so that it just shivers.

To peel and seed tomatoes: Cut out the stem ends, then cover the tomatoes with boiling water and allow to stand for about 20 seconds (unripe tomatoes may take a few seconds longer). Plunge into cold water. With a small sharp knife, start peeling at the stem end. To seed, cut a slice of the stem end or cut the tomato in half, crosswise. Squeeze gently to extract seeds.

CREAMED CUCUMBERS

EQUIPMENT:
Measuring cups and spoons; peppermill; French chef's knife; teaspoon; paring knife; kitchen teaspoon; polyethylene bag; paper towels; ovenproof baking dish; wooden spoon; small saucepan.

INGREDIENTS:

6 medium cucumbers
2 tablespoons wine vinegar
½ teaspoon salt
Big pinch sugar
2 green onions, *minced*

½ teaspoon basil
4 tablespoons (½ stick) butter, melted
Several twists of the peppermill (white pepper)
1 cup heavy cream
Few sprigs parsley, *minced*

To peel, slice, mince, or dice onions, shallots, garlic the easy way—see directions on page 306.

To mince parsley—hold the blade of a heavy French chef's knife at both ends and chop with rapid up-and-down motions, pulling the ingredients back into a pile with the knife as you work.

Preheat the oven to 375° (or moderate) for 15 minutes before baking the cucumbers.

Cut the cucumbers in half, lengthwise, and scoop out the seeds with a tea-spoon. Cut each half into three strips, then cut the strips into 2-inch pieces. Combine the cucumbers with the vinegar, salt, and sugar in a polyethylene bag, turning the bag occasionally so slices are well soaked. Marinate for at least 30 minutes, but longer if possible. Drain and pat dry with paper towels.

Place the cucumbers, butter, basil, and onions with a sprinkling of pepper in the baking dish. Bake, uncovered, for 30 to 40 minutes. While baking, turn the cucumbers over 2 or 3 times with a wooden spoon. Set aside for the moment.

Meanwhile pour the cream into a small saucepan and bring to a boil. Boil until the cream has *reduced* to 1/2 cup. Mix into the baked cucumbers. Add salt and pepper to *taste*. Spoon into a heated vegetable dish. Garnish with the parsley. Serves about 6.

Learn to taste. This makes sense, since one person's salt-and-pepper tolerance can be quite different from another's.

To reduce—simply boil liquid over a high heat until the amount left is what the recipe specifies.

TOMATO AND SWEET PEPPER SALAD

EQUIPMENT:
Measuring cups and spoons; peppermill; paring knife; French chef's knife; heavy skillet; paper towels; medium mixing bowl.

INGREDIENTS:
1 sweet green pepper
1 sweet red or yellow pepper
2 large ripe tomatoes
1/4 cup olive oil
Sauce Vinaigrette (page 44)

1/2 cup green or ripe olives, sliced
1 small sweet onion, *peeled* and *sliced* thin
1/2 teaspoon dried tarragon or 1 1/2 teaspoons fresh, minced

To peel, slice, mince, or dice onions, garlic, and shallots the easy way—see directions on page 306.

Cut the tops off the peppers, slice in two, cut out the ribs and brush away the seeds. Finally, cut into strips. Heat the oil in a heavy skillet, add the pepper strips and cook slowly until they just begin to turn soft. Lift from the fat and drain on paper towels. Combine with the Sauce Vinaigrette and allow to marinate for at least 30 minutes or longer.

Peel and seed the tomatoes, then slice. Arrange on a serving dish. Combine the peppers with the olives, onion, and tarragon and spread the mixture over the tomatoes. Serves about 6.

MERINGUES WITH ICE CREAM

EQUIPMENT:
Measuring cups and spoons; 2 cookie sheets; large mixing bowl; rotary or electric beater; wire whisk; large spoon; metal spatula; wire rack.

INGREDIENTS:

Vegetable shortening

3 egg *whites*

⅛ teaspoon salt

⅛ teaspoon cream of tartar

¾ cup sugar

If you haven't mastered the trick of separating egg yolks from egg whites— see directions on page 305.

To grease a cookie sheet— crumple up a little waxed paper, scoop up a bit of butter and coat the surface of the sheet generously.

Preheat the oven to 275° (or slow) for 15 minutes before baking the meringues.

Grease two cookie sheets and coat lightly by adding several spoonfuls of flour. Working over the sink, tip the pan back and forth so the bottom is well coated. Then turn upside down and give the pan a good bang to knock off any excess. Set aside.

Place the whites in a generous bowl. Sprinkle on the salt and cream of

Beat egg whites only to the stiff, shiny stage. If beaten longer, they become granular.

tartar. *Beat* with a rotary or electric beater until the whites begin to hold a shape. Gradually add the sugar, beating constantly and vigorously until the meringue is very stiff and shiny.

Spoon onto the prepared cookie sheets (you should have about 16 mounds), leaving room for spreading. Bake in the preheated oven for 35 to 40 minutes or until firm when touched. Lift off immediately with a metal spatula and cool on a wire rack.

To serve, place a big spoonful of ice cream (chocolate, peach or whatever your favorite) in one shell and top with another.

Meringues keep extremely well if stored in an airtight container.

Other ways to serve meringues: Fill one meringue shell with Crème Chantilly (whipped cream sweetened with sugar); top with another; toss fresh raspberries in enough superfine sugar to sweeten lightly, then perfume with kirsch to taste. Heap raspberries in one meringue shell, then top with another. Serve plain whipped cream on the side.

THE CAKE PANS

In addition to such standard pans as 8- and 9-inch layers, 8- and 9-inch squares, rectangular pans and cookie sheets, these three important pans belong in your kitchen: the 10-inch tube for angel cake, fruit cakes, etc.; the spring form (8, 9, and 10 inches) which is necessary in making cheese cakes, but is called for many other times; and the very useful 6-cup and 8-cup ring mold.

THE ELECTRIC BLENDER

This remarkable piece of equipment can do almost everything except talk. With many speeds and a powerful motor, it can grate nuts and hard cheeses; crumb bread and crackers; purée fruits, vegetables, fish, poultry; mince parsley; chop vegetables; make Hollandaise and mayonnaise. It also makes drinks such as daiquiris. Keep it right on your work surface so it's always at hand.

TUBE, SPRING FORM
AND RING MOLD.

TECHNIQUES AND MEASURES

To Eat Whole Artichokes, Hot or Cold

Dip the fleshy end of each leaf into the sauce, then scrape off the flesh between your teeth. Eventually, you come to the heart which is covered with the "choke," a hairy center growth. Cut out the choke and eat the heart with a knife and fork, dipping the pieces into the accompanying sauce. To remove the choke before serving—spread the leaves apart carefully so you can reach the interior easily. Then pull out the center cone of leaves, all in one piece. This exposes the hairy "choke." Scrape the choke out with a teaspoon. To present the artichoke with professional style, turn the cone of leaves upside down and place in the hollow of the artichoke.

To Separate Eggs

Have two bowls ready, a large one for the whites, a smaller one for the yolks. Crack the egg sharply on the edge of the bowl, mid-center, to break the shell. Pull the two halves, apart, holding them upright, over the egg-white bowl. The yolk, because it's heavier, will automatically remain in one shell, with the white running out. Switch the yolk back and forth between the two shells until all the white has disengaged itself and dropped into the large bowl. If, by mischance, you should break the yolk and some gets into the white, lift it out with a piece of shell or, failing that, with a piece of paper toweling. The white will not beat up properly if there is even so much as a drop of yolk or other fat.

How to Fold One Ingredient into Another

Folding is of major importance in making soufflés and cakes and there are other instances in cookery where folding is called for. The object is to retain the air which has been beaten into the food that is "folded in"—be it egg whites, meringue, or cream. To fold beaten whites into a soufflé base or cake batter, beat about a third into the base thoroughly, whipping vigorously with a wire whisk. Then, with a rubber spatula, scoop remaining whites on top of the mixture. Cut the spatula down from the center to the bottom of the pan or bowl, then run it along the bottom toward you and against the edge of the pan, rotating the pan as you work. Make sure the spatula reaches to the very bottom and sides of the mixture and brings it up over the top. Keep repeating the process until all whites have been folded in. With soufflés it is not essential to fold in every last bit of whites, but with cakes it is.

For folding in cream, essentially the same method is used, except that you fold it all in at one time.

How to Deep-Fat Fry

Lacking a regular deep-fat fryer with a wire basket, use a deep heavy saucepan with straight sides. The fat or oil should be deep enough to cover the food generously, at least 4 inches, and there should be 2 or 3 inches between the top of the fat and the top of the pan so the hot fat won't bubble over.

Approximate proportions: 1 quart fat or oil to a 3-quart kettle allows you to cook about 3 doughnuts, 3 croquettes, or a cupful of potatoes at a time. Do not fry too much at a time. Deep-fat fry with a basket if at all possible. Slowly lower the basket with the food into the fat. It will bubble up, but will soon subside.

It is important to keep the fat temperature constant. If you are working without a basket, use a large slotted spoon to place food in the fat and to remove it.

Without a thermometer: Heat the fat slowly. Drop a 1-inch cube of 1-day-old bread into it. If the bread browns in 40 seconds, the fat is ready for frying cooked food. If the bread browns in 1 minute, the fat is ready for frying uncooked food. This is true of all foods except French Fried Potatoes. They should be fried when a cube of bread browns in 20 seconds.

How to Hard-cook Eggs

Place the eggs, straight from the refrigerator, in a saucepan deep enough to accommodate them without crowding. Add 5 to 6 cups cold tap water, regardless of the number of eggs, making sure all of the eggs are covered by at least a generous inch of water. Bring up to a rolling boil (220° on the thermometer).

Remove the pan from the heat when water reaches a rolling boil. Cover and allow to stand for 15 minutes. Then immediately plunge the eggs into cold water to stop the cooking.

How to Truss Poultry

To truss a bird (any kind), place it on the table, legs facing you. Fold the wing tips under the body, akimbo, and also pull the neck skin under. Take a good long piece of soft, white string and slip it under the body, holding the neck skin in place. Bring one length of the string along the right side of the body, across the cavity and loop around the left leg; do the same with the other length looping it around the right leg. Then draw the two other together tightly and tie. Clip off the string ends.

How to Clarify Butter

Cut butter into pieces, place in a saucepan over moderate heat. When the butter has melted, skim off the foam that rises to the top and strain into a bowl through several layers of cheesecloth discarding the milky residue at the bottom of the pan. The advantage of clarified butter is that it does not burn readily at high temperature because the milk solids have been removed. Clarified butter freezes well. You'll note it becomes opaque, but it clears up when heated. Wrap properly, however.

How to Peel, Slice, Mince, or Dice Onions, Garlic and Shallots the Easy Way

To peel more than one or two vegetables, drop them into a pot of bubbling water. Allow 5 seconds for garlic or shallots; about

10 seconds for small, white onions; about 5 minutes for large mature onions. Drain, run under cold water, then trim off both tops and bottoms—just enough so as not to disturb the layers. Slip off the outside skin and the first layer with your fingers. Before boiling white onions, make an X with a small sharp knife at the root end to keep them from falling apart.

To slice these members of the onion family or any round vegetable (potatoes, for example), peel, and cut a thin slice off one side. Place, cut side down, on a chopping board. Holding the piece with your left hand, fingers curled under somewhat, slice straight, thick or thin, with a good sharp knife (we like French chef's knives), pushing the slices away as you work. Watch your fingers.

To mince, peel, leaving the root end on. With the root end at your left, using a small sharp paring knife (for garlic and shallots) or a French chef's knife for onions, make vertical slices, down the length, from one side to the other, without cutting through the root, so the slices remain attached. Next make horizontal slices from the right to, but not through, the root end. Finally, cut down the length of the vegetable, across.

To dice, follow the same technique as for mince, cutting in larger pieces.

How to Peel and Section Citrus Fruit

To peel, hold the fruit (orange, grapefruit, lemon, or lime), in your left hand. Cut off all the rind and the white skin, using a sharp, fairly large knife, working around and around over a bowl to catch any juices. Peel right down to the flesh, and if you miss any white skin, cut it off. To section, cut down on both sides of each section as close to the membrane as possible and push the section into the bowl. Remove seeds, if any.

EQUIVALENT MEASURES

A pinch, ½ to ⅓ teaspoon, or as much as can be picked up between thumb and forefinger			5 tablespoons plus 1 teaspoon	=	⅓ cup
3 teaspoons	=	1 tablespoon	8 tablespoons	=	½ cup or 4 ounces
4 tablespoons	=	¼ cup or 2 ounces	16 tablespoons	=	1 cup or 8 ounces

EQUIVALENT AMOUNTS

BUTTER, LARD, MARGARINE OR SHORTENING

1 ounce	=	2 tablespoons or ¼ stick
2 ounces	=	4 tablespoons, ¼ cup or ½ stick
4 ounces	=	8 tablespoons, ½ cup or 1 stick
½ pound	=	16 tablespoons, 1 cup, or 2 sticks
1 pound	=	2 cups or 4 sticks

CHEESE

¼ pound Cheddar or Swiss	=	1 cup, grated
½ pound cottage	=	1 cup
3-ounce package cream	=	6 tablespoons

CREAM

1 cup or ½ pint heavy cream	=	2 cups whipped

EGGS

4 to 6 whole shelled eggs	=	about 1 cup
8 to 10 egg whites	=	about 1 cup
12 to 14 egg yolks	=	about 1 cup

FLOUR

1 pound white all-purpose	=	4 cups, sifted
1 pound cake flour	=	4¾ to 5 cups, sifted

FRUIT

1 pound, 3 medium apples	=	3 cups sliced
1 pound, 3 medium bananas	=	2½ cups sliced
1 medium lemon	=	3 to 4 tablespoons juice*
1 medium lemon	=	1 tablespoon grated rind
1 medium orange	=	⅓ cup juice*
1 medium orange	=	10 to 11 sections
1 medium orange	=	1 tablespoon plus 1 teaspoon grated rind
1 medium grapefruit	=	⅔ cup juice*
1 medium grapefruit	=	10 to 12 sections
1 pint box berries, except gooseberries	=	2 cups

* All citrus fruits, boiled for about a minute, yield a larger amount of juice. The rind cannot be grated after boiling.

PASTA

1 8-ounce package macaroni or 2 cups, uncooked	=	4 to 5 cups, cooked
1 8-ounce package noodles or spaghetti, or 2½ cups, uncooked	=	3 to 4 cups, cooked

RICE

1 cup uncooked long-grain rice	=	3 cups cooked
1 cup parboiled or converted rice	=	4 cups cooked
1 cup precooked rice	=	2 cups cooked
1 cup brown rice	=	4 cups cooked

SUGAR

1 pound brown, firmly packed	=	2½ to 2⅓ cups
1 pound confectioners', unsifted	=	4½ cups
1 pound granulated or superfine	=	2¼ to 2½ cups

UNFLAVORED GELATIN

1 envelope = 1 tablespoon. This amount will "gel" 2 cups of liquid.
(If sugar is used, it should be counted as part of the total liquid.)

CHOCOLATE

1 ounce semisweet chocolate pieces is the equivalent of 1 ounce of any sweet cooking chocolate or 1 square, 1-ounce size, semisweet chocolate

NUTS

1 cup or about 5 ounces, by weight, grated with a hand-operated grater yields 2 cups grated

1 cup or about 5 ounces, by weight, grated in the electric blender yields about 1½ cups grated

PARSLEY

1 cup parsley sprigs = ½ cup minced parsley

INDEX

311

NOTES INDEX

Although some notes are repeated frequently throughout the text,
they are indexed only once, at the point of first mention.

ABOUT THE AUTHOR

HELEN McCULLY is one of the most distinguished food experts in the country. She is the Food Editor of *House Beautiful*, where she has a monthly column and a monthly food feature. She was, for many years, the Food Editor of *McCall's* and has appeared frequently on radio and television. She lives in New York City.